RESEARCH IN APPLIED LINGUISTICS

Becoming a Discerning Consumer

RESEARCH IN APPLIED LINGUISTICS

Becoming a Discerning Consumer

Fred L. Perry, Jr.
American University in Cairo

LEA LAWRENCE ERLBAUM ASSOCIATES, PUBLISHERS
2005 Mahwah, New Jersey   London

P129 P47 2005

Copyright © 2005 by Lawrence Erlbaum Associates, Inc.
All rights reserved. No part of this book may be reproduced in
any form, by photostat, microform, retrieval system, or any other
means, without the prior written permission of the publisher.

Lawrence Erlbaum Associates, Inc., Publishers
10 Industrial Avenue
Mahwah, New Jersey 07430
www.erlbaum.com

Cover design by Sean Trane Sciarrone

Library of Congress Cataloging-in-Publication Data

Perry, Fred L. (Fred Lehman), 1943–
    Research in applied linguistics : becoming a discerning consumer / Fred L.
Perry, Jr.
        p.   cm.
    Includes bibliographical references and index.
    ISBN 0-8058-4684-0 (alk. paper)
    ISBN 0-8058-4685-9 (pbk. : alk. paper)
    1. Applied linguistics—Research.   I. Title.

P129.P47   2005
418′.0072—dc22   2004061932
                                                                  CIP

Books published by Lawrence Erlbaum Associates are printed on acid-free paper,
and their bindings are chosen for strength and durability.

Printed in the United States of America
10 9 8 7 6 5 4 3 2 1

Dedicated to the memory of my parents,
Fred and Ann,
and to my wife, Karen Kay,
who inspires me to do my best

Contents

Preface

The premise of this book is that teachers, administrators, students and others working in applied linguistics need to understand research in the field—they need to be *discerning consumers* of research as well as know how to carry out a research project. The impact of research on our daily lives has greatly increased in recent years. People affected by research include those developing language learning programs, those implementing programs, parents who are involved in their children's education, and students. All of these people and others on whom research in applied linguistics has an impact need to be able to understand it to the point where they are able to evaluate recommendations based on such research.

This book is specifically written for all those who want and need to be consumers of research—administrators, teachers, students, student parents, but especially for M.A. students in applied linguistics. These students tend to be thrown into the deep end of the pool of research from the first day they enter their programs, and they find it necessary to become consumers of research overnight to fulfill the assignments given by their instructors. This text is designed to assist them in getting up to speed. The goal is not to develop just *casual* consumers who passively read bits and pieces of a research article, but *discerning* consumers who will read research reports from beginning to end with a level of understanding that can be used to address both theoretical and practical issues. Once this stage is reached, consumers will no longer look on research journals as forbidding, boring documents that only university professors find interesting. Rather they will regard them as important sources of evidence or counterevidence that can be used in arguing the pros and/or cons of implementing new ideas and methodologies in educational settings.

ORGANIZATION OF THE TEXT

The organization of this book has evolved from more than 18 years of experience in teaching people how to understand research in applied linguistics. This has been one of my major roles at my institution, and one that I thoroughly enjoy. Based on my interaction with various audiences, I have discovered that the format used in more traditional texts on research methodology works best for people who want to learn how to do research, but it is not the most effective for those who initially only want to be consumers. Consequently, I have structured this book differently, although covering many of the same topics found in traditional texts.

The book is organized in two parts. Part I introduces the reader to the fundamentals required for becoming a discerning consumer. Chapter 1 distinguishes between common conceptions of the meaning of research and how it is understood among professional researchers. It also discusses the driving force behind the entire research process: the research question(s)—the question(s) that guide the choices researchers make when planning and carrying out their studies. Chapter 2 is intended to help students get a jump start on how to find research articles, through both traditional and electronic methods. Basic information accompanied by several walk-through examples is provided. Appendix A features detailed instructions on how to write a literature review. These instructions are put in an appendix at the end of the book, rather than in chapter 2, so that readers can complete a literature review after they have become discerning consumers; that is, on completing the entire book. Putting this material in an appendix also allows an instructor to assign reading this material at anytime s/he feels appropriate. An additional aid, Appendix C, provides an annotated list of many of the journals pertinent to applied linguistics.

Part II is structured around the order in which each component appears in a typical research report used by most research journals. Chapter 3, the first chapter of this section, maps out these components along with brief explanations and then examines the functions of the Title, Abstract, and Introduction in a typical study, along with descriptions of criteria used for evaluating these components. Chapters 4, 5, and 6 delineate the different criteria readers need to evaluate the material that is usually placed in the Methodology component of a report: sampling, research design, and data gathering. Here and throughout the text, I attempt to help readers integrate the many aspects of research methodology by synthesizing them into graphic illustrations. This may appear to be somewhat reductionistic—that is, to leave out details some instructors may consider important—but my experience has led me to understand that up-and-coming discerning consumers of research need to first develop a *big picture* schematic view of research before dealing with too many details. Once this overall framework is in place, the consumer will be able to accommodate whatever additional information s/he finds important as time progresses.

In this regard, chapter 4, on understanding sampling, uses two broad sampling paradigms to encompass more detailed sampling techniques. Chapter 5, which deals with research designs, summarizes three related dimensions for classifying research, taking the reader beyond the somewhat limiting quantitative–qualitative debate to provide a more realistic picture of research. The consumer of research needs this wider perspective to understand the range of methods/approaches being used today, often in concert with one another. Chapter 6 provides a conceptual framework to help the reader understand the numerous ways data are collected. Based on this framework, criteria for proper use of these data-collection methods are highlighted, and illustrative studies are reviewed.

Continuing through the standard order of elements in a typical research study, chapter 7 focuses on understanding and evaluating the Research Results section. My intent is for readers to be able to look into the Results section of a research article with enough confidence to critically evaluate whether appropriate procedures have been used and correct interpretations have been made. This chapter is divided into two main sections. The first relates to how verbal data are analyzed and interpreted. The second focuses on numerical data. Because the readers of this text come from a variety of academic backgrounds and levels of mathematical sophistication, when I discuss statistical issues, my goal is not to inundate the reader with more information than a consumer of research needs. I approached this topic in layers according to frequency of use and relevance to the reader. The first layer is presented in this chapter. The next layer is presented in Appendix B containing important information, but less common and a little more complex. In both layers, statistics are approached conceptually. My contention is that consumers of research do not need to know math formulas to understand statistical concepts, but they do need to know why certain procedures are followed, how to interpret them, and whether they are appropriately used.

Chapter 8, the final chapter, provides a set of criteria by which to appraise the Discussion and Conclusion section of the typical research report. Here readers are drawn to examine the logical thinking researchers engage in when interpreting results, formulating answers to the research questions, generalizing to target populations, and discussing how results are applied to practical problems.

SELECTION AND USE OF STUDIES
FOR ILLUSTRATIONS

I have tried to illustrate each major point in the book with at least one research study published in a refereed journal. When choosing these studies,
I followed five criteria in order of priority. First, the study should provide a
clear example of the point being made. Second, it should be as recent as
possible at the time of writing this book. Third, the topics of the research
studies should vary to expose the reader to some of the breadth of the issues
being researched in applied linguistics. Fourth, the studies should come
from a wide variety of journals to familiarize readers with a good sample of
the type of journals available. Finally, studies should not only look at the
teaching and learning of English as a second/foreign language, but also include other languages. After applying all five criteria, the possibilities were
narrowed down considerably.

Although most of the studies used point out how certain criteria were
met on several occasions, I identify where studies might have weaknesses in
relation to the evaluative criteria being discussed. My rationale is that readers' critical skills need to be sharpened to help them develop into discerning consumers of research. It is not enough to simply state that some published studies have certain weaknesses; the reader needs to see actual
examples where such weaknesses did occur or could have occurred. The
key word here is *discernment*, which does not mean *fault finding*. I do not
want readers to become cynics who delight in slamming researchers on every little perceived weakness, but rather to develop a healthy skepticism.
The objective is for readers to gain confidence in their own ability to assess
research so they can evaluate the influence any one study should have on
practical issues of concern. (Any researcher who has published one of the
studies I used for this purpose should not take offense. No study is perfect,
including my own.)

On occasion, I use some humor to lighten up the reading, especially
when dealing with heavy issues. This is risky, I know, because humor, like
beauty, varies in the eye of the beholder. However, I have taken this risk because I think research should not be perceived as a dry, boring affair. My
goal is that every once in a while the reader might crack a smile even when
reading difficult material.

RECOMMENDATIONS FOR USE AS A TEXTBOOK

I have used each chapter of this text with my graduate students while it was
under development. In this sense, it has been *field-tested* As a result, I have
made a number of adjustments based on the feedback from my students to
make the text more effective and user-friendly. The motivation behind this

book was to create a textbook that would provide my students with a solid introduction to the foundations of research methods, with the goal of helping them become discerning consumers. I have found that this frees me, the instructor, from having to lecture about things that students can read for themselves. It also releases class time for more interaction among students, myself, and one another.

The exercises distributed throughout the chapters play an important role. My students come to class having completed their assignments based on the exercises. They are expected to share their work with the rest of the class and respond to questions based on their assignments. Not only does this help individual students apply the criteria being learned on research studies, which match their own interest, it also exposes the entire class to a variety of studies and journals. By the end of the class session, students' exposure to how these criteria have been applied to recent research studies in different journals has grown exponentially.

The strategy that I use for interspersing exercises throughout the chapters, rather than placing them at the end, is based on the notion of the effects of adjunct aids. Based on research I and others did some years ago (e.g., Cunningham, Snowman, Miller, & Perry, 1982; Perry, 1982), we found that interspersed questions and exercises create strategic pauses for students to digest and apply what they have been reading. This creates an atmosphere that encourages readers to engage interactively with the text at the time of reading, when information is still fresh in their minds.

I have also found interspersed exercises to be convenient markers for scheduling the topics for discussion over the semester. I distribute the exercises over 16 weeks of classes (two class sessions per week) in addition to a mini-literature review (10 pages) based on Appendix A, which is the last assignment for my initial research methods class. Each chapter takes different amounts of time due to the varied density of the information in the chapter (e.g., I use seven class sessions to cover chap. 5 on research designs). However, this distributes the number of research studies the students examine in proportion to the topics being studied.

Last, in my course, I have chosen to allow students to select research articles on topics related to their own interest for each exercise, rather than use a lock-step strategy of assigning readers the same article. Although using a lock-step strategy would make things simpler for me as the instructor, in that everyone would have to respond to the same research articles, I have found that many students, especially graduate students, are not interested in topics that I think are interesting! My experience is that giving students the freedom to follow their own interests increases student motivation and appreciation for the course. It also enhances their confidence in their ability to find and work with published research. Finally, it encourages autonomous thinking.

FINAL COMMENTS

My hope is that this book is a useful tool for achieving the goal of helping readers who work with language issues to become discerning consumers of research. Whether it is used as a textbook or independently studied, I believe that anyone wanting to improve his or her ability to understand research will find this book instrumental for achieving this goal. However, it is also important to keep in mind that this is just an introduction with the intention of providing a framework with which to begin one's search for answers to research questions related to language matters.

ACKNOWLEDGMENTS

I could not have imagined when I sat down at my computer in a small apartment in Almaty, Kazakstan, during my first sabbatical, what a challenging journey I was about to undertake to write this book. Now, looking back, I can clearly see that I would not have completed this journey without the assistance of many along the way.

First, I must thank my heavenly Father, without whom I would never have had the energy or perseverance to complete this book.

On a more human level, I owe much to the candid comments of those who have reviewed this manuscript at various stages: Mary McGroarty, Northern Arizona University; G. Richard Tucker, Carnegie Mellon University; Jessica Williams, University of Illinois, Chicago; and a reviewer who wanted to remain anonymous. Without their constructive insights, this book would have never arrived at the end of the tunnel.

In addition, others have been so kind to have edited various editions of the manuscript: several colleagues at the American University in Cairo, Deena Borai and Russanne Hozayen; my daughter, Juleen R. Keevy; my wife, Karen Kay; and a friend who does this for a living, Barbara Martensen—they all helped catch many editorial errors and make constructive comments.

I also want to thank my graduate assistants whom I have had over time to aid me on this book: Hanna Bokhtar, Hayam William Mikhail, Germin Sanad, Heba Saber El Sayed, and Dahlia Hassan Sennara. They have worked hard at providing me extra hands and legs for obtaining and entering data into a large database of information. Also, thanks to Susan Zamora, who initiated the list of journals several years ago, which has now evolved into Appendix C. There are also the many MA graduate students who have been willing to experiment with me on how best to become consumers of research. I trust that they will share the positive emotions of close relatives at the birth of a child.

Last, I want to thank Naomi Silverman, the senior editor, along with her staff at Lawrence Erlbaum Associates, who have given me a world of encouragement and professional advice during this entire process.

If this book meets your needs, as it has with my students, I invite you to work with me in making future editions even better. Please send me any comments; I guarantee they will be taken very seriously and contribute to future changes where possible.

List of Acronyms and Abbreviations

ACRONYMS

AAAL: American Association for Applied Linguistics

ACTFL: American Council on the Teaching of Foreign Languages

AERA: American Educational Research Association

APA: American Psychological Association

CAE: Cambridge Certificate in Advanced English

CIJE: Current Index to Journals in Education

ERIC: Educational Resources Information Center

IATEFL: International Association of Teachers of English as a Foreign Language

IELTS: International English Language Testing System

LLBA: Language Teaching, Linguistics and Language Behavior Abstracts

MLA: Modern Language Association

MLAIB: Modern Language Association International Bibliography

RIE: Resources in Education

TESOL: Teachers of English to Speakers of Other Languages

TIRF: TESOL International Research Foundation

TOEFL: Test of English as a Foreign Language

ABBREVIATIONS

DV: dependent variable
EFL: English as a foreign language
ESL: English as a second language
EV: extraneous variables
FL: foreign language
IV: independent variable
L1: first language
L2: second language
MV: moderating variable
NNS: non-native speakers
NS: native speakers
OV: observational variables

FUNDAMENTALS FOR DISCERNING CONSUMERS

Chapter 1

Understanding the Nature of Research

INTRODUCTION

The amount of research in applied linguistics pouring off the presses to-day is staggering. The Teachers of English to Speakers of Other Languages (TESOL) Web site[1] references 53 journals that specialize in research in ap-plied linguistics, not to mention many other journals that include related articles. Some journals are monthly, others are quarterly. Can you imagine how many research studies are published in just 1 year?

So what is all this research about? Whom is it all for? Is it important? If so, how can we understand it better? Briefly, I answer these questions, but the main purpose of this book is to answer the last question—How can we com-prehend it all?

What Is All This Research About?

A quick answer to this question is that this research tries to provide answers to massive numbers of research questions being generated around the world in the field of applied linguistics. By *applied linguistics*, I agree with the definition given by the Department of Linguistics and Applied Linguistics at the University of Melbourne, Australia, which stated in its Web site,

> Applied Linguistics is concerned with practical issues involving language in the life of the community. The most important of these is the learning of sec-ond or foreign languages. Others include language policy, multilingualism,

---

[1]http://www.tesol.org/pubs/author/books/demystifygrids.html. Retrieved January 10, 2004.

language education, the preservation and revival of endangered languages, and the assessment and treatment of language difficulties.

Other areas of interest include professional communication, for example, between doctors and their patients, between lawyers and their clients and in courtrooms, as well as other areas of institutional and cross-cultural communication ranging from the boardroom to the routines on an answer-phone. (http://www.linguistics.unimelb.edu.au/about/about.html)

In other words, research in the field of applied linguistics covers a vast domain of topics that deals with just about anything where language relates to society.

Who Is All This Research For?

It is for you, the person who, for whatever reason, wants or needs to gain a better understanding about language issues that are important to him or her. This includes the following:

- Master of Arts students in applied linguistics
- Teachers of second/foreign languages
- Administrators of second/foreign language programs
- Parents of students in language programs

Is All of This Research Really That Important?

To answer a question with a question, "Is language important?" Needless to say, language is the backbone of society. It is one of the major characteristics of being human. Without it we would not know the world as we know it today. Literally everything that humanity has achieved would not have taken place without language. Consequently, to study language and all that it means in society is one of the major challenges that I believe we have before us today. For example, significant strides made in applied linguistic research have aided us in the improvement of teaching and learning of languages throughout the world. Hopefully, this will contribute to humanity's understanding of one another and improve the quality of life in an atmosphere of world peace.

If Applied Linguistics Research Is So Important, How Can We Understand It Better?

This book is specifically designed to answer this question. I have divided it into two parts. The first consists of this chapter and chapter 2, which provide you with a foundation for working with the remaining chapters. This chapter introduces the concept of the *discerning consumer* and the meaning of research. The second chapter gives tools for finding research reports based on your own interests. Quickly mastering these simple guidelines will make accessible a wealth of information that can have a major impact on your career.

The chapters in the second part of the book are structured around the typical format used in published research. In them you will be given a set of criteria with which to evaluate each component of a research study. For each criterion, you are given excerpts from published research to illustrate how it is used for evaluation. By the end of the book, you should be able to approach any published study in applied linguistics with confidence to not only understand it, but to evaluate its value for practical applications.

Overview

This chapter attempts to lay a foundation in building a framework for understanding a typical research study. I begin by defining the term *discerning consumer* and then argue for the importance of becoming one. This is followed by an attempt to demythologize how research is perceived by many people and then describe what it typically means to the applied linguistics community. In this description, a schematic understanding of the driving force behind research, the research question, is provided. With this perspective, you will be ready for the following chapters.

WHO IS A DISCERNING CONSUMER OF RESEARCH?

The term *consumer* in the business world means a customer—someone who buys and uses a product. In a similar fashion, the reader of research is a consumer in that s/he uses research for specific purposes. To some degree, the reader of research might *buy into* the research product, if not actually pay money to obtain access to the research study.

There are two basic types of consumers: *casual* and *discerning*. The *casual* consumer is one who passively reads selective pieces of a research article out of curiosity. In the business world, s/he is the window-shopper who looks, but does not buy. However, the *discerning* consumer does more than window-shop. S/he wants to use research for practical purposes; s/he wants to read research reports from beginning to end with a level of understanding that can be used to address both theoretical and practical issues. I use the word *discerning* in two senses: *penetrating* and *discriminating*. In the first sense, the discerning consumer is given the necessary tools to penetrate beyond the surface of the text to analyze the rationale behind the procedures used and interpretations made. In the second sense, the discerning consumer is able to discriminate between strong and weak research studies by applying the criteria that s/he will study in this book to make value judgments.

However, by a discerning consumer, I do not mean a *hypercritical consumer*. The key word here is *discernment*, not faultfinding. I do not want readers to become cynics who delight in slamming researchers on every little perceived weakness and group all research as worthless. Rather, the discerning consumer is one who has self-confidence in his or her own ability to gauge research so that s/he can evaluate the influence a study should have on practical issues of concern. When this objective is reached, research journals will no longer be looked on as forbidding, boring documents that only university professors dare to read. Rather, they will be regarded as important sources of evidence or counterevidence that can be used in arguing the pros and/or cons of implementing new ideas and methodologies in the classroom.

WHY BE A CONSUMER OF RESEARCH?

Many students, teachers, and administrators are looking for practical information that will help them in their studies, teaching, or program development, respectively. They typically do not want to get overburdened with hypothetical theories. They want immediate and practical information that they can use. They want to know how to teach a foreign (or second) language such as English. They want to know what materials to use and what method works best.

However, there is no one way to teach. There is no one set of materials that can be used in every situation. We must make decisions, and these decisions must have some rationale for support. We must decide what, how, and when to teach based on the needs of the learner. We need to know how the learner thinks and feels, and what the best time is for teaching certain material via a certain methodology. To make these decisions, we must gather information, and this information is obtained through reading and doing research.

Unfortunately, I have seen many people in language teaching over the years jump on various bandwagons regarding what to teach, how to teach, and how the learner acquires a language. I have seen various charismatic experts sway audiences of teachers to accept their viewpoint as if it were the absolute truth. However, when the content of what was said was examined, little solid evidence was provided to back up the conjectures. Yet teachers pour out of the conference doors, back to their classrooms, heralding the latest jargon, thinking that they have come on the most revolutionary thing they have ever heard. Programs are changed, new curricula are developed, and training sessions in new methodologies are imposed on the faculty. Yet have we really advanced in our discipline? The answer is often in the negative.

To avoid wasting time, money, and human energy, and to prevent being led down the garden path, I argue that we must attend to what is happening in research. Yes, this will slow things down. People will become frustrated that they must wait for answers. They want quick solutions to their problems. They do not want to delay until the verdict comes in through research. Maybe an answer might never be forthcoming. What then? My response is that if we are unable to see some results based on careful research to guide us, we had better not take this route anyway. Money in education is too limited to go out on wild goose chases to find out 5 years down the road that the latest fad was a waste of time.

To avoid this, we must learn to read research in applied linguistics with a discerning eye. The purpose of this book is to help do exactly this: guide you in becoming a discerning consumer.

THE MOTIVATION BEHIND RESEARCH

To become a discerning consumer, we need to have a clear understanding of the driving force behind the research process. However, we require a working definition of the meaning of research first. Today it has many meanings, but much of what is called *research* would not be considered so by the scientific community. The purpose of this section is to explain how most professional researchers understand research by making contrasts with more commonly used definitions of research.

Demythologizing Research

Research Does Not Mean Searching for Articles to Write Papers. Probably the most common misconception about research is confusing it with papers we were asked to write back in secondary school or during our undergraduate days at university—projects often referred to as *research papers*. Typically, such assignments mean that students go to the library and (re)search for a number of articles from a variety of sources. Then they integrate the gathered information from these articles through summarizing and paraphrasing into papers addressing issues of importance with correct footnoting and referencing. However, the skills used in writing such papers, although important to research, should *not* be regarded as research.

The fact is, the consumer of research will spend most of his or her time in this searching activity. Even the researcher has to spend a lot of time in the library looking up research articles. Both consumer and researcher have to summarize and paraphrase research articles and then integrate them into logical arguments. Both have to document everything and take care in referencing. However, these skills are especially needed at the preliminary stage of information gathering. After this, research begins in earnest.

Working Only in Laboratories With Artificial Experiments. A second common misconception about research is to think that it only involves people in white coats working in spotless, white-walled laboratories running experimental tests on helpless rats or people. Included with this stereotype are graduate students sitting at computers analyzing statistical data with the hope of graduating one day.

These caricatures discourage many people from either reading research or doing it. Fortunately, it is not a true representation of what research is all about. Research is done in many different environments, such as classrooms, homes, schools, and even on the street. Few people wear white coats anymore except in chemical and animal laboratories. Most researchers whom I know would not look any different from many people we see on the street on any given shopping day. As for computers, many people have them in their homes for their children to do their homework or play games. Computers have become so user-friendly now that anyone can use them for all sorts of everyday applications. As for practicality, research results have been applied to help solve some important problems in the language classroom.

The Meaning of True Research

Research is the process whereby questions are raised and answers are sought by carefully gathering, analyzing, and interpreting data. In some cases, answers are hypothesized, predictions made, and data collected to support or discredit hypothesized answers. Figures 1.1 and 1.2 provide a general framework that encompasses the entire research process. Figure 1.1 illustrates the first phase, how research questions are formulated, and Fig. 1.2 summarizes the second phase, finding the answers.

The *heart* of both figures is the *research question*. It is the beginning of the research process and the focus of both the consumer and researcher. Any given research question asks, explicitly or implicitly, either *what* or *why*. The following are examples of how these two generic questions typically manifest themselves:

"What" questions:
What phenomena are of importance?
In what context do these phenomena occur?
What important relationships exist between phenomena?

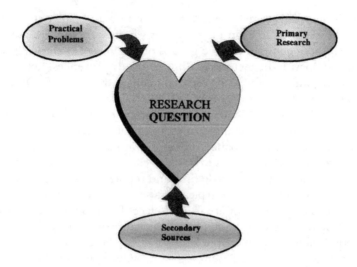

FIG. 1.1. Sources for research questions.

"Why" questions (Causation):
Why do these phenomena occur?
Why do people differ on certain traits?

Identifying Important Questions

The motivating force behind research is the inherent curiosity of human beings to solve problems. We see phenomena around us, and we begin to ask questions: What is something made of? How did it get here? How does one phenomenon relate to another? Does one phenomenon cause another one to exist, decrease, or increase?

Our questions usually arise from several sources. Probably one of the most common sources is from observing *practical problems* (Fig. 1.1) in the language classroom. Every day, teachers and administrators are confronted with issues that require informed answers. For example, Ferris (1995) noted that teachers believe that feedback on student compositions is important based on the fact that they spend a lot of time providing feedback to help their students. This led her to question whether such feedback actually helps students improve their writing. Was this an important question? I would think so because teachers who are strapped for time when correcting homework need to know whether all the time they are taking to give written feedback really makes an impact.

Another question posed by Arva and Medgyes (2000) came from the observed phenomenon that the number of non-native teachers of English as a second/foreign language has exceeded the number of native speakers who teach ESL/EFL. Their main question was whether there were any behavioral differences between the two groups of teachers. Their corollary questions had to do with the factors causing observed differences. Related issues have also become the focus of research promoted by the TESOL International Research Foundation (TIRF).[2]

The second place where important research questions are often identified is *secondary sources.* I discuss these in more detail in chapter 2, but for now textbooks and theoretical papers presented at conferences are examples. These sources are referred to as *secondary* because they summarize other people's research rather than provide firsthand reports by the original researchers. Authors of such literature typically raise questions that need to be addressed. For this reason, they are fruitful places for finding current research questions being asked by the applied linguistics community.

A good example of an application of this type of source in research comes from an article by Carrier (1999). Although published in a research journal, this article is not firsthand research. Instead it is an argument for the need to research the roles that status between native speakers (NS) and non-native speakers (NNS) plays in listening comprehension. Carrier concluded by raising several questions for future research: What differences are there between reactions of NS and NNS listeners due to status? Are these differences due to culture? There are many articles like Carrier's that end with a list of questions for further research.

The third resource for identifying important questions is the place I later suggest we look for answers (i.e., *primary research*).[3] In fact this is one of the most rewarding locations for discovering current questions being asked by the applied linguistics community. The better versed we are in the research literature, the more aware we become of the missing pieces in our framework of knowledge. For instance, we might notice that most of the research addressing a particular question has used a small number of people as subjects. This is not unusual because it is common practice for researchers to use small groups of available students from their own programs as research subjects. On careful examination, we begin to realize that important characteristics of the group of students we teach are not represented in the samples used in previous studies. This raises the question of how to generalize the findings to answer questions related to our students. We might have a suspicion that our group would behave differently. Such reasoning should lead us to be cautious toward making any practical recommendations based

---

[2]www.tirfonline.org. Retrieved January 10, 2004.

[3]*Primary research* is research that is reported firsthand by the person(s) who actually performed the study.

on such research. We would need to look for other studies using samples that are more similar to our students to see whether the same results occur. More is said on this matter in chapter 4.

Issues other than sampling might also lead us to raise important questions from previous research. The type of material used in a treatment, the method for administering a treatment, and the way in which the data were analyzed are often places where gaps might be found. Future research is needed to help complete the bigger picture before our own questions can be answered. I address these issues in the following chapters of this book.

Besides looking for incongruities in research studies, the next best place to look for research questions is in the Discussion/Conclusion section of a study, usually identified by the terms *limitations* and *recommendations for further research*. Major, Fitzmaurice, Bunta, and Balasubramanian (2002), for example, noted in their Discussion section two limitations in their study on the effects of non-native accents used in assessments for measuring listening proficiency. One limitation was in the design of their study, in which they made the assumption that the lectures they used were equal in difficulty. The second limitation was the possibility that the accents they used in the study were not representative of accents used by the majority of university instructors. Research questions immediately arise from these limitations. Based on the first limitation, this question emerges: Would similar findings occur if the difficulty of the assessments for the lectures were not equally difficult? From the second limitation, we might ask: What set of accents best represents the non-native accents of instructors in English universities? Based on these, the next step would be to find whether there were any answers to these questions—which leads us to the following section.

At this point in the chapter, I suggest that you stop and reflect on some of the questions you might have regarding language teaching and/or learning. Complete the following exercise and share the results with colleagues for discussion.

Exercise 1.1

1. Identify a question you have in the area of teaching or learning a language based on:
   a. your own experience.
   b. your reading of a secondary source.
   c. the discussion section of a research article.
2. Why do you think these questions are important for others besides yourself?

Where Are the Answers?

The purpose of research is not only to raise questions, but to provide answers to our questions. Unfortunately, most people look for answers in the opinions of famous people before going to primary research. Such opinions are found in textbooks, published papers, and public presentations. However, before expert opinions can have any weight, they must be supported by research. Regrettably, some opinions are given without supporting research and would be recognized for what they are: educated guesses and no more. They should not be given the same status as statements that are supported by research no matter how famous the person is. However, such opinions can be used as *potential* answers and subjected to research, as indicated by the arrow going to the Proposed Answer oval in Fig. 1.2. To draw a direct arrow from Expert Opinion to Research Question is not allowed, although some people, either intentionally or unintentionally, try to make this leap of faith.

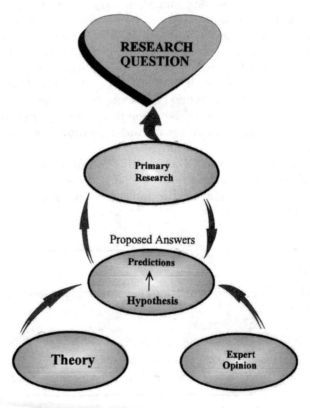

FIG. 1.2.   Sources for answers to research questions.

Theories are especially developed to generate proposed answers, as Fig. 1.2 exhibits. A theory is an attempt to interrelate large sets of observed phenomena and/or constructs into meaningful pictures. In applied linguistics, we do not have any all-encompassing theories that provide explanations for all the phenomena that have been observed in language learning. However, a number of mini-theories, also known as *theoretical models*, like Chomsky's (2000) theory of Generative Grammar, are constantly being developed to tie subsets of constructs together. Some more traditional theoretical models that you may encounter in your reading are Chomsky's Universal Grammar, Krashen's Monitor Model, Selinker's Inter-language Model (Omaggio-Hadley, 1993), and Schumann's Acculturation Model (Schumann, 1986). These and many more are attempts to give meaning to the many observed phenomena that we encounter in applied linguistics.

Occasionally, you will come across studies that compare and contrast various theoretical models. The article previously mentioned by Carrier (1999) did exactly this. She looked at five theoretical models in her search for an answer to the question of why people vary in listening comprehension. I chose three for illustration:

- The Social Accommodation Theory by Giles, Bourhis, and Taylor, which proposes the effects of social status on language behavior.
- Social Interaction Theory by Wolfson, which adds social distance to status and how they affect interpersonal negotiations.
- Interpersonal Perception Theory by Laing, which argues that the perceived relationship with the speaker will affect listening.

Based on her overview of these theoretical models, she proposed that sociolinguistic factors such as status play an important role in the listening comprehension of foreign language (FL) or second language (L2) learners. However, she did not stop there. She continued by mentioning that she had begun a research study to investigate whether her suggestion had any merit.

Previously, I mentioned how theories interrelate various *constructs*. A construct is a concept that a given discipline (e.g., applied linguistics) has constructed to identify some quality that is thought to exist. One of the popular constructs that applied linguists have formulated is *communicative competence*.

Constructs are defined in two different ways: either by using other constructs or by operational definitions. For example, Canale and Swain (1980) defined *communicative competency* with four other constructs: grammatical competency, sociolinguistic competency, discourse competency, and strategic competency. This does not shed too much light on what communicative competency is, except that it is broken down into four abstract components.

Before a construct like communicative competence can be of any use in research, it must be defined operationally. An *operational definition* is one that defines a construct in observable terms. Bachman and Palmer (1996), for example, refined the four constructs of Canale and Swain (1980) with further definitions. For instance, *strategic competency* was defined as consisting of meta-cognitive strategies (note, another construct). However, they operationally defined one of the meta-cognitive strategies *goal setting* as "identifying and selecting one or more tasks that s/he might attempt to complete and deciding whether or not to attempt to complete the task(s)" (Bachman & Cohen, 1998, p. 7). The construct is now defined in such a way that it can be observed and used for research study.

Another construct that has been given a lot of attention in the literature related to motivation (also a construct) is *willingness to communicate* (WTC; MacIntyre, Baker, Clément, & Donovan, 2002). MacIntyre et al. (2002) defined this as "an underlying continuum representing the predisposition toward or away from communicating, given the choice" (p. 538). Again, as you can see, they have defined this construct with another construct, "a *predisposition* toward or away from communicating . . ." (p. 538). Later in the article, they operationally defined WTC as a score on the "McCroskey and Baer's . . . 20-item willingness to communicate scale . . . that asked students to indicate the chances . . . of their initiating a conversation in each of 20 situations" (p. 544). Often constructs are operationally defined in terms of performance on some form of data-gathering instrument.

Going back to Fig. 1.2, when theory generates a potential answer to a research question, the answer is in the form of a theoretical hypothesis. These are theoretical explanations that propose how several constructs relate to one another. For example, in his article, which addressed whether adult second language learners learn grammar differently than children learning their first language, Zhongganggao (2001) presented Bley-Vroman's Fundamental Difference Hypothesis. This hypothesizes that children differ in three ways from adults when acquiring a language: cognitive states, language faculty, and availability of the language acquisition system. If this hypothesis receives sufficient support from research, we might conclude that adult second language learners do not learn grammar the same way children learn their L1 (i.e., without instruction). This would have direct application toward what and how we teach in the classroom.

As Fig. 1.2 illustrates, hypotheses can also come out of previous research. (Note the arrows going back and forth between the hypothesis and primary research ovals.) Often larger theoretical models are not yet available from which to generate hypotheses. However, this does not stop researchers from trying to hypothesize why phenomena occur. When results repeat themselves over a number of studies, hypotheses can be formulated in an attempt to explain them. A study that illustrates this was done by Akamatsu (2002), who investigated what factors in a reader's L1 affected word recognition in L2. Three hypotheses were stated. The first was drawn from Seidenberg's "universal direct access hypothesis" (p. 120), which proposes that there would be no differences due to a reader's L1 orthographical system on recognizing L2 vocabulary. The second and third hypotheses were based on previous research that contradicted the Seidenberg hypothesis. Both of them were variations on the same theme, proposing that a reader's L1 would have an impact on word recognition in an L2.

Hypotheses are of two basic types depending on the nature of the research question. One type is *relational*; that is, if the question asks whether one construct relates to another, the hypothesis would state that there is a relationship. In effect, this means that as one construct changes (or varies), there is some degree of change in the other construct. For instance, a student of mine formulated the hypothesis that a relationship exists between students' attitudes toward writing in English and their proficiency in English as a foreign language, based on a review of theory and previous research. The two constructs in this hypothesis are *attitude toward writing* and *language proficiency*. In other words, this hypothesis proposes that changes in student attitude toward writing occur in conjunction with changes in language proficiency. Note that this hypothesis does not say that attitude toward writing *affects* language proficiency.

An example from research is found in Pichette, Segalowitz, and Connors' (2003) study where they addressed the question concerning the relationship between L1 reading skill (Construct 1) with L2 reading skills (Construct 2). They tested two hypotheses that provide possible answers: Clarke's (1980) short-cut hypothesis, and Hacquebord's (1989) transfer hypothesis. The first, also known as "*the language threshold hypothesis*" (Pichette et al., 2003, p. 87), proposes that the two constructs only relate to one another if the L2 has been adequately developed. The second hypothesis states that the reading skill in both languages is related if the reader keeps active reading in his or her L1.

The second type of hypothesis is *causal*, in that it states that one construct *causes* changes in a second construct. A study that illustrates this was done by Rodriguez and Sadoski (2000), who examined the effects of different learning strategies on L2 vocabulary learning. They used Paivio's (1991) Dual Coding Theory to explain why the mnemonic methods of keyword and contextual produce superior vocabulary learning compared with nonmnemonic rote memory techniques. Briefly, the theory states that information processed at both iconic/echoic (nonverbal) and semantic (verbal) levels is better learned than that being processed at just one level. As an additional note, causal hypotheses can be easily identified by the use of such verbs as *affect, influence, determine, impact, change,* and so on when connecting the two constructs.

Both relational and causal hypotheses are either *directional* or *nondirectional.* These terms are used to specify the precise nature of the relationship between the two constructs. In the case of a relational hypothesis, a directional hypothesis designates whether there is a positive or negative relationship. A *positive relationship* simply means that as one construct increases so does the other one. A *negative relationship* means that as one construct increases the other decreases. If a relational hypothesis does not state clearly whether the relation is positive or negative, then it is nondirectional, meaning that the researchers are not sure which direction the relationship will manifest. The study by Pichette et al. (2003), mentioned previously, clearly had directional hypotheses. They posed that there was a positive relationship between L1 and L2 reading skills in both of the hypotheses they tested. Their results support the Clarke hypothesis, but only partially support the Hacquebord one.

Causal hypotheses can also be directional or nondirectional. If a hypothesis proposes that one construct will cause change in a second construct in a certain direction, then it is directional. However, if it only poses that there will be a change without stating which direction the change will take place, it is nondirectional.

On what bases, you might ask, do some researchers make directional hypotheses and others do not? The answer lies in whether there is a theory or enough previous research to warrant the assertion that the results of the study will show a specific direction. I think you will find most studies have nondirectional hypotheses, if they have them at all.

Hypotheses are usually stated in terms of abstract constructs. Yet as mentioned previously, unless the constructs are defined *operationally,* the hypotheses are difficult to test. When the constructs are transformed into operational definitions, the hypotheses become *predictions* (cf. Fig. 1.2). In this form, the hypotheses can be tested. For example, in the Rodriguez and Sadoski (2000) study previously mentioned, the two levels of the Dual Coding Theory were operationally defined by using the mnemonic techniques of context and keyword methods, whereas the nonmnemonic method was defined as rote rehearsal of new vocabulary. *Retention of vocabulary* was operationally defined as performance on a cued-recall test. They made four predictions based on these definitions, two of which were: (a) the keyword and context methods would produce superior results to the rote-rehearsal group, and (b) the keyword/context combined method would further improve vocabulary learning over the keyword and context methods individually. In this more concrete format, the hypotheses can be tested.

Once the predictions are made, the hypothesis can be tested in primary research (cf. Fig. 1.2). Rodriguez and Sadoski (2000) did exactly this by carrying out their study to test the overall hypothesis. Notice here that I use the phrase *primary research* rather than *published research* in contrast to Fig. 1.1. Primary research is research reported firsthand by the researcher(s). Not all primary research is published; some research is presented orally at conferences, and some never see the light of day. I discuss this more thoroughly in chapter 2.

As you can see in Fig. 1.2, all roads eventually lead to primary research for answering our questions. The results either *support* the hypothesis or *refute* it. Note that I did not say *prove* the hypothesis. *No theory or hypothesis has ever been proved*, although you would not get this impression after hearing some people talk about their pet theory. At best, a hypothesis may be supported, in which case we have a tentative answer to our question, not a conclusive one. If the results fail to support a hypothesis, the hypothesis is then *refuted*, meaning that it can be rejected as a possible answer.

I need to warn you that Fig. 1.2 could be misleading if we are not careful. You might get the impression that one needs all of the elements in this figure before we can answer our questions. In fact all of the ovals in the figure, except the ones for primary research and the research questions, are not necessary. As I explain in further chapters, there are cases where researchers tackle questions without any previous theories or hypotheses. They are going in with open minds, trying to uncover new information without having their perceptions biased by expectations imposed on them by any given theory. This research is exploratory and usually is seeking answers to What type questions. Do not be mistaken, however; just because there is no theory or hypothesis attached, it does not make it inferior. In fact you will find that there is much more exploratory research published than there is research testing hypotheses. More is said about research designs in chapter 5.

In conclusion, the emphasis I want to make here is that there is no other place to find support for possible answers to our questions than from reading primary research. After a thorough search, we might find that sufficient evidence has been presented in answer to our questions. Yet if we find that our questions have not been answered adequately by previous research, we still benefit greatly by knowing that there remains the need for more research. At least we will be prevented from going down the proverbial garden path, wasting time and resources.

In preparation for your own search for studies, the next chapter shows how you can access primary research for yourself. I think you will be surprised when you discover how much is readily available for your perusal.

Before you move on to the next chapter, however, I suggest you work through this next exercise to help you apply the information you have just covered.

Exercise 1.2

1. Define the following constructs (in observable terms):
   a. Motivation
   b. Anxiety
   c. Listening comprehension
   d. Attitude

   How did you define them? With other constructs or operationally?

2. In each of the following hypotheses, first underline the constructs. Then identify whether each hypothesis is *relational* or *causal* and explain your reasoning.
   a. Level of income influences second language acquisition.
   b. The more L2 learners are anxious, the slower they will learn a second language.
   c. The level of motivation will determine how well pronunciation is learned.
   d. The more positive L2 learners feel about the country of the language they are learning, the better they will do in their L2 courses.

3. Using the same hypotheses, determine whether each is directional or nondirectional and explain your reasoning. If it is relational and directional, is it negative or positive?

Key Terms and Concepts

applied linguistics

construct

discerning consumer

hypothesis

    causal

    directional versus nondirectional

    refuted

    relational

operational definition

positive versus negative relationships

prediction

primary research

research versus search

secondary sources

theory

Additional Recommended Reading

The following references provide information on the various topics that are currently being studied along with excellent examples of related studies.

Bonch-Bruevich, X., Crawford, W. J., Hellermann, J., Higgins, C., & Nguyen, H. (Eds.). (2001). *Past, present, and future of second language research: Selected proceedings of the 2000 Second Language Research Forum.* Somerville, MA: Cascadilla.

Breen, M. P. (2001). *Learner contributions to language learning: New direction in research.* New York: Longman.

Byrnes, H. (Ed.). (1998). *Learning foreign and second languages: Perspectives in research and scholarship.* New York: Modern Language Association of America.

Casanave, C. P. (2004). *Controversies in second language writing: Dilemmas and decisions in research and instruction.* Ann Arbor, MI: University of Michigan Press.

Doughty, C. J., & Long, M. (Eds.). (2003). *Handbook of second language acquisition.* Williston, VT: Blackwell.

Ellis, R. (1997). *SLA research and language teaching.* Oxford: Oxford University Press.

Phillips, J. K., & Terry, R. M. (Eds.). (1999). *Foreign language standards: Linking research, theories, and practices.* Chicago: National Textbook Company.

Tucker, G. R., Lightbown, P. M., Snow, C., Christian, D., de Bot, K., Lynch, B. K., Nunan, D., Duff, P. A., Freeman, D., & Bailey, K. M. (2001). Identifying research priorities: Themes and directions for the TESOL International Research Foundation. *TESOL Quarterly, 35,* 595–616.

How to Locate Research

CHAPTER OVERVIEW

In chapter 1, I talked about generating research questions and searching for answers by looking into previous research. This chapter shows how you can find research studies that might provide potential answers to your questions. I first identify some of the main sources where you can find such research along with examples that walk you through the necessary steps for using them. I then give you guidelines on how to distinguish among the different types of published articles and how to weigh their value for answering questions. Finally, I provide you with suggestions for obtaining the articles you need. If this is all new to you, I have supplied a list of journals related to applied linguistics in Appendix B for your perusal to help you get started.

WHERE TO LOOK AND WHAT TO LOOK FOR

Remember the main goal is to find *primary research*. As stated in chapter 1, primary research is the only way we can test proposed answers to our research questions. As mentioned earlier, the amount of research currently published is overwhelming. New journals arrive on the scene practically every year, dedicated to new areas of interest in the research community. Accessing this research can be a real challenge.

Although the amount of research being published continues to increase, do not despair. Today is the day of personal computers and the Internet, which make the task of finding relevant research much easier. If you have not yet developed an appreciation for these two technological advances, I strongly recommend that you take advantage of any training you might be able to get. It is well worth the investment in time and money.

These days you can often sit at your computer at home and access the information you need. Not only are you able to find out what and where studies are published, but you can often download them into your computer for reading and printing. What used to take many hours of work can be done in a matter of minutes. No longer do you have to go to the library to page through gigantic indexes trying to read type so small that you need a magnifying glass. The only disadvantage is that you miss the physical exercise of going to and from the library, not to mention the running around within the library looking for material.

There are three places where you can locate primary research: *preliminary sources, secondary sources,* and *tables of references/bibliographies.*

Preliminary Sources

Fortunately, a number of people have gone to the trouble of preparing sources to help us find research. Publications that lead us to primary research are known as *preliminary sources.* Some of the more traditional ones that can be found in bound copies in most university libraries are *Educational Index, Current Index to Journals in Education (CIJE), Language Teaching, Linguistics and Language Behavior Abstracts (LLBA), Modern Language Association (MLA) International Bibliography, Social Science Index, Psychological Abstracts,* and *Resources in Education (RIE).* Both the CIJE and RIE are produced by the Educational Resources Information Center (ERIC). All of these sources are organized by a set of *keywords* that reveal the focus of the study.

Keywords are useful for locating research articles. If you have an idea about what you are interested in, you can use the substantive words contained in your research question to guide you in looking up related studies. For example, let us say that you have formulated the question: "What is the relationship between anxiety and language learning?" The keywords in your question are *anxiety* and *language learning.* You would then search the earlier sources using these two key terms to locate relevant studies.

However, thanks to the computer age, many of the bound preliminary sources have now been converted to electronic databases[1] and put on *CD-ROM* disks and/or into Web sites on the Internet. *ERIC,* the *LLBA,* and *Modern Language Association International Bibliography* are all on CD-ROM. These can be accessed from a computer if your library has the equipment

---

[1]A database is an electronic storehouse of information that contains references to papers consisting of authors, dates, titles, and abstracts, and how to obtain the material. More frequently, the entire paper can be retrieved through the database.

to run CDs. You can also purchase these CDs with annual upgrades, although they can be costly. These databases and many others are available on the Internet through your library, such as *Academic Search Premier*, *PsychInfo*, and *Sociological Abstracts*. Another database, *JSTOR*, contains some valuable data and goes back as far as the 1800s.

A Walk-Through Example. To familiarize you with the use of an electronic database in your search for studies, I chose ERIC as an example. Although there are many other useful databases, this is the most accessible one on the Internet from almost any location. Moreover, both the *CIJE* and *RIE* have been made available through ERIC on the Internet.

If you are near a computer and have access to the Internet, try following the steps as you read along.

1. Go to the Web site www.eric.ed.gov; you will be taken to the main Web page for ERIC. This screen welcomes you to the ERIC Database, which is the gateway to more research than you will ever be able to read in your lifetime! The database currently contains research from 1966 onward and is updated often.

2. Put the cursor on **ERIC Search** and click the left button on the mouse. This takes you to the **Basic Search** screen.

3. There is a box in which you can type the keyword(s) that you are looking for. Type in the word *anxiety* and click on **Search**. This should result in over 9,000 references.

4. Obviously, there are many research articles in this list that do not relate to your research question. To narrow the list down to articles pertinent to your question, click **Back to Search** and click on **Advanced Search**.

4.1. This screen opens up a number of ways to limit your search. In the **Publication Type(s)** window scroll down and click on **Journal Articles** then click **Search**. By doing this you will limit your search to research that is published in research journals.

4.2. Having done this, I got a list of 3,973 references to research published since 1966 that contain the word *anxiety*.

5. Now type both of your keywords in: *anxiety* in the first box and *language learning* in the next box separated by an *AND*. The word *AND* is an **Operator**. (To get more information on Research Operators click on **Searching Tips**.) When I did this, the computer responded with 130 studies that deal in some way with these two terms from 1966 to 2003.

5.1. However, if you are only interested in research done within a certain time gap, you can click on the year you want to begin and the year you want to end by scrolling down either the **From** or **to** boxes under **Publication Date**. When I limited this search to the years 1990 to 2003, ERIC returned 80 references.

6.   If you choose the **Advanced Search** option you will have more choices to guide your search. You can use more terms, varying your choices of either **Keywords**, **Author** names, **Titles** to articles, and much more. You can also combine categories with the operators *AND, NOT,* or *OR.*

You can view the results either in **Table** or **List** format. The **Table** format gives you the title, author, publication date, ERIC number, and a button for further details, respectively.

Anxiety About Foreign Language Learning among High School Women, Ganschow, Leonore; Sparks, Richard, 1996. EJ527751

In the **List** format, the journal name, publication type, and journal citation are added along with an abstract.

In either format you can click on a **Details** button to obtain additional information, part of which is shown in the following example. I have added in italics some explanations for ERIC's terminology for further explanation.

ERIC #: EJ527751[2]

Title:	Anxiety About Foreign Language Learning among High School Women.
Authors:	Ganschow, Leonore; Sparks, Richard
Descriptors:	Analysis of Variance; *Anxiety; *Females; High School Students; *Language Aptitude; *Language Proficiency; *Memory; *Second Language Learning; Semantics; Test Results; Testing (*Same as keywords used in ERIC's thesaurus*)
Journal Name:	Modern Language Journal
Journal Citation:	v80 n2 p199-212 Sum 1996
Publication Date:	1995
Abstract:	Examines the relationship between anxiety and native-language skill and foreign-language aptitude measures among high school foreign-language learners using the Foreign Language Classroom Anxiety Scale (FLCAS). Findings suggest that skill in one's native language may affect aptitude for learning a foreign language and that

---

[2]The EJ = found in a published journal; ED = a document other than in a journal. The number is used for accession.

the FLCAS may provide an early indicator of basic language problems. (65 references) (Author/CK) (*Initials of
the abstractor; in this case, the authors were also involved*).

Note that an abstract is given with this output. This is extremely helpful
because it gives you a much better idea as to whether this article is related to
your question. To make things even better, you can save this information
on a floppy disk (if you are doing this from the library's computer) and
carry it home to peruse when you have more time on your own computer.
You can also e-mail the retrieved information to yourself, which I prefer to
do. If you are working from your own computer, you can download the information onto your hard drive. Being able to censor through all of the articles that your search produces will save you many hours of rummaging
through a library, only to realize that many of the studies are not what you
wanted.

Once you have listed out all of the studies that you think would be of interest, you can go to the library to read the entire article or send for it
through ERIC. Increasingly, many of the studies are now available electron-
ically and can be downloaded to your computer if your library has sub-
scribed to this service.

The other online databases mentioned previously, such as the *LLBA,
MLA International Bibliography,* and *PsychInfo,* work similarly to ERIC. However, these are not as accessible as ERIC. So far I have only been able to access these databases through university Web sites, which require identification codes and passwords. If you are a student at a college or university, you
might have access to your own institution's Web site or gain access to an
outside Web site to use these databases.

At my university, I used the same keywords and time frame with the
MLA database as used earlier and received 32 references. Again I repeated the same with the *LLBA* database and got 159 citations. In the
latter case, I obtained more references to studies done internationally.
The same search with *PsychInfo* turned up 30 articles. It is always wise to
search several different databases to make sure there is not some important study out there in cyberspace that would be important for the purpose of your search.

Another Working Example. Let us ask the following question based on
our own observations when visiting homes where parents speak only in
their L1 while their children are trying to learn an L2 outside the home:
How do parents' L1 influence their children's learning of an L2? As outlined before, the first thing to do is search for primary research that addresses the
problem. To do this:

1. Identify the search terms. There are two phrases in our question that may guide us: *parents' L1* and *children's learning of an L2*. I used these as the search terms in an ERIC search. The results were zero hits[3]: No articles came up for viewing. Now what do we do?

2. Play with various combinations of words until some combination produces desirable results. A useful tool to aid us at this point is a *thesaurus*, which most databases such as ERIC provide.

2.1. I clicked on ERIC's thesaurus and typed *parent* in the **Keywords** box. When I clicked on the **Search** button, it jumped down to a section with 242 related *descriptors* about parents. I could scroll down this list to find related terms. Another way to do this, which I used, was to choose the **Browse** button back at the **Thesaurus Search**. This displayed a series of alphabetical **letter buttons** that take you to keywords beginning with the letter you choose. I clicked on P and scrolled down until I came across descriptors with the word *parent*. I clicked on **Parent Influence** to find what descriptors were subordinated under this heading. I found two of interest: **Parent Influence** and **Parents as Teachers**. Notice that I could not find **Parent Language**, so I had to think of something that might be related. I entered the two phrases into the first line of the **Advanced Search** separated by the operator *OR* because I wanted the search to use either of these terms, not necessarily both. Had I used *AND*, both words would have had to appear in the same article before the study would have been selected.

2.2. Next, I needed to find some alternative descriptors for *children's learning of an L2*. I tried *children's language learning*, but captured no hits. I began with a broader term by typing *language learning* in the **Keyword** box and acquired 57 references. I chose **Language Proficiency** and clicked it. From the results, I selected three alternatives: **Language Aptitude**, **Language Fluency**, or **Language Proficiency**. I typed them into the second line in the **Advanced Search** screen separating them with *OR*s. Between the two boxes, I used the operator *AND*. In Box 2.1, I provide a summary of three searches using these terms with three different limiting conditions.

The previous sample exercise helps you realize that phrasing questions may need some imagination if you are to produce fruitful literature searches. I dare say that if a question has any importance, there will be primary research to be found. By playing around with the thesaurus, you will be able to unleash a wealth of material out there in cyberspace. The following exercise gives you another opportunity to put the prior procedures into practice.

---

[3]A *hit* is database language for finding a reference to a paper.

BOX 2.1
ERIC Search Summary

ERIC Advanced Search with **no delimiters**:

Input
Line 1: parent influence or parent as teacher (AND)
Line 2: language aptitude or language fluency or language proficiency (AND)

Results
62 documents found (25 returned) for query : (parent influence or parent as teacher) AND (language aptitude or language fluency or language proficiency)

Advanced Search with **one delimiter**:

Input
Line 1: parent influence or parent as teacher (AND)
Line 2: language aptitude or language fluency or language proficiency (AND)
Limit to Journals

Results
15 documents found (15 returned) for query : (parent influence or parent as teacher) AND (language aptitude or language fluency or language proficiency) AND (080) :publication_type) AND (1965< Publication_Date &lt2003)

Advanced Search with **two delimiters**:

Input
Line 1: parent influence or parent as teacher (AND)
Line 2: language aptitude or language fluency or language proficiency (AND)
Limit to Journals for years 1998 to 2002

Results
2 documents found (2 returned) for query : (parent influence or parent as teacher) AND (language aptitude or language fluency or language proficiency) AND (080): publication_type) AND (1997< Publication_Date &lt2003)

Exercise 2.1

1. Write down a question you think is important for teaching another language.
2. Underline the key phrases.
3. Do an initial search using ERIC or some other database.
   a. How many articles did it turn up? Too many or too few?

   b. If too many, add delimiters to reduce them down to a manageable size. If too few, go to the next step.

4. Look into the ERIC Thesaurus, or the thesaurus of the database available to you, and identify related terms to the ones you have chosen. Plug those into the Search boxes and repeat Steps 1 to 3.

5. When satisfied with your search, print out your results with a report on how you obtained the final list.

Secondary Sources

Besides primary research, your search using preliminary sources will turn up another category of literature referred to as *secondary sources*. As mentioned in chapter 1, secondary sources are ones that refer to or summarize primary research through the eyes of someone other than the person(s) who did the study. For this reason, they are valuable places to find references to primary research. These are commonly found in the form of literature reviews, position papers, and books.

Literature Reviews. One of the most useful secondary sources is a well-written literature review. This is an important piece of work that summarizes a number of primary studies related to a particular research issue. A well-written review tries to make sense out of all the research done in a given area. It compares and contrasts various studies and identifies areas that still need more research. I advise people to first look for reviews of research when trying to find out what research has already been done on a topic and what researchers have concluded so far.

An example of a well-written research review is found in Sparks and Ganschow's (2001) article, "Aptitude for Learning a Foreign Language" in the journal, *Annual Review of Applied Linguistics*. They provided a useful overview of research on foreign language aptitude and how it was measured before 1990. I found this article through an ERIC *Advanced Search*, where I typed the keywords *review* AND *language learning*.

Some journals only publish research reviews. The *Annual Review of Applied Linguistics* is dedicated for this purpose in applied linguistics. It comes out once a year, and each volume contains reviews around one general theme in the discipline. Another journal that contains only reviews is the *Review of Educational Research*, which occasionally contains reviews of research related to issues in applied linguistics. Research reviews are also published in journals that contain primary research.

Let me interject a warning here regarding working with secondary sources. There is no substitute for firsthand reading of primary research. This means, for instance, that we cannot rely on summaries of research studies in secondary sources such as a literature review. The reason is that the reviewer selects information only relevant to his or her review and leaves out the rest. The selection process might have a particular bias that influences the spin that the reviewer puts on the information s/he is summarizing. Using this material in our own work would perpetuate this bias and misrepresent the original study. I strongly recommend that you do not yield to any temptation to short-cut the process, but that you take the extra effort to track down the articles you want to examine and read them for yourself.

Position Papers. Another type of secondary source commonly found are position papers. Often they resemble literature reviews, but with a much more focused purpose. In these, writers argue their particular viewpoints or positions on various issues. For example, one of the articles I found in the literature search I did previously as an exercise (without restricting my search to *journal* articles only) was Clapham's (2000) article entitled, "Assessment for Academic Purposes: Where Next?" This was published in a research journal, but it was not primary research. Rather in her article, Clapham argued that, for international tests of English, testing English for specific academic purposes should be abandoned due to the effects of background knowledge. She cited a number of studies to warrant her viewpoint.

Because position papers are not primary research, researchers cannot use them as direct evidence to support answers to our research questions. The reason is that they usually draw the proposed answers (i.e., formulated hypotheses) out of the research studies they cite (cf. Fig. 2.1). Yet the research they cite cannot then be turned around to support their positions (represented by the dotted curve line). In other words, the same research cannot be used for both things: proposing answers and justifying answers. If I generate a hypothesis (i.e., possible answer) from existing data and then

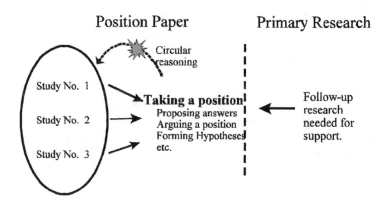

FIG. 2.1. Relation between a position paper and primary research.

turn around (the dotted curve line) and use the same data to support my hypothesis, I have fallen into the trap of circular reasoning (Giere, 2004). There is nothing wrong with the first part (i.e., generating a hypothesis based on existing research), but I cannot use the same data to support the hypothesis from which it was derived. To test a hypothesis, I must do subsequent research to find support, as illustrated on the right side of the vertical dotted line in Fig. 2.1.

Let me also reiterate here that we cannot use a position paper to support a possible answer on the basis that the person giving the paper is famous or an authority in his or her field. Somewhere we seem to have picked up the notion that because someone is famous, what s/he says must be true. Unfortunately, many people have been led down many a wrong path by relying on someone's fame or charisma. Therefore, unless these famous *someones* back up what they say with solid research, they are just giving their own opinions, which cannot be used as evidence.

As with literature reviews, we cannot substitute position papers for personally reviewing primary research with our own eyes. In presenting her argument, Clapham (2000) summarized several primary research studies to generate her suggested answer. The temptation for us is to use her summaries rather than take the time to find the primary studies and summarize them ourselves. However, we cannot use such summaries as substitutes for summarizing primary research ourselves because it is not uncommon to only focus on information for the specific purposes of the position paper. Important information critical for our purposes may have been left out.

Books.   The third secondary source that can provide information about previous research consists of published books. Typically, books are used to provide people with foundations for the issues being considered in a given area. In the process of doing this, they cite and summarize large quantities of primary research. Yet again the discussion of such research has been run through the cognitive filter of the author(s) and cannot be relied on as unbiased. Such material can help us become aware of existing research, but they cannot substitute for firsthand reading of such studies.

Tables of References/Bibliographies

Other profitable places to find research studies, often overlooked, include tables of references/bibliographies of research articles we already have found. Often I find *benchmark* (or seminal) studies this way. A benchmark study is one that either sparked interest in a particular issue or marked a pivotal directional change in the way research moved on a given subject. One tactic I use to identify a benchmark study is frequency of citation. When you notice that just about every article you read cites a particular study, you can be sure that it is an important one in the history of the area you are investigating.

IS ALL PRIMARY RESEARCH OF EQUAL WEIGHT?

I have stated that primary research is the only place where we can find evidence to answer our questions. However, not every piece of primary research that you find in your database search is of equal weight for supporting a proposed answer to a question. Figure 2.2 lists the various venues in which primary research can be found. The higher the venue is in Fig. 2.2, the more weight it has. Two criteria are directly relevant to the weight: (a) whether the submissions for publication are refereed, and (b) whether the referee is blind toward who wrote the study. A referee is usually someone who is either at the same academic level (thus the term *peer evaluation*) as the person submitting the study for publication or higher. They are considered by the journal publishers to have enough experience in research to give meaningful evaluations. A *blind* referee is one who does not know the researcher's identity when reviewing the article.

There are three general venues: published research, conference presentations, and databases. Under published research, there are three types of journals plus doctoral dissertations. Journals are divided into blind/non-

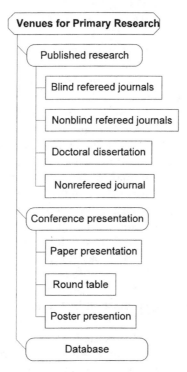

FIG. 2.2. Levels of weight given to research in different venues (the higher, the more weight).

blind refereed or nonrefereed. Most journals have editorial boards that review every manuscript submitted for consideration before being accepted for publication. Yet the rigor to which a manuscript is evaluated varies with the journal.

To aid in determining the weight of any given study, the TESOL organization has surveyed 53 journals on its Web site, listing a number of criteria for rating journals (http://www.tesol.org/pubs/author/books/demystify-grids.html). The TESOL Web page reported that all but 2 of the 53 journals require referees, and 1 sometimes does. Regarding whether the referees were blind, all but 11 of the 53 used blind referees. Consequently, more weight should be given to studies that have been critiqued by qualified referees who are blinded than those that have not received this scrutiny. I suggest that you look at this Web page to familiarize yourself with the various journals and features about them. It also provides you with a more detailed explanation of the qualities of each journal.

Notice in Fig. 2.2 that I placed Doctoral Dissertations higher than Nonrefereed Journals. The reason I did this is that doctoral dissertations typically go through rigorous screening by a doctoral committee and are not accepted until everything is in good order. These dissertations are available, although not as readily as articles in research journals. They are also typically voluminous, which makes them much more difficult to work with. They can be ordered on microfiche, which saves on postage and storage, but requires a microfiche reader. Eventually, some of these are summarized and submitted for publication in research journals. However, you might not want to wait that long.

Primary research can also come in the form of papers read at conferences (cf. Fig. 2.2). If you have ever attended any conference related to applied linguistics (e.g., AAAL, IATEFL, TESOL, etc.), you will find many sessions where primary research is presented: At Paper Sessions, researchers present 15- to 20-minute summaries about their research; at Round Tables, various researchers present short summaries of their research on a common theme and are available for questions; and at Poster Sessions, researchers (often graduate students) exhibit their studies on poster boards and are available to explain their research to anyone interested. Notice in Fig. 2.2 that I put them in order based on the degree to which they are critiqued. Although there is some degree of scrutiny applied before papers are accepted at conferences, research presented at this venue does not have the same weight as a study published in a journal. The reason is that they have not gone through the same degree of rigorous evaluation prior to presentation. Yet some work presented at conferences is usually evaluated by discussants and certainly by those who hear the presentations. The problem for the consumer is that s/he does not hear or read these evaluations unless s/he is present at the time of the presentation.

Least weight is given to any primary research that appears in a database which has neither been published in a journal nor presented at a conference. Some databases provide references for books, theses, dissertations, speeches, viewpoints, reports, conference papers, as well as primary research. They do not require any of these works to be published or presented at conferences. Therefore, some primary research referenced in them has been submitted by the researcher so that others might see what s/he has done. For example, individuals can submit summaries of their research to ERIC, which references them for all to see and even provides full text copies at the minimum cost. A case in point is Watts' (2001) study on the use of register in the Spanish language classroom that is found in ERIC. From what I can see in the reference, it has not been published as of yet nor presented at any conference. However, it is available through ERIC's *Document Reproduction Service's* Web site, www.eric.ed.gov, free on a pdf file.

This is not to suggest that articles such as Watts' are not useful research. There is a lot of important research that has not been published or presented at conferences. However, because it has not gone through some form of peer review, it cannot carry the same weight as research that has. As you develop into a discerning consumer, you can review these articles for yourself and determine their value for answering your questions.

A third criterion you want to keep in mind when weighing the value of a research study for answering your questions is recency. Studies that are 10 years old or older do not usually carry the same weight as more recent studies unless they are seminal studies. When searching, you will want to begin with the most recent and work your way back. The most recent research will bring you up to date on what is happening.

The order of recency usually goes like this: conference presentations, research journals, and secondary sources, respectively. The first is the most recent. If you are trying to get the latest research on a topic, the place to go is a research conference where people are reporting their own research, often still in progress. You can usually obtain complete research studies directly from the author(s) at these conferences. If the author does not have full reports or has run out of them, s/he is usually more than happy to send you a copy. Such conferences as TESOL, AAAL, IATEFL, and AERA are full of sessions where the most recent research is presented. There are also a number of regional conferences where fresh research is presented.

Less recent are journal articles that may appear anywhere from 6 months or more from the time the research has been accepted for publication. Referring back to the TESOL Web site cited earlier, most journals take 6 months to 1 year before an article is published; the *ESP Journal* takes from 1 to 2 years. Remember that the study may have been completed much earlier than that, therefore the actual data could be 3 to 4 years old before you see the study in print.

The least recent research is material cited in secondary sources. Under this classification, literature reviews and position papers are less dated than books. The review cited earlier by Sparks and Ganschow (2001), for example, reviewed studies as recent as 2000. In contrast, books have older references simply because it takes much longer to publish a book than to get a literature review or a position paper presented.

DIFFERENTIATING PRIMARY FROM SECONDARY

One problem my students complain about is the difficulty in identifying primary research from position papers and even literature reviews when searching preliminary sources. My suggestion is that the first thing to examine is the title of the article. For example, in the following reference from my ERIC search, Astington and Jenkins (1999) informed us that their article is primary research by using the term *longitudinal study* in their title.

> A Longitudinal Study of the Relation between Language and Theory-of-Mind Development, Astington, Janet Wilde; Jenkins, Jennifer M., 1999, EJ595688

However, we cannot detect whether the following ERIC reference is a primary research article from the title:

> An Oral Interview Procedure for Assessing Second Language Abilities in Children, Carpenter, Kathie; And Others, 1995, EJ511944

Are the authors collecting data or presenting a case for a particular oral interview procedure? In this case, we need to go to the next step of reading the abstract usually provided by the preliminary source. In our example, we would click on the Details button for EJ511944, which provides an abstract of the article as seen next. Here we look for key phrases that will give us a clue regarding the nature of the article.

> ABSTRACT: This article presents the goals, design, and pilot-testing results of a new oral interview procedure for eliciting a representative sample of spontaneous Japanese *language abilities* from children aged 5 through 10. Pilot results show that the procedure elicits a language sample that is superior in quality and quantity to other existing Japanese language *assessment* instruments for children. (JL) (*Note: As mentioned previously, the initials identify the abstractor.*)

The phrase in the abstract that shows that the article is a primary study and not a position paper or review is, "This article presents . . . results."

Not every abstract uses these exact words, but something is said to the same effect.

The next ERIC reference does not reveal what type of article it is in the title either:

> Preference Organization in Oral Proficiency Interviews: The Case of Language Ability Assessments, Lazaraton, Anne, 1997, EJ539358

Yet the following abstract clearly informs us that Lazaraton is arguing that the construct of *self-deprecation* in assessing one's own language ability is an important variable to investigate. She makes no reference to collecting data or stating any results. This is most likely a position paper.

> ABSTRACT: Focuses on a phenomena emerging from examination of a corpus of language interview data, representing a type of institutional talk evaluating the English *language ability* of international students for the purposes of elective English-as-a-Second-Language course placement. This phenomenon is the students' self-deprecations of their own English *language ability*. (17 references) (CK) (*Note: There were 17 references cited in this paper.*)

A third ERIC reference cited next that does not reveal the nature of the paper in the title is Sparks and Ganschow's (2001) article, to which I have already made reference. This title is so general that it could be anything. However, the abstract immediately states that it is a review of research.

> Title: Aptitude for Learning a Foreign Language.
>
> Author: Sparks, Richard; Ganschow, Leonore
>
> Publication_date: *2001*
>
> Journal_citation: Annual Review of Applied Linguistics; v21 p90-111 2001
>
> Abstract: *Review* research on foreign language aptitude and its measurement prior to 1990. Describes research areas in the 1990s, including affective variables, language learning strategies, learning styles as contributors to aptitude and aptitude as a cognitive construct affected by language variables. Reviews research on individual differences and the importance of phonological and orthographic processing for foreign language *learning*. (Author/VWL)

HOW TO OBTAIN RESEARCH ARTICLES

Although finding references to research articles has become much easier, there continues to be the major challenge of getting access to the actual journal articles. If the article you want to read is published in a journal, the first place to inquire is your nearest university library. If it does not subscribe to the journal, it might be able to obtain the article for you from another library through interlibrary loan. Finding a good library that has helpful staff is like finding a gold mine.

If you do not have access to the articles through a library, ERIC gives you information where you can order any article it has in its database for a small charge. I recommend you order microfiche rather than a paper copy because it is cheaper, easier to post, and saves trees. You can read the microfiche at your nearest library on the microfiche reader, although you want to first make sure there is one available.

WHAT JOURNALS ARE RELATED TO APPLIED LINGUISTICS?

There are many research journals that can be used for different areas of interest in the field of applied linguistics. The reason is that applied linguistics is multidimensional; that is, many different disciplines are related to this broad field. You will find research related to applied linguistics in journals dealing with anthropology, computer assisted learning, linguistics, psychology, sociology, and many more areas.

To give you a good head start, several of my graduate students have worked with me to put together a list of journals with brief descriptions of their stated purpose to aid you in your search. These will give you a good idea of the variety of journals and their purposes. I recommend that you check to see how many of these are easily accessible to you. They are found in Appendix C.

To apply what you have been reading, I recommend the following exercise. The objective is for you to train your eye to look for terminology that will speed up your ability to distinguish among the various types of literature you will encounter in your searches.

Exercise 2.2

1. Choose a topic related to applied linguistics that interests you.
2. Go to one or more preliminary sources and select several references to articles related to your topic.
3. Examine the titles of these and try to determine whether they are primary studies, position papers, or literature reviews. What terminology helped you decide?
4. Now look at the abstracts given by the preliminary source and try to confirm whether your decisions were correct. What statements provided you with further information regarding the nature of the study?
5. Last, decide from the title and abstract whether each article you have listed is relevant to the topic you chose.

Key Terms and Concepts

delimiter
keyword
literature review
operator
position paper
preliminary sources
primary research

Additional Recommended Reading

Hock, R. (2004). *Extreme searcher's Internet handbook.* Medford, NJ: Information Today.
O'Dochartaigh, N. (2001). *The Internet research handbook: A practical guide for students and researchers in the social sciences.* Thousand Oaks, CA: Sage.

THE MAJOR COMPONENTS
OF PUBLISHED RESEARCH

Chapter 3

Understanding the Framework of a Primary Research Article

CHAPTER OVERVIEW

Research articles typically follow a standard format for presentation in research journals. I have used this format to organize the following chapters. The purpose of this chapter is to provide you with an overview of this framework as an introduction to the rest of the book. I begin by describing what a typical research study looks like with a brief explanation of each component. The first three parts—title, abstract, and introduction—are discussed more fully in this chapter, whereas separate chapters are dedicated to the remaining components. I provide you with examples of current research from different journals and have interspersed some exercises to help you develop an overall schema of the basic structure of a research article.

THE FRAMEWORK OF A RESEARCH ARTICLE

Most research articles adhere to the following format:

1. Title
2. Author(s) and institution(s)
3. Abstract
4. Introduction

5. Methodology (Method)
6. Results
7. Discussion/Conclusion
8. References

The Title

Although many readers might not think the title is very important, it is in fact critical. Titles either attract potential readers or dissuade them from reading the article. A well-written title should give enough information to inform the consumer what the study is about. It might suggest what the research question is or even what hypothesis is being tested, but there should be no doubt what issue is being investigated.

The title should also indicate what type of article it is. There should be no necessary guessing as to whether the study is primary research, a review of the literature, or a position paper. For example, there is little doubt what Tsang's (1996) study is about, entitled "Comparing the Effects of Reading and Writing on Writing Performance." It is a primary study that examines the differential effects of reading and writing on writing ability. In contrast, Zhongganggao's (2001) paper entitled "Second Language Learning and the Teaching of Grammar" is unclear as to whether it is primary research or a position paper. It could be either. The reader has to go to the abstract or body of the introduction to find out which it is.

At the same time, the title should not require unnecessary reading. Some titles are short and succinct, clearly telling the readers what they want to know, such as Tsang's (1996) study mentioned earlier. Others can be quite long and unnecessarily complex, such as (in my opinion) the study entitled "Word Translation at Three Levels of Proficiency in a Second Language: The Ubiquitous Involvement of Conceptual Memory" (de Groot & Poot, 1997). Although this title clearly indicates what the study is addressing and that it is a primary study, it probably could have done without the final phrase, "The Ubiquitous Involvement of Conceptual Memory." However, I am getting off topic into the art of title writing.

In summary, the three criteria to look for in a title are: focus of the study, type of article, and succinctness. The first two are the most important because they quickly inform you whether the paper is what you are searching for. The third is more of a stylistic issue, which you should keep in mind if you ever have to entitle a paper of your own. Take time to do the following exercise to apply these criteria to some example titles that I have supplied, and then apply the criteria to other articles from your own search.

Exercise 3.1

Look at each of the following titles of real studies and answer the following:

1. What is the study's
   a. focus?
   b. research question?
   c. hypothesis?
2. Can you tell if the article is a primary study, a position paper, or a literature review? Explain your reasoning.

Titles:

- Learners' perceptions of listening comprehension problems (Hasan, 2000)
- Preliminary findings of a format-based foreign language teaching method for school children in the Basque Country (Azpillaga et al., 2001)
- Finding out about students' learning strategies by looking at their diaries: A case study (Halbach, 2000)

The Abstract

The abstract in a research article is written by the author(s) of the study. This is not always the case with the abstract written in preliminary sources, such as ERIC. For this reason, the abstract in the article is usually much more reliable to identify the content of the study.

A well-written abstract should summarize five essential things to help the reader know what the study is about: (a) purpose of the study, (b) source(s) from where the data are drawn (usually referred to as participants), (c) the method(s) used for collecting data, (d) the general results, and (e) general interpretation of the results. Some abstracts may contain more than these things, but unfortunately some abstracts do not contain some (if not all) of these essential elements.

With this information, the consumer will know from the abstract whether the article is of interest. To illustrate, I extracted the prior five pieces of information from the abstract of a study by Treiman, Kessler, and Bourassa (2001), which looked at whether a child's spelling ability is affected by knowledge of his or her own name. The following is a copy of the Abstract from their study with the essential information summarized in Table 3.1.

We analyzed spellings that were produced by children in kindergarten (N = 115), first grade (N = 104), and second grade (N = 77) in order to determine whether children's own names influence their spellings of other words. Kindergartners overuse letters from their own first names (or commonly used

TABLE 3.1
Analysis of an Example Abstract

Essentials	Content
Purpose of the study	This paper investigated whether knowledge of one's own name affected a child's spelling ability.
Sample	115 kindergartners, 104 first graders, and 77 second graders.
Method used for collecting data	They analyzed the children's spelling in comparison to the spelling and length of the children's names.
Results	Kindergartners differed from the older children in three ways, which they listed.
Interpretations of results	The results support the notion that knowledge of one's own name is involved in becoming literate.

nicknames) when spelling. Kindergartners with longer names, who had more own-name letters available for intrusions, tended to produce longer spellings than did children with shorter names. Moreover, the spellings of kindergartners with long names tended to contain a lower proportion of phonetically reasonable letters than did the spellings of children with short names. These effects appeared to be confined to children who read below the first grade level. The results support the view that children's own names play a special role in the acquisition of literacy. They further show the children choose in a way that reflects their experience with the letters. (p. 555)

As you can see, this abstract provided enough information to decide the relevance of the study for the reader's purpose.

There is nothing like firsthand experience to get a better grasp of the prior discussion. The following exercise provides you with a framework for analyzing and evaluating research abstracts.

Exercise 3.2

Task: Find a recent research study of interest and examine the **abstract** carefully. Fill in the Abstract Analysis Grid below and answer the following questions:

Abstract Analysis Grid

Essentials	Content
Purpose of the study	
Sample	
Method used for collecting data	
Results	
Interpretations of results	

1. What other information is in the abstract? Summarize in your own words.
2. Was the abstract succinctly written?
3. Was it easy to understand?

The Introduction of a Study

The introduction is the *brains* of the study. In it we should find the topic being investigated, why it is important enough to be studied, the research question, any theory being considered, any hypothesis being proposed, and any predictions made. In addition, constructs and special terminology should be defined that will be used throughout the study.

Typically, the introduction should provide historical context to the issue being investigated and bring in any theory that may be relevant to the reader. Often this is referred to as the *literature review* of the study (although not necessarily referred to as such), in that it summarizes and references a number of articles to introduce the reader to the study. However, this is not a literature review, such as referred to in chapter 2, which is a complete document that provides a broad overview of research and thinking on a given area. Rather, a literature review within the introduction of a study is a highly orchestrated, logical argument consisting of a number of statements to provide the reasoning behind the study. With each statement, a study is summarized and/or referenced for support of the statement. At the end of the argument, there should be a conclusion in the form of at least one research question and possibly a hypothesis or several hypotheses. Hypotheses, in turn, should be operationally defined and translated into predictions.

In the discipline of logic (Giere, 2004), a statement is either true or false and is used in a logical argument as one of the premises of the argument (see Appendix B for a more detailed explanation). Each statement needs to be supported by findings from at least one study to warrant the statement as a premise of the argument. If no support is provided, the statement is no more than a hypothesis and needs to be tested before it can be used as a premise in any argument. For example, if I want to make the statement "Women are better language learners than men" as one of the premises of my argument, I had better cite at least one study to back this up. If there is no primary research to back this statement up, it cannot be used as one of the premises of my argument. It becomes a hypothesis that needs to be tested in a study of its own.

The support for each statement will be in the form of at least one reference to a study that you can look up to see whether the statement has support. If there is no reference to a study after a statement, the statement should be treated with suspicion. Statements without support weaken the overall argument.

However, not every reference that follows a statement is a research study. Sometimes references only cite the opinion of someone else. A well-written paper lets the reader know in the text whether the reference is a study or an opinion. If you are not sure, look at the title in the full reference section to see whether you can identify which one it is. If that does not work, and you are really curious, you need to look at the abstract of the study provided in one of the preliminary sources (e.g., ERIC) or the study.

To illustrate the argument process, one of my graduate students and I analyzed the introduction section of Sasaki and Hirose's (1996) study entitled "Explanatory Variables for ESL Students' Expository Writing." Our analysis is presented in Box 3.1.

As can be seen in this example, the authors built their argument so that the reader can understand why this particular study was needed. After every premise, they supplied references to studies that provided support. If they had not, the argument would have been flawed. This is important when the goal of the argument is to lead the reader to a hypothesis that the researcher wants to propose.

A detailed analysis of the argument in the introduction is not something the consumer will do every time s/he reads an article. However, to help develop a mindset for reading introductions in this fashion, I suggest you do the following exercise. It is not an easy exercise, but you will find that it focuses your mind more than usual when you read an introduction to a study. After doing this several times, you will find that you will be doing this automatically.

Exercise 3.3

Task: Use a recent journal related to applied linguistics. Find a research study of interest and examine the introduction carefully. Perform the following tasks:

1. Outline the argument with the main points (cf. Box 3.1).
   a. List the premises of the argument.
   b. Indicate what support is given for each premise by citing one reference to a primary research study. If there is no supporting reference, indicate this.
   c. State your opinion on how well you think the points logically relate to one another.
   d. Are there any gaps in the logic? If so, what are they?
2. Identify the conclusion of the argument that should be in the form of questions and/or hypotheses/predictions.
3. State your opinion on how well you think the conclusion logically relates to the preceding argument.

BOX 3.1
Analysis of the Argument for a Study

The problem: Writing in EFL.

The argument:

Context: There is a controversy regarding what influences writing in EFL. A number of factors have been under investigation, namely, the student's writing strategies, writing ability in L2, proficiency and knowledge of writing in L2, and instructional background.

1st premise: Mixed results have been found regarding whether writing strategies relate to the quality of writing in L2 (cf. Hall, 1990 vs Pennington & So, 1993).

Subpremises:

1) Learners use the same writing strategies in both L1 and L2 (Cumming, 1989). Another study yielded contradictory findings (Raimes 1987).

2) Some have hypothesized that learners have a composing competence that allows them to write in both L1 and L2 (Kraples, 1990).

3) The correlation between writing ability in L1 and the quality of L2 writing has not been clearly demonstrated (cf. Cumming, 1989 vs Carson, Carrell, Silberstein, Kroll, & Kuehn, 1990).

2nd premise: It is also not clear whether L2 linguistic proficiency affects the quality of L2 composition (cf. Pennington & So, 1993 vs Raimes, 1985).

3rd premise: Knowledge of L2 writing conventions helps L2 writers (Raimes, 1985).

4th premise: L2 writing instruction affects the learner's L2 composition (Mohan & Lo, 1985).

Subpremise: Some writing strategies of L2 can be taught (Spack, 1984).

5th premise: All of the above studies did not look at all of the factors at the same time.

The conclusion: A study needs to be done that examines all of these factors at once.

Hypotheses: Based on the previous premises, this study will test the following six hypotheses, all related to Japanese EFL students:

1) L1 writing ability together with L2 proficiency will affect quality of L2 composition.

2) The quality of L2 composition is not necessarily affected by meta-knowledge of L2 composition.

3) L1 writing ability correlates with L2 proficiency.

4) Good writers utilize "good writers' strategies" identified by researchers.

5) Good writers are fluent writers.

6) Good writers write confidently in both L1 and L2 and have previous L2 experience in writing.

Methodology

The *methodology* (or *method*) section consists of the skeleton of the study. If it is well written, others should be able to replicate the study exactly. The ability to replicate a study is the principal criterion used to judge the quality of this component of a research report.

The methodology section tells us who was studied, what was studied, and how the information was collected and analyzed. The following outline lists the typical subsections found under this heading. Studies vary in what subsections they include under the methodology section, but the information contained in the following subsections should be presented in some manner. The following chapters discuss many of these subsections in detail, but I provide a brief definition for each in the following:

- Sample
- Research design
  - ▶ treatment(s) (optional)
    - ▪ techniques (optional)
    - ▪ materials (optional)
- Data-collection procedures
  - ▶ instruments (optional)
  - ▶ observational methods
- Procedures followed

Sample.   This subsection of the methodology section describes the participants/subjects or the objects of the study from which the data were gathered. A well-written sample section provides as much detail as needed about the participants/objects. It should also explain the rationale used for selecting the participants so that the reader may be able to assess whether the resulting data are valid for the purpose of the study.

In a study using participants, for example, Zahar, Cobb, and Spada (2001) described their participants as 144 Grade 7 male ESL students. They continued by providing information about the fact that they had been placed in different ESL levels, how much class time they had completed prior to the study, and their language background. With this information, the reader can decide whether the results of the study are applicable to the question under consideration.

However, there are studies that look at *objects* rather than participants, such as when a discourse analysis study is being done on a corpus of text. de Beaugrande (2001) used a position paper (i.e., the object) as his data source when he compared three different methods of discourse analysis: systemic functional linguistics, corpus linguistics, and critical discourse analysis. de

Beaugrande was not interested in the who, but the what (i.e., the corpus of the text, rather than the person who wrote the position paper).

Another example of using objects is in Al-Khatib's (2001) study, which looked into pragmatic issues in personal letter writing related to culture. His data source was a corpus of 120 personal letters written by students at two Jordanian universities to a hypothetical friend in the UK.

Chapter 4 expands more on a number of important issues regarding the sample subsection of which the consumer will want to be aware. Although this segment of the study, on face value, appears to be somewhat routine, these issues will either add or distract credibility to the study's results.

Research Design.   The research design subsection, often referred to as *design*, explains the overall structural design used in the study. There are a number of designs available, and each one has its appropriate use. Each has its strengths and weaknesses depending on how well the data answer the research question(s).

In a well-written design section, the *variables*[1] of the study are clearly identified and defined. In fact the term *construct* is usually replaced by the term *variable*. If something does not vary, it is not a variable. For example, *language ability* is a construct that varies (i.e., people vary in language ability). Therefore, it is referred to as variable when used in a study, regardless of whether the word *construct* is used. Gender is a variable in that it has two possibilities: male and female. Examples of other possible variables are nationality, language proficiency, method of instruction, and so on.

Variables can have different classifications. A variable may be *independent, dependent, moderating, observational,* or *extraneous.* How a variable is classified depends on the role the variable plays in a study and the type of research design being used. In other words, the same variable can be independent in one study, dependent in another, moderating in a third, observational in a fourth, and extraneous in a fifth. To make things more challenging, research studies vary in how many of these different types of variables are present. A study may only have observational variables, independent and dependent variables, and so on.

Although I explain more about variable classification within the context of my discussion of the different research designs in chapter 5, let me give you a brief overview of these different types of variables. An *independent variable (IV)* is regarded as the *variable of influence*—that is, it *affects* the variation (or change) in another variable. The variable being influenced (or changed) is labeled the *dependent variable (DV)*, in that its variation *depends* on changes in the independent variable. These two variable labels are found in research designs that look at causation and prediction. The way

---

[1]A *variable* is simply something that varies, usually corresponding to one of the constructs in a study.

you can identify the two variables is to note which one is thought to affect (i.e., impact, change, cause, influence, etc.) the other. The one doing the affecting is the independent variable, and the one being affected is the dependent variable. Often you can spot them in the title of the study. For example, the title of Treiman, Kessler, and Bourassa's (2001) study is "Children's Own Names Influence Their Spelling." The IV is something related to children's own names. In operational terms, the IV was the awareness of children to the spelling of their own names. The DV was the spelling ability of children for other words.

A study can have more than one independent variable and/or dependent variable as well. For instance, the Zahar et al. (2001) study entitled "Acquiring Vocabulary Through Reading: Effects of Frequency and Contextual Richness" indicates two IVs, frequency and contextual richness, and one DV, vocabulary acquisition.

Some research designs have what is referred to as a *treatment* or maybe even several treatments. This is usually done when the researcher(s) *manipulates* an independent variable and looks at its effect on a dependent variable. The treatment may involve some *technique* as demonstrated in Norris, Mokhtari, and Reichard's (1998) study, where they examined whether children improved their writing skills by drawing pictures prior to the writing task. In this case, *drawing pictures* would have been the treatment.

The treatment might also consist of some type of *material.* The material can be in the form of written, audio, or visual information presented to the subjects. This is illustrated by Koolstra, van der Voort, and van der Kamp (1997), who did a study over a 3-year period where they looked at the long-term effects of TV on the reading ability of elementary students in the Netherlands. Their material consisted of two types of TV programs, which constituted the treatments.

Also related to the IV and the DV is the *moderating variable (MV)*. As the name suggests, this variable works as a go-between from the IV to the DV; that is, it moderates the effect that the IV has on the DV. Figure 3.1 shows the intermediate role the MV plays in a study. For instance, in the study by Zahar et al. (2001), the two IVs were *frequency of word occurrences* and *richness of context.* The DV was *vocabulary acquisition.* However, they used an MV as well: *learner proficiency.* In other words, they wanted to know whether the effect of the two IVs on the DV was different depending on different levels of language proficiency.

Extraneous variables (EV) are any variables that the researcher does *not* want to influence his or her DV other than the IV. As Fig. 3.1 illustrates, these variables are lurking around a study trying to creep in to distort the results. In some studies, the researcher may not want his or her data influenced by differences in such variables as gender, age, level of language proficiency, intellectual development, and so on. The design of the study, if planned appropriately, should keep the influence of these variables at bay.

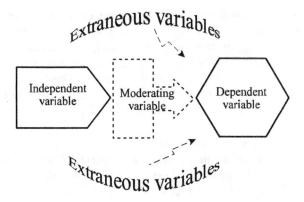

FIG. 3.1. Relationships among variable types.

Chapter 5 provides a detailed description of many types of EVs that can mess up a study. A well-written study mentions what EVs threaten the results and states what was done to prevent their effects.

Observational variables (*OV*) are variables that are observed without looking at the effects of one variable on another. These variables are mostly used to answer the What's out there? research questions. The data recorded on these variables are usually in the form of frequency of occurrence and/or detailed verbal descriptions. A study by Buckwalter (2001) provided a clear example of a study that solely examined observational variables. It was clear from the title that her principal variable of interest was repair sequences that occur when people in dialogue try to correct discourse when an error has been made. Her main goal was to identify who in a dyadic discourse identified the problem, and, second, who made the correction. Data were in the form of verbal description and frequencies.

Identifying variables of a study is not a straightforward task. For this reason, I have included the following exercise to give you an opportunity to identify variables and classify their types in studies that you have found. I suggest that you use Fig. 3.1 as a guideline for making your decisions.

Exercise 3.4

Task: Use a recent journal related to applied linguistics. Find a research study of interest and examine the introduction and methodology sections carefully. Perform the following tasks:

1. Locate the variables in the study.
2. Classify the variables according to the previous definitions.
3. Provide a rationale for your classifications.

Data-Collection Procedures. This subsection explains in detail how the information is collected for the purpose of a research study. Most studies involve either instruments and/or observational procedures.

Instruments specifically relate to the devices used to collect the data. These are usually in the form of surveys or tests. They can be presented in written, audio, or visual format. Responses can be gathered via paper-and-pencil tests, computer administered tests, video camera, or audiotape recorder.

Other studies may not involve any data-gathering instruments, but may involve personal observations of subjects or objects. These studies typically use video or audio recording to keep a record of the data in case there is need for validation, but the actual data collection is done by an observer or a group of observers.

In some studies, confusion between the instruments and the materials used in the treatment can occur if the reader is not careful. One might think of the material as the stimulus that elicits the behavior that is measured or observed by the instrument. For example, Storey (1997) examined the cognitive processing that subjects went through while taking a *cloze* test (i.e., a test consisting of a text with missing words). The cloze test was not the instrument of the study, however, but rather the material used to elicit the subjects' think-aloud responses that were audiotaped. Whether the subjects got the items on the test correct was a secondary issue to the study. The data of interest were the participants' verbal responses. As with other sections of a study, more needs to be said about data gathering. Chapter 6 provides a more detailed discussion on this.

Procedures Followed. This subsection is a detailed explanation of how the complete study was executed. In some studies, the data-collection procedure subsection and this section are the same. The procedures subsection describes when and how the treatments (if any) were administered, when and how the instruments (if any) were given, and/or when and how observation methods were used. The main criterion for judging the quality of this subsection is whether we have enough information to replicate the study if need be. In the Zahar et al. (2001) procedures section, we are told that they gave their subjects 45 minutes to complete the Nation's Vocabulary Levels Test (i.e., the instrument) in its paper-and-pencil format. The amount of time they gave the students to complete the task and the amount of time subjects were exposed to the instrument were important to know. The reason is that if anyone wanted to replicate this study, s/he would also have to limit their participants to the same time constraints. To give you a feel for what has just been discussed, I recommend you doing the following exercise.

Exercise 3.5

Task: Use the same research study that you used for Exercise 3.4. Examine the methodology section carefully. Complete the following tasks:

1. Briefly summarize the procedures that the researcher(s) went through to collect their data.
2. Estimate whether you could replicate this study if you had the facilities. If you could not, explain what pieces of information you would need to repeat this study.

Results

In this section, the results of any data analysis are given. Depending again on the nature of the research design, different methods are used to try to make sense out of the data. One common method is to use statistics. Often many readers jump over this section, thinking it is only for the mathematically inclined. However, one of my goals in chapter 7 is to help the consumer of research not to be intimidated by strange Greek symbols, tables full of numbers, and graphs full of lines.

Not all studies have results sections filled with statistics. In some studies, what I later refer to as *qualitative studies*, the results section contains verbal data consisting of detailed descriptions of what was observed. Researcher(s) spend extended amounts of time gathering large quantities of verbal data, with the main purpose of identifying patterns and trends that will guide in answering the research questions of the study. Occasionally, some descriptive statistics are used to help illustrate these patterns. More is said about the issues involved in this type of analysis in chapter 7.

The results section of a study is important and should not be avoided. The strengths and weaknesses of a study can often be found in the choice of a data analysis procedure that affects the results. Conclusions based on faulty results cannot be used to answer our research questions. Chapter 7 expands the results section more. It compares how verbal and numerical data are treated and the criteria that need to be used when evaluating whether they have been properly used.

Discussion/Conclusion

The final section of a research study discusses the results and concludes the study. If the discussion is exceptionally lengthy, the conclusion may be separated from it. Here is where the results are interpreted in light of the research question(s) being asked and/or any hypothesis being tested. A well-written discussion/conclusion section also relates the findings of the study to previous research that has been done and to any theorizing that has been going on regarding the research topic. In addition, the author(s) should evaluate his or her own study by pointing out its strengths and weaknesses. This section characteristically concludes with what further research needs to be done and suggestions on how it might be done. Chapter 8 spends more time describing what constitutes a well-written discussion section.

Key Terms and Concepts

abstract
data-collection procedures
instruments
material
methodology section
observational methods
premise
research design
subjects/objects
treatment
variables
   dependent
   extraneous
   independent
   moderating
   observational

Additional Recommended Reading

Giere, R. N. (2004). *Understanding scientific reasoning.* Graton, CA: Wadsworth.
Porte, G. K. (2002). *Appraising research in second language learning: A practical approach to critical analysis of quantitative research.* Philadelphia, PA: John Benjamins.

Chapter 4

Understanding Where Data Come From: The Sample

CHAPTER OVERVIEW

The first subsection in the methodology section of a study typically informs the reader where the data come from (i.e., the sample). You might ask, "What is so important about a sample of participants that we have to spend a whole chapter on the topic?" As I hope you see while reading this chapter, what initially appears to be an insignificant portion contained in the methodology section of a study proves to be one of the foundation stones on which the study is evaluated regarding its usefulness.

The purpose of this chapter is to provide you, the consumer of research, with an overall understanding about the importance of and the thinking that goes on when choosing a sample. I first provide some initial definitions of terminology, which are essential for understanding the rest of the discussion. These definitions are followed by two segments that discuss the two major sampling paradigms found in research in applied linguistics. The choice of paradigm, as you might suspect by now, is guided by the research question being asked by the researchers. The chapter ends with a discussion of the ethics of using human participants in a research study.

SAMPLING TERMINOLOGY

The *sample* is the source from which data are drawn to answer the research question(s) and/or to test any hypothesis that might be made. The sample consists of one or more *cases*. In most studies, the cases are made up of human beings referred to as *subjects* or, more currently, *participants*. For example, Su (2001) used 122 Chinese and English native speakers in a study investigating the effects of discourse context on sentence processing.

In other studies, the cases might be inanimate *objects* from which the researcher extracts his or her data. Examples are *corpora* of verbal discourse, such as an accumulation of newspaper articles, or when researchers cull their data from transcriptions of taped dialogues. Spencer-Oatey (2002), for instance, used 59 records of incidents involving social interactions from 14 Chinese students when looking at the motivation involved in the management of rapport. Although she mentioned that 14 students were involved, the real data source, or objects, from which the data were drawn was the 59 records of the incidents.

Sometimes the reader can be confused as to what makes up a sample, as seen in the Spencer-Oatey (2002) study. However, one of my students found another study that was even more challenging. Kamhi-Stein (2000) compared the amount and quality of student participation between traditional face-to-face classrooms and Internet Web-based discussion groups in a TESOL teacher education course. Although 20 student participants were surveyed, 12 of the 20 were interviewed, eight classroom discussions were videotaped, and 253 Web bulletin board discussions were analyzed. Now for the $64 million question: Who and/or what makes up the sample? The answer is determined by which source of data is used to answer the research question(s). So the answer is, all of the above. Data were drawn from each of these sources. For reasons outlined next, there were different uses that demanded different combinations of participants/objects to answer different questions.

SAMPLING PARADIGMS

There are basically two sampling paradigms used for gathering data. The first I call the *information-rich paradigm*. The second is the *representative sample paradigm*. As the names suggest, the first type tries to get samples that are rich with the information the researcher is trying to uncover, whereas the second attempts to obtain a sample that is representative of a larger group.

Whether a sample paradigm is appropriate depends on the purpose of the study. If the purpose is to *generalize* the findings to a larger group of people, then sampling strategies need to be used that ensure *representativeness*. They focus on obtaining samples that best *represent* the larger group of individuals to which the findings will be applied. If the purpose is to do an in-depth analysis of some phenomenon, a sample needs to be selected that maximizes relevant information—that is, to obtain information-rich samples.

It seems that many journals do not require researchers to provide clear explanations for why they are using particular sampling strategies. I have my students examine, among other things, whether the authors of the studies they review explain how and why the samples were chosen. On one occasion, only 5 out of 35 studies reviewed by my students clearly provided a rationale for selecting the samples they used. This finding is not characteristic of any one journal. These 35 papers covered 20 different journals. Although this finding may not come from a representative sample of studies, it suggests that journals need to require researchers to include this information in their reports.

The Information-Rich Paradigm: Sample Strategies for Maximizing Information

Typically, but not necessarily, studies that use the information-rich sampling paradigm have small sample sizes. These can range from one participant/object, as in a case study, to larger numbers. However, with this approach, the emphasis is always on the *quality* of the information taken from the sample, not the quantity. One particular genre of research methodology, *qualitative research,* uses this type of sampling paradigm almost exclusively. I discuss this approach more fully in the next chapter.

A number of sampling strategies have been developed for the purpose of getting information-rich data. Gall, Borg, and Gall (1996, pp. 231–236) summarized 15 *purposeful sampling strategies.* Patton (1990, pp. 169–183) used *purposeful* to indicate that the sample is chosen deliberately to supply the most information possible regarding the research question. While reviewing these, I found a fair amount of overlap among the 15 strategies and extrapolated two common guidelines from them.

1. *The sample should provide a very good example of the phenomenon that is being studied under conditions relevant to the research question.* As an example, Borg (1998) purposely chose only one teacher to study a teacher's personal perspective as to how his own pedagogical system influenced his grammar teaching. He clearly justified his choice of subject by stating:

> The teacher whose practice is discussed here was a 40-year-old native speaker of English who had been involved in TEFL for over 15 years and who held qualifications in TEFL at both the certificate and the diploma levels. He was one of the most highly qualified and experienced teachers in his institute and was chosen for this study on the basis of his reputation as a professionally committed L2 teacher. (p. 11)

In other words, this teacher, in Borg's opinion, was an appropriate person to study because he could provide the information needed—this subject was *information-rich.* The value of using this type of sampling paradigm is seen in Borg's following discovery:

> During the course of the study, however, it became clear that the teacher's pedagogical system could not be adequately understood without reference to the factors that influenced its development and application, and a focus on these factors was consequently added to my research design. (p. 10)

Often during an intense time of information gathering from one or a few participants, the researcher becomes aware that something else needs attention. This type of design allows the researcher to make midstream changes in his or her design when this happens. Such changes in the middle of a study are not usually made in more quantitative designs.

2. *The number of cases should be manageable given the logistical constraints.* The rule, *the more the better,* holds true in most qualitative research as well as quantitative research, although for different reasons. As stated previously, the purpose of qualitative research is to do in-depth investigations that need information-rich samples. Obviously, the *more* information-rich data obtained, the better.

Guardado (2002), for example, used four families in his study, which investigated the loss and maintenance of Spanish children living in Canada. He clearly stated the criteria he used for selecting these families. Two families were chosen on the basis of having "at least one child over the age of six, fluent in English" (p. 348) whose proficiency in Spanish was low. The other two families needed to have a child of similar age who was fluent in both languages. Then he unambiguously gives his rationale for his sampling strategy—"to ensure obtaining both L1 loss and maintenance perspectives" (p. 348). Larger numbers than this can be selected for the sample, but the paradigm selected will always be based on gaining the best information possible to address the research question.

Although researchers using the information-rich paradigm are not generally concerned with *generalizing* their findings to larger populations, they are usually hoping that the interpretations of their data can be *transferred* to other situations. With a sample of one, for example, Borg did not try to generalize his findings to all teachers. However, his findings were suggestive for similar situations and certainly promising for further research. More is said about the issue of transference in chapters 5 and 7.

Before going to the next sampling paradigm, complete the following exercise so that you can get firsthand experience looking at a study that has used the information-rich sampling paradigm. Later you will be asked to note the differences between the study you find for this exercise and the one you use for Exercise 4.2. The more you see here will help in the later comparison.

Exercise 4.1

Locate a study of interest that used the information-rich sampling paradigm and complete the following:

1. Summarize the purpose of the study and the research questions under investigation.
2. Did the study use participants or objects?
3. Summarize the characteristics of the sample.
4. Did the researcher(s) provide a rationale for making the selection? If so, summarize it.
5. Did the data help generate any theoretical hypotheses? (You will have to look in the results and discussion sections to find this.)
6. Summarize why you think the sample fits the information-rich paradigm.

The Representative Sampling Paradigm

In the representative sampling paradigm, the goal of the researcher is to generalize the findings and interpretations of the study to a larger population. The sample is a portion of a larger population. The word *population* usually means everyone in a country or city. In research, this word has a more technical use; although similar, *population* means *all* the members of the group of participants/objects to which the researcher wants to generalize his or her research findings. This is referred to as the *target population*. In other words, the criterion for defining a target population is determined by the group of people to which the researcher would like to generalize the interpretations of the study. For example, the population might be all learners of English as a foreign language (EFL), or it might be a more limited group of all learners of EFL who attend an English-medium university. For another study, the target population may be entirely different.

Typically, having access to the entire target population to which researchers want to generalize their findings is impossible. For example, having access to all learners of EFL who attend English-medium universities throughout the world is, in practice, impossible. However, the researcher may have access to English-medium universities in his or her own country. Whatever is available for use becomes the *experimentally accessible population* (Gall et al., 1996). It is to this population that the findings of a study can be directly generalized, not to the entire target population. The only time a researcher could make inferences from the findings of his or her study to the target population is when s/he can show that the experimentally accessible population possesses similar characteristics as the larger target population. For the rest of the book, I use the phrase *target population* with the understanding that I am referring to the *experimentally accessible* population.

Selecting a representative sample is important for making use of the findings of a study outside of the confines of the study. This is because the degree to which the results of a study can be generalized to a target population is the degree to which the sample adequately represents the larger group—the degree to which a sample represents a population is determined by the degree to which the relevant attributes in the target population are found in the sample.

Figure 4.1 illustrates the relationship between the sample and the population. I have used different graphic symbols to represent different attributes of a population. These attributes could be gender, age, level of education, level of language proficiency, and so on. Notice that the attributes in the sample (A, B, C, D, F) almost match exactly the attributes in the population; however, Attribute E is missing in the sample. In this case, the sample is not 100% representative of the population, but it is very close. Most likely we could conclude that the population was representative enough to make *tentative* generalizations. However, there would always remain caution due to the missing Attribute E.

The degree to which findings of a study can be generalized to a larger population or transferred to similar situations is referred to as *external validity* (or *transferability*; Miles & Huberman, 1994). To achieve this type of va-

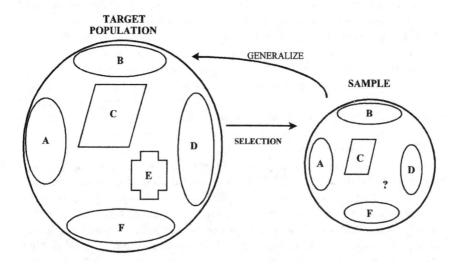

FIG. 4.1.   Illustration of a sample partially representing a target population.

lidity, researchers must demonstrate that the samples they use represent the groups to which they want to apply their findings. Otherwise, without this important quality, the findings are of little use outside of the study. The more representative the sample is to the population, the higher the external validity. In other terms, the more similar the characteristics of the sample is to other situations, the better the transfer of conclusions.

Identifying the target population is not always easy. For example, Silva (2000), looking at pragmatic issues and bilingualism, used a number of different groups of participants in her study. Her research questions refer to Brazilians and American non-native learners of Portuguese and their understanding of the phrase "Why don't you?" In her hypotheses, she restricted the Brazilians to be those who have lived in the United States for less than 1 year and those who have lived there for "longer periods." In her sample subsection, labeled *participants*, she provided detailed information regarding her participants. There were 117 Brazilians (68 females and 49 males, average age 30 years). Of these 58 knew little English with no experience living in the United States, while 59 had lived in the United States. There were 90 Americans (46 females and 44 males, average age 33), 44 who lived in Brazil, and 46 who were non-native speakers (NNSs) of Portuguese who were living in the United States. We get an idea of who the target population is in her Conclusion and Implications section when she stated, "Data have shown that Americans living in Brazil are much closer to Portuguese monolinguals . . . than Brazilians living in the US for 3 years or more" (p. 173). However, a little later she stated, "Findings from the present study clearly demonstrate that monolinguals constantly adjust the way they deal with their L1 in both linguistic and pragmatic terms" (p. 173). As a result, we are not quite sure who the target population is. Does it consist of Americans living in Brazil, Americans studying Portuguese in the United States, Brazilians with more than 3 years in the United States, and monolingual Brazilians? Or is it all monolinguals who are learning a second language? Then again, does the researcher want to generalize her findings to all the groups that these subgroups represent?

The problem of researchers not identifying their target populations is not uncommon in published research. However, without this information, the consumer cannot evaluate whether correct generalizations are being made.[1]

An additional note is that choosing a representative sample is not only used for quantitative research. Some qualitative studies also seek this quality in their samples. To illustrate, Storey (1997) used 25 first-year/first-semester female students from the Hong Kong Institute of Education to be

---

[1]I believe that all journals should add to their criteria for publication a clear statement that identifies the target population if the researcher plans to generalize his or her findings.

"as representative as possible of new entrants to the institution" (p. 219).
We can assume from this statement that all the entrants to the Hong Kong
Institute were females.

Sampling Strategies for Making Generalizations

There are many strategies used to achieve a representative sample. Because
the manner in which a sample is chosen is so important, published studies
in applied linguistics should inform the reader how the samples were selected. The following is a list of the more common sampling strategies and
the rationales used to warrant them.

The most desired strategy, yet rarely achieved, is *simple random* sampling. This method attempts to ensure that every member of the target
population has an equal opportunity for being chosen. If successfully obtained, such samples can control unwanted influences from extraneous
variables. As mentioned in chapter 3, these are variables that could impact
the variables being studied and produce spurious results. The reason simple random sampling controls the impact of these nuisance variables is
that it dissipates their effect throughout the sample. For example, if a researcher is not interested in whether males behave differently than females, yet gender could affect the dependent variable in some undesirable way, the researcher would want to ensure that the sample consisted of
approximately half males and half females. One way to do this is to obtain
a sample randomly. If the sample is randomly chosen (and large enough),
there is a high probability that both genders will be equally represented,
which would wash out any gender effect when the data from the two
groups were combined.

However, simple random selection on its own does not guarantee a representative sample; sample size is also a consideration. Obviously, a sample of one person would not represent a population of language students
even though randomly selected. The target population might consist of
males and females, but a sample of one is not representative because only
one of the genders is represented. If the sample of one is a male, but the
dependent variable does not behave with males as it does with females,
then the findings would be misleading. To avoid these two problems, you
need to use a larger sample. The maxim in research that aims to make
generalizations is *the larger the sample, the better.* In chapter 7, when I discuss
some statistical issues, I show the relationship between sample size and the
risk of getting a nonrepresentative sample. Suffice it to say here that the
larger the random sample, the greater the probability of getting a representative sample.

The negative impact of overall small sample size is exacerbated if there is any *attrition* (i.e., loss of participants).[2] An example of how this might work is Taguchi's (1997) study, which looked at the effects of reading a passage repeatedly for slow, beginning L2 readers. The research design used required three subgroups for reading ability level, among other things. Sixteen participants were used in the total sample, and they were divided into three groups: "Three students were assigned to Level 3, six students to Level 4, and seven students to Level 5" (p. 104). The chance that such small subgroups were representative of a larger group is questionable based on sampling error.[3] However, related to the topic at hand, one subject was excluded for not responding appropriately. Fortunately, this happened for Level 5, where there were seven participants. Had this occurred for Level 3, the cell size would have been reduced to two subjects, making this level even less representative.

When the sample size is too small and/or *simple* random sampling cannot be done, other sampling strategies need to be used. This is especially true when the population consists of subgroups such as males/females, various language proficiency levels, and different ethnic backgrounds, which the research wants to control. In this scenario, one of two forms of *stratified* random sampling can be used: *proportional* or *nonproportional* (Gall et al., 1996).

Proportional stratified random sampling attempts to choose cases that represent the proportion of each of the subgroups. For example, suppose a foreign language program is made up of three language levels: low, intermediate, and advanced. In the low and high groups, we have two classes of 15 each. In the middle group, we have six classes of 15. If a researcher were to sample 30 students using the simple random procedure, s/he could easily end up with a sample that would not represent these proportions. If the main intent were to generalize the findings to the whole group in that particular foreign language program, the sample would need to reflect these proportions. Therefore, a representative sample should have approximately 20% from each of the low and high groups (i.e., 30/150) and 60% from the middle level. To ensure that these proportions are obtained, the researcher would randomly select six participants (20%) from the low group and six from the high group. The remaining 18 would be randomly selected from the intermediate level. Now s/he would be able to make valid inferences from the sample to the target population.

---

[2]For effects of small samples, see www.unf.edu/dept/fie/sdfs/selecting_programs_2004. ppt. Retrieved June 7, 2004.

[3]For sample size and sampling error, see www.davidmlane.com/hyperstat/sampling_ dist.html. Retrieved January 10, 2004.

However, if the main intent were to compare the subgroups with one another, the researcher needs to have equal numbers of participants for each group. To do this, s/he should use a *nonproportional stratified random sampling* strategy. That is, the researcher will randomly sample the same number of participants from each of the levels. In the previous example, it would mean 10 participants from each level.

The following study exemplifies the use of the nonproportional stratified sampling strategy. Arriaga, Fenson, Cronan, and Pethick (1998) compared the language skills of low- and middle-income toddlers. They compared all of the 103 toddlers (approximately equal sexes) available to them in the low-income group with three independent random samples from a larger pool of middle-income participants. Although the proportion of middle income to low income was almost 10 to 1, they randomly chose three samples of 103 from the middle-income pool. They chose three different samples to ensure that they did not, by chance, obtain an atypical sample from the middle-income toddlers pool. However, they also made sure that they had the same number of males and females as the low-income group by randomly selecting from the middle-income group the same number of boys and girls for each set of 103 middle-income participants. With these samples, they could make reasonable comparisons between the two income levels.

In practice, having access to all members of the entire population is often impossible due to time or financial constraints. Instead researchers access participants from a population that is available. This strategy is referred to by Gall et al. (1996) as *convenience sampling.* For example, if my target population is all learners of EFL who attend an English-medium university, but I only have access to a sample from learners of EFL who attend the English-medium university where I teach, I use this group because it is convenient.

Whether one can apply their findings from a convenience sample to a larger target population depends on how well one can show that the sample corresponds to the larger population on important characteristics. This is done by providing clear descriptions of how the sample shares these features. Often the researcher gathers this information through surveys and tests prior to the implementation of the study.

From the many studies that I and my students have seen, our conclusion is that the majority of studies use *convenience sampling* when selecting samples. One such study that clearly used a convenience sample was done by Byrnes, Kieger, and Manning (1997), who investigated teachers' attitudes toward students from different language backgrounds. They selected 191 regular-classroom teachers who participated in teacher-education courses taught in three states in the United States: Arizona, Utah, and Virginia. Most likely, the teacher-education courses were either taught by the researchers or someone close to them. However, Byrnes et al. also stated that, although their sample was one of *convenience*, an effort was made "to reflect a range of language-diversity experiences that teachers might encounter" (p. 639). Clearly, they were establishing a link between their sample and the target population to which they want to generalize their findings.

I think it is safe to say that when a study does *not* identify how the sample was selected—and many do not—we can assume that the method used was convenience sampling. For instance, Baker and MacIntyre (2000) examined the role gender and immersion play in L2 on nonlinguistic outcomes such as attitude, motivation, and anxiety. They provided a concisely written description of their participants by stating the numbers of males or females, whether they were in immersion or nonimmersion settings, and the age range of each group. The participants were taken from Grades 10, 11, and 12 and were all studying French. However, nothing is said about the manner in which the sample was chosen. Neither is anything said as to whether all of the participants came from the same school. I assume they did. I have to also assume that the participants must have been conveniently available to the researchers for use in the study. Nevertheless, knowing this information helps understand the degree to which we can generalize results to the larger population of male/female high school students who are immersed/nonimmersed in the French language.

Closely related to convenience sampling is the use of volunteers as a sampling strategy. *Volunteers* are participants who have been solicited and have agreed to participate in a study. They differ from a convenience sample in that they are not under any obligation to participate in the study, whereas the former usually consists of students who are required to be participants of a research study as partial fulfillment of their courses. Volunteers are often paid for their services, whereas participants in convenience samples are not. When all attempts fail to find participants using other strategies, using volunteers is often the only way researchers can go.

However, research has shown that using volunteers frequently leads to a sample that is not representative of a target population (Gall et al., 1996). Findings have shown that in the West (Gall et al., 1996), volunteers tend to be better educated, more motivated, more outgoing, higher in need achievement, and from a higher socioeconomic level. Gall et al. pointed out that if any of these qualities could possibly impact the variable(s) under investigation, you would have to treat the findings of the study with some reservation.

Dehaene-Lambertz and Houston (1997) provided us with an example of using volunteer participants and some of the problems that can occur. Based on previous research findings suggesting that infants can differentiate between native and foreign languages, the researchers assessed the amount of linguistic information infants required to make this discrimination. In their first experiment, the sample consisted of 14 infants from American-English-speaking parents living in Eugene, Oregon, and 12 from French-speaking parents from Paris. Parents had to sign a consent form for their children to participate in this study. The researchers went on to report that they had to exclude 14 participants due to participants not being able to complete the study (nine American-English and five French). The question immediately arises as to whether the remaining families who volunteered their 2-month-olds possessed qualities that would enhance or distract from the listening test that was administered. In addition, would there have been different results if the 14 infants who were excluded continued in the study? Dehaene-Lambertz and Houston realized this and answered these questions by doing a second experiment reported in the same paper.

Another study done by Onwuegbuzie, Bailey, and Dailey (2000) illustrates the attention that must be given to the makeup of volunteers to increase the likelihood of obtaining a representative sample. Their study examined the age-old issue of finding what variables best predict foreign language achievement. One hundred eighty-four students studying various foreign languages at a U.S. midsouthern university volunteered to participate in the study. They were required to sign an informed consent document, which is now required by law in the United States for anyone participating in a research study. The researchers then listed a number of descriptive statistics that revealed information about their language proficiency, level of course, age, level in the university, program major, course load, previous language training, countries visited, and percentage of family whose L1 was not English. The researchers apparently wanted the reader to have enough information to judge whether their participants are fairly representative of foreign language learners at the university level. The researchers were careful to explain in their Discussion section that their findings were just "a step nearer" to supporting the notion that language achievement can be predicted given the right cognitive and motivational information.

Let me encourage you regarding your attitude toward studies using volunteers or convenience samples. You should not think that such studies have little value. Rather, you need to take the findings from such studies with the understanding that they need to be replicated with different samples. I think it is safe to say that few studies use samples that pass all of the criteria for a good sample. For this reason, the consumer needs to look for similar studies using different samples to see whether the results are repeated. If so, you can have more confidence in the answers to your questions.

In summary, whatever sampling paradigm a researcher uses, s/he should give attention to precision in describing why a sample was chosen and what steps were taken to ensure that the best sample was selected. The more precise the description, the more credence can be given to the interpretation and application of the results. For further reading on sampling theory, I recommend Gall et al. (2002) and Krathwohl (1998).

In Exercise 4.1, you were asked to find a study that used an information-rich sampling paradigm. Exercise 4.2 provides an opportunity to find a study that used the representative sampling paradigm. After completing this exercise, compare the results of the two exercises. Note the similarities and differences.

Exercise 4.2

Select a study of interest that used a representative sampling strategy. Summarize the following:

1. The purpose and the research question(s) of the study.
2. Were participants used or objects?
3. The sample used in the study:
   a. The target population to which findings were intended to be applied. You will most likely have to infer this from the questions, hypothesis, or discussion section.
   b. The experimentally accessible population.
   c. How the sample was chosen (e.g., simple random method, volunteers, etc.).
   d. The size of the sample.
   e. Characteristics of the sample.
4. Evaluate the sample:
   a. Was the sample size large enough? Defend your answer.
   b. Was the sample representative of the target population? Defend your answer.
5. Compare your work with your results from Exercise 4.1.

ETHICS IN SAMPLING OF HUMAN PARTICIPANTS

When using human participants in a study, there are several ethical issues that must be addressed. The main concern is to protect the rights and privacy of human participants. This issue is so important that the U.S. government set up a commission in 1974 that produced the Belmont Report in 1979. In 1991, many U.S. government agencies adopted a number of regulations to protect human participants (American Educational Research Association, 2000). In fact they established the Office for Protection from Research Risks inside the Department of Health and Human Services to monitor any misuse of participants.[4]

In essence, these guidelines can be summarized in the following statement: "The 'rights' of a research subject include reading and discussing the informed consent with study staff, answering any questions, voluntary participation, and a right to information about the study's procedures, risks, and benefits" (American Educational Research Association, 2000, ¶ 5).

There are some situations where these rules do not have to apply:

1. Research conducted in established or commonly accepted educational settings.
2. Research involving the use of educational tests, surveys, interviews, or observation of public behavior.
3. If the human participants are elected or appointed public officials or candidates for public office.
4. Research involving the collection or study of existing data, documents, or records.
5. Research and demonstration projects which are conducted by or subject to the approval of Department or Agency heads, and which are designed to study, evaluate, or otherwise examine public benefit or service programs. (American Educational Research Association, 2000, ¶ 5)

As seen in these five exceptions to the rule, there is a lot of latitude that will keep researchers from being overly tied up in red tape. However, it is important that participants are protected from research that violates their rights to privacy.

As I conclude this chapter, I trust that you have gained a healthy appreciation regarding the need for a researcher to provide a clear description of the sample s/he uses in her or his study. The sample subsection should describe detailed characteristics of her or his sample and indicate the conditions under which it was selected. The two main criteria are, first, whether you are able to identify the sampling paradigm(s) that a researcher uses and the reason(s) for its use. The second is whether you have enough information to decide whether the findings of the study can be generalized/transferred (cf. Fig. 4.1) to the target population or similar situations. The choice a researcher makes will guide how you evaluate the conclusions and applications suggested from the findings of the study. In addition to these basic criteria, the researcher needs to point out what precautions were taken to ensure the safety and confidentiality of any human participants.

---

[4]If you are interested in getting more details regarding this, I suggest that you go on the Internet to the site of the Department of Education, www.ed.gov/offices/OCFO/humansub.html. From there you will be able to locate a number of documents that spell out clearly what these regulations are.

The final thought is, although the sample subsection in a research article may consume little space, the implications have profound effects on the rest of the study.

Key Terms and Concepts

attrition

case

convenience sampling

experimentally accessible population

external validity

information-rich paradigm

objects

participants

proportional/nonproportional stratified random sampling

purposeful sampling

representative sample paradigm

sample

simple random sampling

stratified random sampling

target population

volunteers

Additional Recommended Reading

The following references provide access to further information regarding sampling.

Gall, M. D., Borg, W. R., & Gall, J. P. (2002). *Educational research: An introduction* (7th ed.). Upper Saddle River, NJ: Pearson Education.

Krathwohl, D. R. (1998). *Methods of educational and social science research: An integrated approach* (2nd ed.). New York: Longman.

Peters, P. (Ed.). (2002). *New frontiers of corpus research: Papers from the Twenty First International Conference on English Language Research on Computerized Corpora, Sydney 2000.* New York: Rodopi.

Sampling for qualitative research designs. See Kerlin, B.: http://kerlins.net/bobbi/research/qualresearch/bibliography/sampling.html. Retrieved January 7, 2004.

Sampling for quantitative research designs. See Lane, D. M.: http://www.davidmlane.com/hyperstat/sampling_dist.html. Retrieved January 10, 2004.

Sampling for survey research designs. See National Center for Educational Statistics: http://nces.ed.gov/statprog/2002/appendixb4.asp. Retrieved January 7, 2004.

Understanding Research Designs

CHAPTER OVERVIEW

The research design, as mentioned in chapter 1, is the overall plan for carrying out a research study. This design is like the blueprint for building a house. Its purpose is to guide the researcher in constructing the strongest and most efficient structure to provide the most useful data to answer the research question(s). Just like a poorly designed blueprint, which results in a house full of problems and possible collapse, a poorly designed research study produces results containing many flaws and, consequently, little practical use.

The goals of this chapter are to help you understand the technicalities of the design subsection of a study and be able to determine whether the appropriate design was used. There are a number of different research designs that are currently being used to answer a wide variety of questions. This is where things can be a little confusing, and remembering them all can be somewhat overwhelming. In addition, there might be several "best" research designs to answer the same question. For this reason, one needs to develop a discerning eye. As you will see, one should judge a design's suitability by whether it answers the research question.

To aid in accomplishing the previously stated goals, I have divided this chapter into three sections. Section 1 provides a conceptual framework for classifying various types of research designs to help reduce the confusion. Section 2 describes in more detail the various research designs used for finding answers to the two basic research questions: *what* and *why*. Section 3 discusses the factors that can interfere with the results of a study under the heading of *internal validity*. Examples of published research are given to illustrate the main points of the discussion.

SECTION 1: CLASSIFYING RESEARCH DESIGNS

Life would be so simple if we had only one kind of everything, but it would also be very boring. In keeping up with the rest of life, research does not provide just one simple type, nor even a choice between only two types. Rather, research can be classified, at least, by three intersecting continua: *Basic–Applied, Qualitative–Quantitative,* and *Exploratory–Confirmatory* (see Fig. 5.1). Although these continua are independent from each other, any given study can be classified somewhere on an intersection of the three. This means that a study would appear at some point out in the three-dimensional space, represented by Fig. 5.1. Each continuum is first defined with an explanation showing how a study can be located on it. Then an example is given on how one study can be classified on all three continua simultaneously and what this might look like in three-dimensional space.

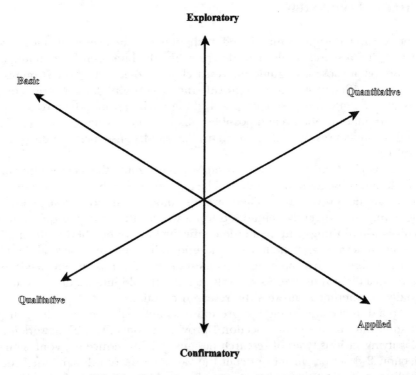

FIG. 5.1.   Design continua for classifying research.

The Basic–Applied Continuum

This continuum represents research that ranges from the highly theoretical (Basic) to the very practical (Applied). At the Basic end of the continuum, research is hypothetical, dealing mainly with highly abstract constructs. These studies are not, at first sight, very appealing to the classroom teacher who is looking for immediate ways to improve his or her students' learning. Nevertheless, these studies are important for looking at the underlying linguistic, psychological, or sociological mechanisms that might be eventually applied in the classroom. In fact, one might argue that this type of research reveals the theoretical foundations on which all other research rests. For example, unless we have demonstrated in Basic research that the brain processes information in a certain way, it would be difficult to promote a teaching method that elicits this type of brain processing.

Some studies can be identified immediately from their titles as Basic research. For example, Clark and Plante's (1998) study entitled "Morphology of the Inferior Frontal Gyrus in Developmental Language Disorder Adults" appears to be at the end of the Basic continuum. Based on the title, it does not look too useful for the language classroom teacher. This does not mean, of course, that this research is of little value. The findings might be useful for identifying possible brain disorders, which affect language usage, as well as stimulating ideas about treatment. Hence, in line with our first impressions, I placed it near the Basic end of the continuum as shown here.[1]

Basic ⟵―――――――⟶ Applied

At the other end of the same continuum is Applied research. As you would expect from the previous discussion, research that is directly applicable to the teaching/learning situation would be placed here. Studies that deal with teaching methods, or ones that try to address immediate problems in the classroom, would fit at this end of the continuum.

To illustrate, Fukushima (2002) explored the effects of having L2 students do an audiovideo project on learner empowerment, autonomy, and real-life applicability, along with any pedagogical implications. Classifying this study on the Basic–Applied continuum is quite simple: I would put it very close to the Applied end as shown here.

Basic ⟵―――――――⟶ Applied

---

[1]There is no precise correct point to place these studies. We are only estimating their placement.

However, some studies might be considered in between these two extremes. If a study is built on a heavy theoretical base, yet has clear practical implications, it would fall somewhere in the middle. For example, Hu (2003) examined the effect of phonological memory and phonological awareness on learning vocabulary in a foreign language. *Phonological memory* was defined as the ability to repeat nonwords. *Phonological awareness* was explained to mean, "the ability to attend to, detect, and manipulate the sound units of one's native words independent of their meanings" (p. 432). On first blush, this study does not appear to relate to anything that would interest language teachers. However, Hu concluded that the findings of the study have important implications and offered several specific recommendations for the language teacher. Based on this, I would place the study near the middle of the continuum.

The prior discussion illustrates that the consumer of research should read research along this continuum. One type is not more important than another. For this reason, journals contain research covering the entire spectrum of this continuum (e.g., *Journal of Phonetics*).

The Qualitative–Quantitative Continuum

The Qualitative–Quantitative continuum has received a lot of attention over the past 20 years, usually accompanied with much controversy. When you read articles dealing with this debate, you might think that this is not a continuum, but two distinct armed camps. However, as you become more familiar with the research available, you will find that many studies are neither purely qualitative nor quantitative. This is in line with Larsen-Freeman and Long (1991), who described these two terms as two ends of a continuum that have different data-collecting procedures along with different degrees of subjectivity in interpreting data. My students' findings concur with this opinion, in that they have classified many studies somewhere between the two ends of this continuum.

The problem is that epistemological issues regarding the nature of reality have been wedded with these two methodologies, resulting in the polarization of a number of researchers into *camps*. I agree with Miles and Huberman (1994), however, who stated, "We believe that the quantitative–qualitative argument is essentially unproductive . . . we see no reason to tie the distinction to epistemological preferences" (p. 41). Therefore, I am not going to address the related philosophical issues of positivism and postpositivism in this book because I do not believe they are important for the consumer of research at this time. However, if you are interested in reading more about this, I recommend chapter 1 of Tashakkori and Teddlie (1998).

I try to use the terms *qualitative* and *quantitative* in ways that separate them from this philosophical spat—getting into epistemology is not necessary. However, you should be aware of the designs and methodologies that are typically associated with quantitative and qualitative approaches. Familiarization with these methods enables consumers of research to be eclectic and versatile—ready to digest whatever research method comes their way. Only then will the consumer be better able to find potential answers to research questions.

The two ends of this continuum mostly have their origins in different disciplines. Quantitative research has come mainly from the field of psychology, where there has been heavy emphasis on the use of statistics to make generalizations from samples to populations, thus the label *quantitative methods*. However, most methods under qualitative research have originated with anthropologists and sociologists who rely heavily on verbal description rather than numbers. Consequently, quantitative research is characterized by the use of numbers to represent its data, and qualitative research is characterized by verbal descriptions as its data.

I would add, in light of the discussion in chapter 4, that sampling paradigms also help distinguish between the two. Quantitative research frequently uses sample strategies for generalizing findings to larger populations, whereas qualitative research works to uncover information from information-rich samples.

Although some mistakenly think that qualitative research does not use any numbers or statistics, this is not necessarily so. A number of qualitative studies involve numbers in the form of frequencies of occurrence of certain phenomena and are analyzed by such statistical methods as chi-square. In fact a number of books have been written (e.g., Agresti, 1996; Leonard, 2000) describing statistical procedures for qualitative research.

Another misunderstanding regarding the differences between qualitative and quantitative approaches is that the former is atheoretical, whereas the latter is not. Although most qualitative research studies do not begin with theoretical hypotheses, developing theory (or, to be more precise, a theoretical hypothesis) is often their goal. For instance, an approach referred to as *grounded theory*, which arose out of anthropology, has become part of the qualitative research repertoire in applied linguistics. The express goal of this method is to develop a theoretical hypothesis from descriptive data as the data accumulate from the ground up. A good example of how such a theory is developed is Spielmann and Radnofsky's (2001) qualitative study, which looked at tension/anxiety in the language learning classroom. They clearly stated, ". . . our goal was to develop a *grounded theory*—one that is inductively based on the data rather than deductively derived from a predetermined hypothesis—on the role of tension in the process of instructed L2 acquisition" (p. 260).

So what is *qualitative research*? Miles and Huberman (1994, pp. 5–8) defined what they thought common features across different manifestations of qualitative research are. I have extracted and summarized them in the following list. Data are gathered:

- in natural settings,
- through concentrated contact over time,
- holistically—"systematic, encompassing, integrated,"
- from deep inside the situation with preconceived notions held in check,
- by the researcher who is the "main 'measurement device,' "
- to analyze for patterns, comparisons, and contrasts,
- with interpretations constrained by theoretical interests and/or "internal consistency," and
- consisting mainly of verbal data.

In other words, any study that is done in a real-life setting, involving intensive holistic data collection through observation at a close personal level without the influence of prior theory and contains mostly verbal analysis, could be classified as a qualitative study.

However, there are differing opinions as to what constitutes qualitative research. Gall et al. (1996) listed under their section on qualitative research such things as case studies, along with a list of 16 research traditions that are typically referred to as *qualitative research*. Among these are methods such as ethnography, protocol analysis, and discourse analysis—all commonly used methods in applied linguistics. Wolcott illustrated over 20 strategies in his famous tree diagram (Miles & Huberman, 1994, p. 6). Tesch organized 27 strategies into a flowchart under four general categories (Miles & Huberman, 1994, p. 7). Nunan (1992) included ethnography, case studies, introspective methods, and interaction analysis in his book. Johnson (1992) limited her book to case studies and ethnography. Interestingly, the TESOL Web site[2] lists only three strategies under the heading of qualitative research: case studies, conversational analysis, and ethnography.

Consequently, it is difficult to provide a simple overview of all of these qualitative research strategies for the up-and-coming consumer. Other texts are better designed to do this (e.g., Denzin & Lincoln, 2000; LeCompte, Millroy, & Preissle, 1992). In the following, however, I use the three general strategies that are mentioned in the TESOL Web site, and I have added a fourth—protocol analysis—mentioned by Gall et al. (1996).

---

[2]http://www.tesol.org/pubs/author/serials/tqguides2.html#qual. Retrieved January 10, 2004.

These strategies are commonly used in applied linguistics for the purpose of introducing qualitative research strategies.

Case Studies.   Case studies are frequently found in applied linguistics research. Gall et al. (1996) defined a *case study* as,

> the in-depth study of instances of a phenomenon in its natural context and from the perspective of the participants involved in the phenomenon. A case study is done to shed light on a phenomenon, which is the processes, events, persons, or things of interest to the researcher. Examples of phenomena are programs, curricula, roles, and events. Once the phenomenon of interest is clarified, the researcher can select a case for intensive study. A case is a particular instance of the phenomena. (p. 545)

Notice that the focus of a case study is on a specific phenomenon. Lam and Lawrence (2002), for example, did a case study that focused on "changes in teacher and student roles in a computer-based project" (p. 295) as the phenomena in a single Spanish foreign language classroom. They used a number of procedures to collect their data: observations, focus groups, questionnaires, and interviews. The data they worked with were mainly verbal. Being a case study that involved only one intact[3] class, the researchers recognized that their findings were not generalizable to larger populations. However, they believed that their findings were valid to transfer important implications for teaching and for stimulating future research.

Ethnography and Conversational Analysis.   These next two approaches are listed in the TESOL Web site. In my opinion, they are two ends of a continuum under the qualitative research banner. On the ethnography end, data are gathered from a number of sources (e.g., notes from observations, interviews, transcriptions of video and audio recordings, etc.), resulting in large quantities of information. The verbal data are examined carefully for any reoccurring themes, coded, reduced into groups of related information, and organized into patterns perceived by the researcher. Interpretations and conclusions are warranted with thick descriptions[4] of the data in the form of quotations from audiotapes, excerpts from interviews, and various documents for the purpose of triangulation.[5] Researchers typically begin their studies with research questions, but hold any preconceived hypothesis in abeyance until all the data have been processed.

---

[3]Intact groups are clusters of people who are found in natural settings, such as a classroom.

[4]A detailed description of the context and procedures of the study.

[5]The combination of different methods and data to validate interpretations.

On the other end of the continuum is *conversational analysis* (CA),[6] which uses one source of data, normally in the form of transcripts from audio-tapes. Lazaraton (2003) explained that,

> CA insists on the analysis of real, recorded data, segmented into turns of talk that are carefully transcribed. Generally speaking, the conversation analyst does not formulate research questions prior to analyzing the data. The goal is to build a convincing and comprehensive analysis of a single case, and then to search for other similar cases in order to build a collection of cases that represent some interactional phenomenon. (p. 3)

Lazaraton continued by stating that the CA procedure approaches the study from a totally inductive perspective by not relying on any prior knowledge about the context of the participants. She added that they seldom use any coding system and do not condense the data into groupings.

After perusing through a number of qualitative research studies, I found few that would fit all the criteria for a CA study. However, there are many studies that share some of the characteristics with CA, but also use methods from ethnography. In other words, they may only focus on a narrow set of data, such as transcripts, without triangulation, but they begin with pre-formulated research questions and may even have some theory guiding their interpretations.

An example of a study that I would place on the qualitative end of the qualitative–quantitative continuum and somewhere between ethnography and CA is one done by Goh (2002), who studied how listening comprehension techniques interact with one another. She selected 2 participants out of 80 ESL students, 1 male and 1 female. Based on scores from a standardized listening test, one participant was high and the other low in listening proficiency. Each participant was exposed to listening passages with built-in pauses. At each pause, the participant verbally reported how s/he was trying to comprehend the passage. These verbal reports were tape-recorded and later transcribed. Weekly listening diaries were also examined. Goh then took the verbal data and analyzed them using a verbal protocol procedure developed by Ericsson and Simon (1993) for distinguishing between actual tactics used versus general knowledge about strategies. The results section of Goh's article consisted of a detailed written description of how the verbal output by the two participants was classified and interpreted. No generalizations were made to any larger target population regarding the findings for tactics used by the two participants. I would place this study on the continuum as follows.

---

[6]See Nunan (1992) for an interesting comparison among discourse analysis, interactive analysis, and conversational analysis.

Qualitative ⟵——————⟶ Quantitative

Protocol Analysis. This fourth approach mentioned by Gall et al. (1996) has its origin in the field of cognitive psychology. Gall et al. defined it as "asking individuals to state all their thoughts as they carry out a challenging task, so that the researcher can obtain a holistic overview of their cognitive activity as recorded in their verbal reports" (p. 596). This is commonly known as the *think-aloud* approach. Similar to other qualitative procedures, audiotapes are made as participants think aloud. The tapes are transcribed and analyzed. This was the method mentioned earlier (Goh, 2002) in collecting data. I provide another example later in this chapter and give further attention to this method in the next chapter.

At the other end of this continuum is the *quantitative approach.* As mentioned earlier, studies located toward this end might test hypotheses or only try to gather information. However, one thing that is characteristic of most quantitative studies is that they try to generalize the results to some target population. As is shown in chapter 7, customarily when researchers use inferential statistics,[7] they plan to make inferences from a sample to a population.

An example that I would place toward the quantitative side of the continuum is Sanz's (2000) study, which examined whether bilingual education affects the learning of a third language. The first indicator as to the nature of this study is apparent in the title, "Bilingual Education Enhances Third Language Acquisition: Evidence From Catalonia." Such a statement strongly suggests that the study will try to generalize the findings to those trying to learn a third language. The next indicator is found in the Participants section (i.e., the Sample), where Sanz used 201 students from two private Jesuit schools. Because no mention is made of how she chose these schools, we must assume that they used a convenience sample. However, she went into detail to provide evidence that these two schools were representative of a population of similar schools. The third indicator is that she used inferential statistics to analyze her data. Consequently, this study should be positioned near the quantitative end of the continuum as shown here.

Qualitative ⟵——————⟶ Quantitative

Often you will find studies that fall somewhere in the middle of the continuum. They land in between the two extremes depending on how much of each methodology they use. These are referred to as *mixed-method approaches* (Creswell, 2002; Tashakkori & Teddlie, 1998, 2003), which combine both qualitative and quantitative methodologies in one study. The following study illustrates this point.

---

[7]I discuss all statistical terminology in greater detail in chapter 7.

Kamhi-Stein (2000) clearly stated in her study that she used both qualitative and quantitative methodologies. She investigated the effect of World Wide Web-based bulletin board discussions on student participants. Of her three research questions, one had to do with finding "quantitative differences between students' participation" (p. 430), and another wanted to know about the qualitative differences. In her Data Analysis section, Kamhi-Stein had two subsections: one for quantitative analysis and another for qualitative analysis. Similarly, in the Findings (i.e., Results) section, she reported on both quantitative and qualitative findings. As you would expect, I place this study right in the middle of the continuum.

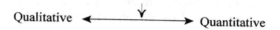

Qualitative ←————————→ Quantitative

The Exploratory–Confirmatory Continuum

The third independent continuum is labeled *Exploratory–Confirmatory* (Fig. 5.1). The main characteristic of this continuum is whether a study is trying to find evidence to support (i.e., confirm) a hypothesis or explore some phenomena prior to the development of any hypothesis.

On the confirmatory side of the continuum, Silva's (2000) study sought to answer two research questions. The first had to do with the comparison between NNS' and NS' emotional response to directives that begin with *Why don't you?* The other had to do with the relationship between longevity in an L2 environment and pragmatic transfer of these emotions. To answer these questions, she proposed two hypotheses. The first, relating to the first question, predicted that "American NNSs of Portuguese will fail in their judgments of appropriateness of directives in the frame *Why don't you* in their L2, due to their influence of their L1 pragmatic competence" (p. 163). The second predicted that "Brazilians who have lived in the US for longer periods of time will not be as accurate as the Brazilians who have lived in the US for not more than a year . . ." (p. 163). Silva designed the study to collect data to test these hypotheses. Her study can easily be plotted near the confirmatory end of the continuum as shown here.

Exploratory ←————————→ Confirmatory

The other studies cited in this chapter so far (i.e., Fukushima, 2002; Goh, 2002; Kamhi-Stein, 2000; Sanz, 2000; Spielmann & Radnofsky, 2001) did not test any hypotheses. They were exploratory. They attempted to find out what was happening without trying to support any particular hypothesis. They should all be located toward the exploratory end of the continuum.

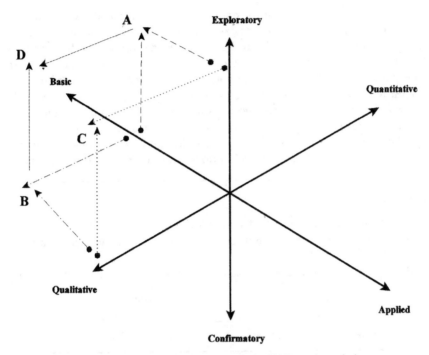

FIG. 5.2.   Example of classifying a study (Goh, 2002) on three design continua.

As Fig. 5.1 illustrates, the three continua intersect. This means that any given study can be plotted along all three continua at the same time. I have tried to show how this might be done in Fig. 5.2 with Goh's (2002) study. Point A shows where the study represents the point of intersection between the Basic–Applied and the Exploratory–Confirmatory continua. It is an exploratory study that is quite basic. Point B at the intersection of the Basic–Applied and Qualitative–Quantitative continua adds that the study is qualitative and quite basic. Point C at the intersection of the Exploratory–Confirmatory and Qualitative–Quantitative continua means that the study is qualitative/exploratory. You have to use your imagination a little to see where a study intersects when all three continua are taken into consideration. Point D attempts to show this, although it is difficult to display a three-dimensional graph on a two-dimensional piece of paper. The study is qualitative, exploratory, and quite basic.

After all of this discussion, I hope you understand that using *only* one of these continua is somewhat simplistic for describing research. The picture is even more complicated than this. For the moment, I have used these three continua to illustrate that there is more to a research study than what we might first be led to believe.

You might ask why this information is important for the consumer to know. The importance lies in the fact that a researcher's system for choosing procedures and an interpretative framework for his or her study is based on how his or her study is designed. For the consumer, knowing where a study intersects on these continua provides an overall framework for understanding the remainder of a study.

To help you become more familiar with the classification system just outlined, do the following exercise. As you read research with this system in mind, you will develop an understanding of why researchers do what they do. You will also realize when a researcher does something out of the ordinary.

Exercise 5.1

1. Find a recent study that interests you.
2. Plot the study on the three different continua based on your perusal of the study.
3. Provide a rationale for each placement based on what you find in the study.

Basic _____	Applied
Exploratory _____	Confirmatory
Qualitative _____	Quantitative

SECTION 2: QUESTIONS AND DESIGNS

Most research methodology books can give the impression that various research designs are independent from one another by the way they present them (i.e., a chapter per method; e.g., Gall et al., 1996; Johnson, 1992; Locke, Silverman, & Spirduso, 1998; Nunan, 1992). However, in my opinion, a more useful way to understand research designs is by organizing them around the type of research question under investigation.

As outlined in chapter 1, the two generic questions found in research literature center around *What* and *Why*. The second section of this chapter is structured around these generic questions and their subquestions. For each question type, I present the most common research designs found in applied linguistics research.

The WHAT Questions

What Phenomena Are Important?   To answer this question, researchers use designs that are usually classified as either Qualitative/Exploratory or Quantitative/Exploratory. These designs can be placed anywhere on the

Applied–Basic continuum. In such studies, there is no hypothesis to test. Rather the researcher is trying to gather information not known previously. The purpose might be to develop a hypothesis during the investigation or fill in missing information, but it is not to confirm an existing hypothesis.

To illustrate, Pailliotet (1997) did a (qualitative/exploratory/applied) case study using one Asian language minority student to try to fill in missing information "about personal experiences of ethnic and language pre-service teachers" (p. 675). She collected her data over a 2-year period using personal observation field notes, audiotaped semistructured interviews, the participant's written work for assignments, and interviews with people somehow related to the participant. While collecting these data, Pailliotet was careful to transcribe everything. She then analyzed the verbal data by looking for changes and/or consistencies. The final stage was to interpret the data.

A second example of a Qualitative/Exploratory study was the one by Spielmann and Radnofsky (2001) who used an ethnography with grounded theory design. As previously mentioned in this chapter, the purpose of their study was not to test a hypothesis, but to generate one from the ground up. Spielmann and Radnofsky sought to gain more insight into the notion of *tension* as an important factor in language learning separate from the construct *anxiety*. The culture that Spielmann and Radnofsky studied was a beginning French class at Middlebury College Language Schools. It supplied the researchers with an information-rich situation in that it is regarded by many as a place where students are under a lot of pressure to learn a language quickly. The two researchers had ample access to the students, faculty, staff, and the facilities due to their previous involvement in the school. To collect data, they used "a palette of standard naturalistic techniques" (p. 265), consisting of interviews, observations, informal and formal interactions, document analysis, and more. They recorded everything, including questions and interpretations, in the form of an extensive notation system. Due to the overwhelming amount of material collected, they only reported "a fraction of the data" (p. 266). Such restrictions are characteristic of studies of this kind due to the space limitations imposed by journals.

However, quantitative designs are also used to answer What questions. Sanz's (2000) study, as you might remember, examined whether bilingualism influenced the learning of a third language. Although she was specifically looking at the interaction of bilingualism with learning a third language, she gathered numerical data on a number of variables (e.g., IQ, age, economic status, motivation, attitudes, etc.) to eliminate their effects as extraneous variables on the variables of interest. A quick glance at her Results section confirms the quantitative nature of this study. The fact that the study did not have a hypothesis shows that Sanz was exploring for information that was not yet known.

Before moving on to another research question with its corresponding research methodologies, do the following exercise to provide yourself with firsthand experience in examining an article that applies the prior discussion.

Exercise 5.2

Find a recent study that tries to answer the following question: What phenomena are of importance (i.e., **NOT** correlational, nor cause/effect)?

1. Classify it on the three continua.
2. State the research question(s).
3. Identify the variables in the study.
4. Summarize the methodology of the study by explaining in your own words how the researcher(s) designed the study to answer the research question(s).

What Simple Relationships Exist Between Phenomena?   Except for research that only wants to identify and describe phenomena, all other research is in one way or other looking at relationships between phenomena. Some researchers want to know if there are any simple relationships between constructs. However, by *simple*, I do not mean the relationships are unimportant or lack complexity. Here the term means a relationship between only two variables. Many simple relationships have profound implications for the language classroom.

A synonym commonly used for a simple relationship is *correlation*. This is not to be confused with the term *correlation coefficient*, which is a specific statistic used to indicate a correlation (i.e., a type of simple relationship).

Research on this question can be classified anywhere on all three of the classification continua. It can be confirmatory or exploratory, qualitative or quantitative, basic or applied. Different from the previous What question, the researcher may have a hypothesis to test for answering the question. Following the research question "What relationships exist?", for instance, s/he may hypothesize that a relationship between certain variables does exist. The researcher could do this based on theory or the findings of previous research.

The most common design used to examine simple relationships gathers data on two or more variables and then correlates each pair of variables using various statistical procedures. Carrell and Wise (1998), for example, explored whether there were simple relationships among prior knowledge, topic interest, and second language reading in the first of their three research questions. Using a simple correlational procedure, one of their findings revealed no meaningful relationship between prior knowledge and topic interest, contrary to expectations.

Another study done by Ehrman and Oxford (1995) illustrates the use of the shotgun[8] method to find relationships among variables. The purpose of their study was to find which of over 20 variables correlated with end-of-training speaking and reading performance. Interestingly, they found that all of the variables correlated, some stronger than others. The advantage of this method is that a lot of relationships can be explored at the same time.

Regarding correlational studies, however, I want to reiterate an important principle here: **Finding a relationship between two variables is not enough to conclude that one variable causes the other to change.** Ehrman and Oxford (1995) could not (and did not) conclude from their data that the variables they found to correlate with end-of-training performance actually *caused* the differences in performance. For instance, they found that belief about self correlated positively with end-of-training performance on both speaking and reading. They might have been tempted to suggest from this finding that if a student's belief about him or herself (i.e., self-esteem) can be improved, the student will learn more. However, they were careful not to fall into this trap. The reason becomes apparent in that, based on these data, one could also say that if a student's ability to speak and read in another language were improved, his or her self-esteem would increase. The reason that both interpretations are possible is that correlations are symmetrical (i.e., Variable A correlates with Variable B in the same way that Variable B correlates with Variable A). But now I am getting into issues that I discuss more fully in chapter 7.

Ehrman and Oxford (1995) explained that their "ultimate purpose is to provide learner profiles for use in diagnoses of learning difficulties, student counseling, teacher training, curriculum design, and prediction of language of language learning success" (p. 67). They were careful to state that it was their ultimate purpose, which suggests that the findings of their study were part of a preliminary step in a process that requires more research, other than simple correlations, before they convert their intentions to recommendations.

There are a number of other ways that relationships are explored, but they relate directly to certain statistical procedures. Consequently, I reserve further discussion for chapter 7 when dealing with different statistical methods.

---

[8]That is, a number of variables are analyzed at the same time with the hope that some relationships will be found.

I recommend that you take this opportunity to do the following exercise to give you another example of a study looking for simple relationships. To help you locate one more quickly, I suggest you look for the keyword *relation(ship)* in the title.

Exercise 5.3

Find a recent study in a research journal that investigates the following question: Are there any important simple relationships between phenomena?

1. Classify the study on the three continua.
2. What relationships were being examined?
3. State any hypothesis and/or prediction made (if any).
4. Identify the variables in the study.
5. Summarize the methodology of the study by explaining in your own words how the researcher(s) designed the study to answer the research question(s).

The WHY Questions

Once we begin to understand what phenomena are out there or what relationships exist between variables, we begin to ask *why*. Why do people vary in the phenomena we observe to be important to a particular issue? Why do certain variables relate with one another? The essence of this type of question is causation. Causation indicates a more specific type of relationship between variables than only a *simple* relationship. Causal relations delineate how variables (i.e., constructs) affect other variables. Why do some people learn languages better than others? What makes people good readers? Does using computers affect the way people write? If only we could discover why, we might be able to help improve desirable abilities and discourage undesirable ones in language learning.

To refresh your memory from chapter 3, the variable(s) suspected of causing variation in another variable(s) is the *independent variable(s)*. The variable(s) being influenced by the independent variable(s) is the *dependent variable(s)*. Sometimes the intent of the researcher is made clear in the title of a study and the variables are easily identified. Kobayashi (2002) expressly stated in her title, "Method Effects on Reading Comprehension Test Performance: Text Organization and Response Format," that she is exploring a causal relationship. From this title she informs the reader that she is examining whether text organization and response format influence examinees' performance on tests of reading comprehension. Other researchers might use terms in their titles such as *impact, influence, improve, change, role of,* and so on when they are investigating whether variables cause changes in other variables. But they are all referring to causation.

Such studies have at least one independent variable and at least one dependent variable. The study just mentioned (Kobayashi, 2002) has two independent variables (text organization and response format) and one dependent variable (reading comprehension). Some studies might even have more than one dependent variable. I cite some examples later.

Research into causal relationships is not restricted to any one end of the three continua discussed in Section 1 of this chapter. Causal studies can be Basic or Applied, Exploratory or Confirmatory, Qualitative or Quantitative. The key characteristic of this type of study is that it is looking for one or more causal relationships.

Causal Qualitative Studies.   Some mistakenly believe that causal relationships can only be studied using quantitative approaches. However, Miles and Huberman (1994) clearly described how causal relationships are studied using qualitative research designs. A study that illustrates this is one by Wesche and Paribakht (2000), who asked why a particular enhanced reading method worked better than *reading only* for learning vocabulary. The independent variable was reading method and the dependent variable was vocabulary acquisition. To answer this question, the researchers deliberately used three think-aloud[9] techniques to maximize the information they were seeking. They used 10 volunteers from the same institution who had the same level of ESL. By analyzing the verbal output of each of these participants and identifying commonalities, Wesche and Paribakht were able to identify possible causative factors that make the difference. I classified this study as *qualitative/exploratory/applied* on our three intersecting continua.

Causal-Comparative Designs.   On the more quantitative side, one common research design that is used to examine causal relationships is the *causal-comparative* design. However, as is made apparent, the findings from this design might suggest cause/effect, but they cannot answer for sure whether the variation in the dependent variable is being caused by the independent variable. The reason is that the nature of the independent variable prohibits the researcher from manipulating it.

Let me first illustrate the causal-comparative method with an actual study. MacIntyre et al. (2002) investigated the causal relationship between two independent variables (sex and age) and four dependent variables (one at a time): willingness to communicate, anxiety, perceived competence, and L2 motivation. Part of the title of the study, "Sex and Age Effects

---

[9]Think-aloud is a protocol analysis procedure where participants are required to talk about what they are thinking. Usually they are video- or audiorecorded while talking.

on . . . ," strongly indicates a cause-and-effect study. However, the research-ers did not manipulate the independent variables. Sex and age cannot be manipulated. They are taken as is; males and females are found in nature at given ages. The sex and age of a participant is a given. In other words, if an independent variable is found already in existence and is not manipulated by the researcher, as is the case with sex and age, the research design is la-beled *causal-comparative.*

Why does this make any difference, you might ask? The reason is that, by not being able to control or manipulate the independent variable, other variables associated with this variable might be the real cause behind any variation in the dependent variable rather than the independent variable it-self. Take *age,* for example. MacIntyre et al. (2002) found, among other things, that willingness to communicate in French as an L2 increased from 7th to 8th grade (i.e., their operational definition of age), but leveled off between 8th and 9th grade. However, can they conclude that difference in age, although only between 7th and 8th grade, *caused* the increase? Not with much confidence. The reason is that some other variable could have contributed to the change between the 7th and 8th grade at the particular school where the participants attended other than age. Did something hap-pen during this 2-year span other than the participants getting older? Most likely a lot happened. For this reason, MacIntyre et al. cannot—and did not—make strong causal conclusions based on their study, which used a causal-comparative design.

For practical or ethical reasons, many independent variables cannot be manipulated. For example, if a researcher wants to know whether eco-nomic status influences language learners' use of reading strategies, s/he cannot manipulate the economic status of the participants. In other words, s/he cannot choose random groups of people who have no economic stat-us and then randomly assign each group where s/he increases or decreases participants' economic level. Each participant already comes from an eco-nomic level when s/he participates in the study. So, the researcher takes random samples from each economic group and then examines whether they differ on what reading strategies they choose (i.e., the dependent vari-able). As with sex and age, the difficulty here is that economic groups differ in a number of other ways that might influence how they choose reading strategies.

The validity of any causal conclusions based on results from a causal-comparative study increases with the amount of care the researcher takes when designing the study. For this reason, you need to attend carefully to how the researcher tries to control for any competing alternative explana-tions for the potential results. MacIntyre et al. (2002) were careful to inform the reader that the three grade levels were housed in the same building, and the participants came from the same community and had similar previous

exposure to French as an L2. This information rules out that any age difference was due to the grade levels being housed in separate buildings or representing students from different communities. However, it would have been
helpful if they would have also reported whether any special events had occurred for the 7th graders that were different for the 8th graders to rule out
any other possible factors that may have produced differences.

Now let us see whether you can find a causal-comparative study for your
own by doing the following exercise. The keywords to look for in the title,
abstract, or research questions in the introduction of the studies you peruse
are: *effect, impact, influence,* and so on, along with variables that cannot be
manipulated, such as sex, age, language level, nationality, and so on.

Exercise 5.4

Identify a recent study from a research journal that answers a WHY question
using a causal-comparative design.

1. State the research question.
2. Identify the independent variable(s) and the dependent variable(s).
3. State any hypotheses and predictions made (if any).
4. Study the introduction and methodology section. In your own words, explain why you think this is a causal-comparative study.
5. Identify any strategies used for controlling for any alternative explanations
   of the results.
6. How strong were the researcher's conclusions? In your opinion, were they
   justified?

Experimental and Quasi-Experimental Designs.   As you might expect, if
there are variables that cannot be manipulated, there are other variables
that can be. Designs that manipulate independent variables are grouped
under the heading *experimental* or *quasi-experimental.* Both experimental and
quasi-experimental research designs involve manipulating the independent variable(s) and observing the change in the dependent variable(s). The
goal of this genre of design in comparison to others is that researchers try
to *control* changes in the variance of the independent variable(s) without allowing the intervention of other unwanted variables. In one of the simpler
designs, there is one group of participants that gets the treatment and another group that does not (i.e., the control group). For example, Demirci
(2000) used one treatment group consisting of 170 native Turkish speakers, one control group of 25 native Turkish speakers, and another control
group of 25 native English speakers. She manipulated pragmatic bias (the
independent variable) in sentences containing reflexives to see whether

choice of possible antecedents (the dependent variable) was affected. The treatment group received the pragmatic biased sentences, but the control groups did not.

The difference between experimental and quasi-experimental research has to do with how the sample is selected. If the samples for the treatment and control groups are randomly selected, the design is experimental. If not, it is quasi-experimental. This is an important difference because any sample that is not randomly sampled could be biased, and thereby could unintentionally allow extraneous variables to affect the results of the study. *Bias*, here, has a specific meaning. If there is a systematic difference in the makeup of either the treatment or control group that might affect the results of the study, other than the treatment variable, the samples are biased.

Demirci's (2000) study, mentioned earlier, would be classified as quasi-experimental because the samples were not randomly chosen. Although this was not mentioned in the study, it can be inferred from the fact that nothing was said about how the sample was chosen. If this is the case, then the question arises as to whether there were any important differences between the treatment and control groups other than receiving or not receiving the treatment.

Purely experimental studies are uncommon in applied linguistic research mainly because it is difficult to randomly select participants from experimentally accessible populations (cf. chap. 4). There are two characteristics that identify them: whether the independent variable was manipulated by the researcher(s) and whether some form of randomization was used in selecting the participants. One example is a study by Martin, Claydon, Morton, Binns, and Pratt (2003), which investigated the effects of orthographic and phonological strategies on children's ability to decode words developmentally. The researchers randomly sampled 191 children from Grades 1 to 10 from four high schools and five elementary schools in differing socioeconomic areas in Southern Tasmania. By doing so, they increased the external validity (cf. chap. 4) of generalizing the findings of the study to the target population. Second, the researchers manipulated two independent variables: modality in which words where presented (visual vs. oral) and instruction type (phonological vs. orthographic). This study is clearly classified as experimental.

Random selection of participants is sometimes substituted by another randomization procedure called *random assignment.* Instead of randomly selecting participants from a pool of possible participants, the treatment is randomly assigned to participants who may have been part of a convenience sample. Note, however, that this use of randomization does not necessarily increase the external validity of the study. The researcher might assign treatments randomly to participants within intact groups, such as classrooms. Such groups are not usually representative of a larger target population to which generalizations can be made. Conclusions, therefore, may not be directly generalizable to the target population.

Swanborn and de Glopper (2002) provided an example of the benefits of using random assignment in an experimental study. They examined the effects of reading purpose on learning incidental vocabulary from the context of a reading passage. They randomly assigned one of four reading purposes to each of 223 sixth-grade students in nine schools in the Netherlands. Obviously, it would have been practically impossible to randomly select these students, take them out of school, bring them to some research center, and place them in one of four groups based on the four reading purposes. Swanborn and de Glopper took care to test the reading comprehension ability of the participants to check whether the sample represented the national norms so as to provide evidence for external validity.

Experimental/quasi-experimental studies come in a variety of designs. I counted over 12 designs presented in chapters 12 and 13 of Gall et al. (1996). The reason there are so many different designs is that there are many extraneous variables, other than the independent variable(s), that might cause the dependent variable to vary. Each design tries to control a specific set of these unwanted variables. I do not go into detail here, but suffice it to say that each design is defined by various combinations and ordering of the treatment and control groups along with random or nonrandom sampling. If you would like more detail, I recommend Gall et al. or Krathwohl (1998).

SECTION 3: INTERNAL VALIDITY

When discussing cause and effect in research, no matter where the study fits on the three continua discussed in Section 1, the internal validity of the study is of critical importance. The extent to which extraneous variables affect the change in the dependent variable is the extent to which the internal validity is influenced. Whereas *external validity* relates to the degree to which findings can be generalized/transferred to populations or situations (cf. chap. 4), *internal validity* is concerned with the degree to which the results of the study are due to the independent variable(s) under consideration and not due to anything else. Researchers favoring more qualitative approaches use the term *credibility* to mean the same thing as *internal validity* (Miles & Huberman, 1994).

Internal and external validity are not mutually exclusive. The degree to which a study lacks internal validity limits the degree to which the findings can be generalized to a target population (i.e., external validity). In other words, for a study that looks at causation, internal validity is a necessary requirement for external validity. Obviously, if the changes in the dependent variable are not due to the independent variable, then you certainly cannot generalize any findings to some target population. Nevertheless, having internal validity is not sufficient for establishing external validity. That is, a study might be designed so that the independent variable is the only thing that could cause change in the dependent variable. Because the sample is not representative of the target population or comparable to any other situation, the results of the study cannot be generalized/transferred to that population or situations. The following may be of some help.

As previously mentioned, there are a number of extraneous factors that can affect the results of a study that will lower the internal and external validity of a study. Gall et al. (1996) gave a good overview (chap. 12) of the work done by Campbell and Stanley (1963), Cook and Campbell (1979), Bracht and Glass (1998), and others that try to identify most of the extraneous factors that can play havoc when exploring causal relationships. They listed 12 factors related to internal validity and 12 factors under external validity. Miles and Huberman (1994) presented a similar list of factors from a qualitative research perspective in their chapter 10 (viz. Sections B and C).

I reworked these lists to remove redundancies and make things more manageable. I have also subordinated some of the factors to show how they relate to one another. As a result, I list 14 threats to internal validity along with 9 subordinate ones. I illustrate these extraneous factors with the research minefield presented in Fig. 5.3. A well-designed study will weave around these hazards to capture a more accurate picture of how the independent variable(s) influences the dependent variable. The following is a brief explanation for each of the 14 *mines* with examples of studies that have either avoided or hit them.

History is one of the possible mines to avoid. It refers to the influence of events that take place at different points in time on the dependent variable other than the independent variable. Any study that takes considerable time to be completed can be affected by this if care is not taken. For instance, suppose a researcher is running a study on improving the L2 of young children using some new teaching methodology over a period of several months. During that time, a new bilingual (L1/L2) TV program is put on national TV. If the researcher found any difference between the treatment and control groups, could s/he be certain that the results were only due to the new methodology? Could the new methodology have interacted with the new TV program in such a way as to produce the results? Had the program not appeared when it did, the new methodology might not have produced the same results. Consequently, the researcher could not be sure what caused the changes in language behavior, if any were observed.

Longitudinal studies (i.e., studies that are done over a period of time) are vulnerable to the History mine. An example is the study done by Azpillaga et al. (2001), who investigated the effects of a teaching method involving

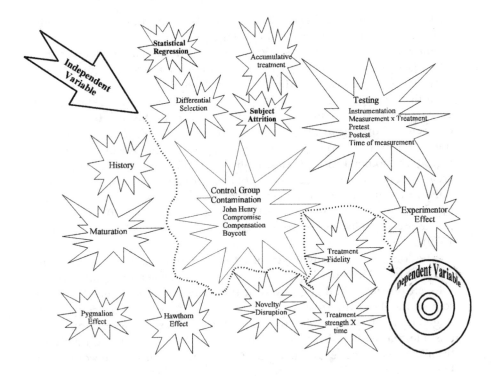

FIG. 5.3.   The research minefield.

drama on a class of students learning English as a third language over a 2-year period. The independent variable was the teaching method: dramatized format versus nondramatized format. The dependent variable was achievement in English as measured by aural comprehension and oral production tasks. The sample consisted of fifty 8- to 9-year-old, 3rd primary-level students from 10 schools for the experimental group and 20 of the same age and level from four other schools with the same linguistic and sociogeographical makeup for the control group. The study began in 1993 and was completed in 1995. Although the researchers were careful to describe many factors about the study, they did not report whether there were any significant events or changes in policy that took place during this 2-year period. Because both the experimental and control groups were in the same region, such changes, if there were any, would have most likely affected them equally. Yet some historical events can interact with a treatment in different ways than with the control group and produce results that otherwise would not have happened. To give more confidence to the results of longitudinal studies, it is always wise for a researcher to inform the reader if anything of possible importance had occurred historically. Even if nothing happened, this should be reported so that the reader is made aware that this precaution was attended to.

Maturation is similar to History, but deals with the natural changes that take place over time in the participants other than what is under study. Such areas as physical coordination and strength, emotional states, and cognitive structures change as people grow older. Studies that take place over longer periods of time are potentially subject to this interference. For example, according to Piaget, young children who are at the pre-operational (Ormrod, 1995) stage, between the ages of 2 and 6, "confuse psychological phenomena with physical reality" (p. 175). In the next stage, concrete operational (6–11/12 years), children are able to think logically, but only with visible concrete objects. If Piaget's thinking is valid, we would have to take great care in the use of visual objects when using them to examine language ability of children across these stages (cf. Perry & Shwedel, 1979).

The longitudinal study by Azpillaga et al. (2001) should not have had this problem. Their participants were all the same age and would have developed physically and cognitively at the same pace. However, if there is something about the treatment that interacts with certain developmental stages, then different results could be found. In this study, for example, is it possible that early pubescent children respond to drama more than children who have not yet reached that change in their lives? We would only know if someone did such a study.

Differential selection can occur whenever a researcher does not randomly select his or her samples when forming different groups for comparison purposes. Any preexisting differences between groups caused by choosing dissimilar participants could result in differences between groups not due to the variable being investigated. The classical situation where this might occur is when two intact classrooms are used: one for the treatment group and the other for the control group. Chances are that there are preexisting differences between the classes. Accordingly, these prior differences, and not the treatments, could account for any difference in the dependent variable between groups.

Azpillaga et al. (2001) did not use random sampling to select their participants for their study, but they were careful to match their participants on several criteria. They had teachers select five students from their classrooms: one shy, one trouble-maker, and three normal for both the treatment and control groups. They also took measures on a number of variables such as attitude and intelligence so they could check for any differences between the experimental and control groups. In fact they found differences between the two groups and controlled for these differences using statistical procedures. These procedures are necessary when participants are not randomly sampled in a quasi-experimental design.

The results of Demirci's study (2000), previously referred to, might have been influenced by *differential selection*. Remember, she had 170 in her treatment group and two groups of 25 for her two control groups: one from the same source as the 170 and the other from a humanities course in a U.S. university. They were not randomly selected as far as we know. However, a possible problem might have arisen if differences between groups were due to the effects caused by the difference in size of the groups: 170 versus 25 and 25. Aware of this, Demirci argued that, at least for the 25 Turkish participants coming from the same department as the 170, there should be no difference. But the chances that the 25 are similar in characteristics to the 170 participants in the treatment group decrease when the samples are not randomly sampled, although they come from the same department.

Statistical regression is a fancy name for a phenomenon found in research where participants chosen from two opposite ends of an ability continuum, usually based on performance on some test, have a high probability of scoring closer to the middle of the continuum on the second testing without any outside help. This movement of scores toward the middle is referred to as *regression toward the mean* or *statistical regression*. This can manifest itself when a researcher selects participants who initially score very low on a language ability test and tests them again after administering some form of treatment to raise their ability level. Any increase in performance after the treatment could not be conclusively attributed to the treatment because it might be due to the statistical phenomenon of regressing upward toward the mean (i.e., the middle of the ability group). Why does this happen, you might ask? The reason is that test scores are not exact measurements of a person's ability. Many people who initially do badly on a test may have done badly for a variety of reasons—maybe they were not feeling well or something disturbing happened on the way to the test. If they had taken the test on another day, they might have done better. This is just one possible explanation of this phenomenon.

However, in the case of qualitative research, the extreme cases might be exactly what the researcher is focusing on (Miles & Huberman, 1994). If s/he is trying to obtain a sample that contains information-rich information to answer the research question, then this strategy is the correct one. Statistical regression is not a factor.

Subject attrition (also known as *experimental mortality*) occurs when there is a loss of participants during a research study. This can affect the results and be misleading because attrition does not commonly occur randomly. People who drop out of a study often differ from those who remain in ways that distort research findings. For example, a researcher might lose some beginning-level EFL learners from his or her sample because they lose interest and drop out. This might leave the study not only with proportionally more participants of higher ability levels, but with participants who have higher motivation. A study that might have been affected by attrition was done by Wallinger (2002), who investigated the effects of block scheduling on learning a foreign language. *Block scheduling* is a nontraditional format that varies the classroom schedules during the instructional week. Wallinger was able to obtain 66 classes from various high schools that had a French program for Grade 9. She began the study with classes that could be grouped into three different scheduling strategies. The number of classes in each group were 23, 23, and 20. However, she reported that six classes did not complete the study. The problem was that all six were from the same scheduling strategy, which later produced some important differences. The question immediately arises whether this particular scheduling had something to do with the classes dropping out. If so, these data are important to the findings.

Sometimes researchers drop participants from groups to produce equal numbers in each group, often referred to as a *cell*. The reason they do this is that many statistical procedures are easier to interpret when there are equal cell sizes. However, you want to check whether participants are dropped randomly. If this is done, there is less chance that a bias may occur. Another caveat is that, when dealing with smaller numbers of participants, the loss of even one participant can have a significant impact on the results. The conclusion is that when you read a research article, give attention to any irregularities in the sample. There should be clear documentation to show that the results of the study were not contaminated by any participant attrition.

Control group contamination is important to consider. Many studies use control groups in their designs. Typically, a control group is one that does not receive the novel treatment, which is the focus of the study. For instance, a new method for teaching vocabulary might be compared with a traditional method.[10]

However, this effect could better be referred to as *competing group contamination*. The reason is that some studies compare differences between groups, possibly without a control group. These studies have several competing treatment groups. In such studies, the following discussion is still applicable.

The Azpillaga et al. (2001) study, discussed previously, is used in the following discussion as a platform for illustrating the four ways a control group can affect the results of a study. Recall that they compared two methods of teaching a third language: dramatized format versus nondramatized format. They noted that the only difference between the treatment and con-

---

[10]Just a note of warning here. What constitutes a *traditional* method varies with each study. You should examine whether the traditional method is clearly defined so that you know exactly what is meant by *traditional*. By doing so, you can understand to what the novel method is being compared (cf. *treatment fidelity* later in this chapter).

trol groups was "using a different method" (p. 38). Yet they stated that each of the four groups of participants used in the control group "differed from group to group because there was no coordination between these schools" (p. 38). In contrast, the treatment given to the eight groups coming from eight different schools was tightly constrained to ensure no variation in the treatment.

Control group contamination can take four different directions. They are:

1. *Control group rivalry (John Henry effect):* When the behavior of the control group is different because it is trying to outdo the treatment group, you cannot be sure the results are due to the treatment(s), i.e., the independent variable(s). This condition might occur if the control group were explicitly labeled "the control group." Not only might extra effort come from the participants in the group, but the person supervising the control group, such as a teacher, might apply extra effort to compete. The thing to look for is whether the researcher has specified what measures were taken to protect from this effect. A careful researcher will take precautions to keep the groups' identities a secret and report them in his/her study.

In the Azpillaga et al. (2001) study, care was taken to mention that the four schools from which the control group was selected came from the same sociogeographical location as the eight schools used for selecting the treatment group. Although there was no mention of the possible *John Henry* problem, had the control group heard about what was going on in the nearby schools, they may have been challenged to compete. This would have been a possible explanation had there been no difference between the experimental and control groups. However, the experimental group outperformed the control group, so this was not a problem.

2. *Experimental treatment diffusion (Compromise):* When the control group gains knowledge of the factor(s) making up the treatment condition(s) and employs this factor(s) in its own situation, the results are corrupted. The extraneous variable here is *not* competition, as in (1), but rather the inclusion of the treatment factors in the control group due to knowledge about what constituted the treatment. This often happens when the control and treatment groups are in close proximity and have time to get to know what the other is doing. Care should be taken to reduce the possibility of participants from the two groups discussing what the other is doing.

Looking at the Azpillaga et al. (2001) study, we can conclude that this did not happen, although there might have been common awareness of what was happening in the experimental treatment. Similar to the John

Henry effect, this problem might have been of concern if there had been no difference between the treatment and control groups, or if the control group outperformed the treatment group.

3. *Compensatory equalization of treatments:* When attempts are made to give the control group extra material or special treatment to make up for not receiving the experimental treatment, you no longer have a true control group. In fact you would have a new treatment group.

The temptation to provide the control group with extra help arises when there is a possibility that the treatment group will have an advantage over the control group in some real-life situation. To illustrate, if a researcher were comparing some new method of teaching grammar (treatment group) to the traditional way (control group) grammar was being taught during a real language course, s/he might be tempted to give the control group some extra material or help so that they would not be at an unfair disadvantage at the end of the course. However, in doing so, the differences between treatment and control could be distorted, making the results uninterpretable. Again because the experimental group outperformed the control group in the Azpillaga et al. (2001) study, this most likely did not occur.

To prevent *compensatory equalization of treatments* from happening, a researcher should use someone to supervise the control group who is unaware of the advantage the treatment group might have during the study. In addition, s/he should allow time after the experiment to help the control group catch up with those in the treatment group so that the control group is not unduly penalized. A well-written study will report how this problem was addressed.

4. *Demoralization (boycott) of the control group:* This potential contaminator occurs when participants in the control group resent the special treatment given to the treatment group and lower their performance. This is the opposite of the John Henry effect. If participants in the control group, for example, learn that those in the treatment group have access to computers to help them increase their writing ability while they have to use paper and pencil, their envy might cause them to refuse to cooperate with their instructor. To prevent this, some strategy needs to be used to convince the control group that it is not being deprived.

Here the Azpillaga et al. (2001) study might have had a problem. Because the schools used for both the treatment and control groups were in the same sociogeographical location, the control group might have become demoralized if it had news that it was not getting the new interesting drama format method. In turn it might have given less effort to learn than normal. This offers an alternative explanation for the inferior performance of the control group in comparison with the treatment group. Because Azpillaga et al. did not state whether they tried to prevent this, we are left with this alternative explanation regarding their findings.

Testing refers to ways in which measuring the dependent variable(s) can distort the results of a study. Under this heading, I listed five sources to which the consumer of research needs to pay attention.

1. *Instrumentation* relates to the type of instrument used to measure performance on the dependent variable(s). This can occur if two different types of instruments are used and the performance of the two are compared with each other. For example, if one test of English proficiency were used (e.g., a multiple-choice test) as a pretest and another test of English proficiency (e.g., an essay test) were used as a posttest, you would not know whether any change in test score was due to increase in ability or difference in the difficulty level between the two tests. Unless the two tests are parallel in all possible ways, the results between the two tests cannot be compared.

2. *Measurement–treatment interaction* is similar, but in this case the results are only found when using a particular type of measure. To illustrate, we might only be able to find certain effects of a novel method for teaching grammar in an EFL context with multiple-choice exams, but not with tests of written compositions. Any attempt to generalize results from only one type of measurement to all types would be groundless.

Almost every study using only one type of instrument to measure the dependent variables could be accused of having this problem. Zahar et al. (2001), for example, used the same test format for pretesting participants' prior knowledge of the targeted vocabulary as well as for the posttest after the treatment. The format followed the test design of the Nation's Vocabulary Levels Test (cited in Zahar et al., 2001, p. 547), in which participants matched words to definitions. The discerning reader should ask whether the same results would have been found if other measures of vocabulary retention had been used. This is not to suggest, however, that the findings of this study are insignificant. They are important, but they are only part of the puzzle. To bolster their conclusions, this study should be replicated using other vocabulary assessment formats to see whether the findings are replicated. Zahar et al., in fact, clearly warned the reader in their Note 3 that this type of assessment format has inherent reliability problems. As you see in the next chapter, if there are reliability problems, there are validity problems.

3. The *pretest effect* is caused when a test given before the administration of the treatment interacts with the treatment by heightening participants'

awareness of the importance of certain material. If this happens, the performance on the test given after the treatment (i.e., the *posttest*) would be
higher than if there were no pretest. The question here is whether the pretest alerts the participants to components in the treatment to which they
would not normally pay much attention. The only way we would know
whether this occurred would be if we had another treatment group that did
not take the pretest and compared their performance on the posttest with
that of the pretest/treatment group. If there was no difference, then we
could conclude that there was no pretest effect.

The Zahar et al. (2001) results might have been influenced by this. They
used the exact same test for assessing the prior knowledge of 30 vocabulary
words in their pretest as they did for their posttest after the treatment.
There was a 13-day interval between the pretest and the onset of the treatment due to a vacation to control for memory. The researchers stated:

> There is little likelihood that they [the participants] would have had further
> exposure to any of the test words. The delay was also intended to allow a lapse
> between seeing the words in the test and seeing them again in the story, re-
> ducing any possibility that test words would have been learned from the pre-
> test definitions rather from the story itself. (pp. 549–550)

Obviously, they were aware of this possible threat to the internal validity
to their study. On the one hand, they avoided the problem of instrumentation mentioned earlier by using the same test. However, had they used an
additional group that did not take the pretest prior to the treatment, they
could have tested whether there was any pretest effect. That is, if no difference between the two treatment groups (i.e., pretest with treatment vs.
treatment without pretest) on the posttest was found, they would have clear
evidence that the pretest did not interact with the treatment.

4. *Posttest effect* can also have an effect on the treatment. Unwittingly, the
researcher might design his or her posttest so that it helps participants *make
associations* between different concepts at the time of taking the test rather
than during the time of treatment. Had another test been used, these associations might not have been made, and the conclusion would be that the
treatment had no effect.

Most likely you have experienced this effect when taking an exam some-
time in the past, like most of us. It is known as the *click of comprehension* effect. As participants take the posttest, suddenly something in the test brings
things together in a way that the participants had not thought of previously,

but this effect was something that the treatment was supposed to have done prior to the posttest, not during it.

This effect might be seen when the posttest is an oral interview given after a treatment that tries to improve students' oral language ability. If the interviewer is not careful, something that she or he says may actually teach the interviewee some correct form of spoken language that was not previously known. The interviewee then uses the newly learned form in answering the question, thus giving the impression that the treatment made the improvement. To avoid this, the interviewer must ensure that the target issues being assessed are not used inadvertently when asking questions.

5. *Time of measurement effect* relates to timing. Many studies apply whatever measurement they are using immediately after the completion of the treatment. To conclude that such results can be interpreted to mean that the treatment also has long-term effects would be misleading. For us to make such an inference, we would have to have an additional measurement with an appropriate time interval.

To control for this effect, some studies administer the test without warning a week or more later. Rodriguez and Sadoski (2000) provided an example of how to control for this effect. In their study, they compared four mnemonic methods to aid students in acquiring new vocabulary. Each of the four treatment groups was first instructed how to use a mnemonic method and then, in a separate session, given 15 new vocabulary words to learn. Half of each of the groups were given an immediate test, and half were given the same test 1 week later. Participants were previously randomly assigned to these groups. By doing this, the researchers could clearly see whether there was a time of measurement effect. In fact they found that there was. The immediate test group performed higher than the delayed test group. However, more important, one mnemonic method (context/keyword) was found to be superior to only one of the three other methods (keyword) when tested immediately after the treatments, but outperformed all of the other methods 1 week later in the delayed task. Had they only given an immediate test, they would not have found that the context/keyword method had longer term effects on retention than the other methods.

The ***researcher effect*** can also be a source for data distortion, which in turn weakens the internal validity of the results. If the results are determined by who does the experiment or who does the interview, the results are questionable. This problem often occurs when the researcher is the one who is either administering the treatment or collecting data that depend on his or her judgment. A study that exemplifies the care needed to avoid this effect is Bejarano, Levine, Olshtain, and Steiner's (1997), which examined whether training in interaction strategies increased the quality of communication in small-group language learning situations. They correctly described how and why they chose the two teachers used in their study "in order to minimize teacher effect" (p. 208): one for the experimental group and the other for the control group. Had the researchers administered the treatment and control, they might have done things in such a way that the results would have been influenced in the direction they predicted.

Another way the researcher can affect the results is simply by being there while collecting the data. Just the presence of a data gatherer can distort the way in which participants behave or think. The data gatherer may be a tape recorder or a video recorder, not just a human. Wesche and Paribakht (2000) used a research assistant and a tape recorder in their study to collect think-aloud data from their participants. Most likely the participants were desensitized[11] to their presence by the time the actual study took place because they had spent substantial time together during training. Had the researchers not planned this desensitization period prior to actual data collection, the results of the study would be suspect. However, one wonders whether the participants would have responded the same way had there been no research assistant or tape recorder.

Consequently, you need to pay attention to who applies the treatment/ control and/or who does the data gathering. If the author(s) of the study is the one applying the treatment, while another administers the control, the results are questionable. If the researcher is directly doing the data gathering, there should be at least one other person checking to make sure the data are objectively gathered. More is given about this in chapter 6.

The *Pygmalion effect* is a type of researcher effect. This effect is caused by the change in the researcher's perception of the behavior of the participants caused by his or her expectations of the participants' performance. For instance, if the data collector thinks that the participants they are observing are high-ability students, they might be more lenient (or demanding) in their observations than if they thought the participants were low ability. Any time participants have been divided into ability groups such as high/middle/low L2 language proficiency and the data collector is aware of this, there is a danger of this effect. The danger is even greater if the type of data collected requires any form of qualitative judgment on the part of the data collector. The researcher needs to take precautions that the data collectors are unaware of the ability level of the participants they are observing and clearly state what precautions s/he has taken in his or her report.

The *Hawthorne effect* occurs when participants behave differently because they know they are in a research study. In a normal classroom environment, the same results would not be found. This problem is usually

---

[11]Desensitization occurs when the participants' behavior is no longer affected by the presence of the data-collection system, whether human or mechanical.

dealt with by masking from the participants the fact that they are involved in a study. To illustrate how this effect might influence the results of a study, I use a study by Gray (1998). He looked at the effects of using interactive student diaries to help teacher trainees understand the students' learning dynamics. However, he requested the students to stay beyond the class period to write in their diaries. Contrary to his expectations, he reported that the students "were clearly flattered at being asked to contribute to the training program" (p. 31). Consequently, the issue arises as to whether the quality of the diaries would have been the same had they been written in a normal classroom setting.

Treatment intervention can affect the results of a study in at least two undesirable ways: **novelty** and **disruption**. Some treatments are so new that their novelty affects the results on the dependent variable. For example, if a study is looking at the effects of using computers to teach L2 grammar in comparison with normal classroom teaching, the students in the computer group may be more motivated to do well because of the novelty of using computers. This novelty may wear off after sustained exposure to computers and their motivation drops. In this study, the improvement would not have been due to the effectiveness of computers, but the motivation level of the students caused by something new in the classroom. To avoid this effect, a study needs to have a *cooling-off period*, where the novelty wears off before any measurements are made.

Not all things new are an advantage, however. Disruption in performance can be due to participants being unfamiliar with the new intervention being tried. Using the computer example from before, many participants who have not acquired good keyboarding skills may perform more poorly than those using traditional paper and pencil. These results would mask any advantage the computer might have over traditional methods.

The Azpillaga et al. (2001) study may have been influenced by some of these issues. The researchers recognized this problem in their Discussion section by noting that the treatment group differed from the control group in several important ways. First, the material used was novel and focused around the treatment method. Second, they suggested there might have been a project effect that created a group dynamic among the teachers that they thought favored the treatment group. Last, they recognized that the fact that only the treatment group was video recorded could have put added pressure on that group to do better. They noted that those involved in the treatment group were more motivated than those in the control group. I take my hat off to these researchers for cautioning the reader by being candid about these matters.

Accumulative treatment effect (*multiple-treatment interference or order effect*) is the result of the accumulative effect of the particular order in which treatments are presented. Some research designs administer several treatments to the same participants. When this happens, care needs to be taken that the particular order in which the treatments are given do not influence the results. The most common way to control for this effect is using what is called a *counterbalanced* design. This is a simple procedure whereby the order of the treatments are varied across participants so as to attenuate the effects of order.

A study that exemplifies this procedure was done by Mehnert (1998), who looked at the influence of giving L2 German speakers different amounts of planning time on their speech performance. Two tasks were given to the participants over a 2-week period. "Order of task was counterbalanced across participants in each group to control for practice effects" (p. 89). *Practice effects* means the effect of taking one task on the following task. To *counterbalance* meant that some participants received Task A before Task B, and other participants got the opposite order. By counterbalancing tasks, Mehnert controlled for the effects of order when the data were combined.

Treatment fidelity has to do with whether the treatment was administered in the correct manner as defined by the researcher (Gall et al., 1996). Studies that use people other than the researcher as the treatment administrators are in danger of the treatment not being administered correctly. If the treatment is not properly given, the results cannot really answer the research question. However, if the researcher does the implementation him or herself, the researcher effect could play a role. To ensure treatment fidelity and avoid researcher effect, the researcher needs to train people other than him or herself to the point where the people are able to administer the treatment at the same level as the researcher.

Bejarano et al. (1997) realized this danger in their study so they trained their teachers who were involved in the treatment and control groups in the use of group work. They followed up their training with evaluating lesson plans and teacher logs of what actually transpired in the classrooms to ensure that both groups used the same level of group-work techniques.

Treatment strength–time interaction is concerned with the time needed for the treatment to have any noticeable effect. Some treatments require more time than others. This potential problem especially relates to studies that deal with teaching methodology commonly found in applied linguistics. Time is needed for most innovative methods to take effect, which means that these studies need more than 1 or 2 weeks before testing whether an innovation works.

When the results find no effect for a new method being tried out, the reader needs to ask whether there was enough time in the research design to allow the treatment to work. This may have been a factor in the Rodriguez and Sadoski (2000) study. The different treatment groups were given only one session to learn their respective mnemonic strategy followed by another session where they were given 15 new vocabulary words to learn. They found differences between the different mnemonic methods. However, if some of the mnemonic strategies had been given more time for participants to use, would the results have been the same? The researchers did point out that maybe their instructors needed more training time, but it is also possible that their participants needed more training time to learn how to use the strategies.

As you can see from the previous list of the many things that can cause differences in the dependent variable other than the independent variables, it is a wonder anyone tries to answer the question, Why? However, rather than turning you into a cynic, rejecting any research as a waste of time, I hope that you have come to appreciate the challenge researchers face when trying to tease out the answers to the Why question. Yes, you should have reservations, but in a healthy sort of way. You should take the results and interpretations of any one single study with a degree of caution, knowing that there most likely is a weakness or two. However, this should encourage you to find more studies that address the same question to find whether the results agree. If you find a number of studies producing similar findings, you will have more confidence regarding any answers. In addition, when you find a study that is designed in such a way that it avoids all of the mines mentioned earlier, you will find yourself admiring the study as if it were a famous painting in the Louvre. Maybe that is taking it too far, but you will appreciate them more when you come across them.

In conclusion, there are many variations in the types of designs you will encounter in your readings. In many cases, you will even find combinations of designs included in one study. There is nothing to restrict a researcher from using whatever s/he believes will best answer the research questions.

There has been a lot of material covered here, and you will probably not remember it all the first time through. I certainly did not. However, as you continue to read research, you may want to review this chapter now and again to refresh your memory regarding the rationale for using certain techniques. As you do this, you will sharpen your skills at becoming an effective, discerning consumer.

However, before moving on to the next chapter, take the time to do the following exercise. It gives you an opportunity to find a study that answers the Why question and apply what you have read. This should be easy to find because these studies often have terms in their titles that suggest causation between constructs. I have developed an instrument to help you catalogue the information you will be seeking: It is called the *Internal Validity Evaluation Inventory*.

Exercise 5.5

Find a recent study from a research journal that answers a Why question using an experimental/quasi-experimental design.

1. State the research question(s).
2. Identify the independent variable(s) and the dependent variable(s).
3. State the hypotheses and/or predictions made, if any.
4. Study the introduction and methodology section. In your own words, explain why you think this is an experimental or quasi-experimental study.
5. Using the Internal Validity Evaluation Inventory at the end of the chapter, rate the risk level of any one of the possible threats to internal validity. Summarize any precautions the researcher(s) took to prevent any of these effects.

Key Terms and Concepts

accumulative treatment effect
applied research
basic research
case study
causal-comparative design
compensatory equalization of treatments
confirmatory research
control group contamination
conversational analysis
correlational study
counterbalanced design
demoralization
differential selection
ethnography
experimental design
experimental treatment diffusion
exploratory research
external validity
grounded theory
Hawthorne effect
history
instrumentation

intact groups
internal validity
John Henry effect
longitudinal study
maturation
measurement–treatment interaction
posttest effect
practice efforts
pretest effect
Pygmalion effect
qualitative research
quantitative research
quasi-experimental design
random assignment
researcher effect
shotgun method
statistical regression
subject attrition
thick description
think-aloud technique
time of measurement effect
treatment fidelity
treatment intervention
treatment strength/time interaction
triangulation

Additional Recommended Reading

The following references elaborate on the topics in this chapter in more detail.

Creswell, J. W. (2001). *Educational research: Planning, conducting, and evaluating quantitative and qualitative research.* Upper Saddle River, NJ: Prentice-Hall.

Creswell, J. W. (2002). *Research design: Qualitative, quantitative, and mixed methods approaches.* Thousand Oaks, CA: Sage.

Denzin, N. K., & Lincoln, Y. S. (Eds.). (2000). *Handbook of qualitative research* (2nd ed.). Thousand Oaks, CA: Sage.

Duff, P. (in press). *Case study research in applied linguistics.* Mahwah, NJ: Lawrence Erlbaum Associates.

Huberman, A. M., & Miles, M. B. (2002). *The qualitative researcher's companion.* Thousand Oaks, CA: Sage.

Johnson, B., & Christensen, L. B. (2003). *Educational research: Quantitative, qualitative, and mixed approaches, research edition* (2nd ed.). Upper Saddle River, NJ: Pearson Education.

Lazaraton, A. (2002). Quantitative and qualitative approaches to discourse analysis. *Annual Review of Applied Linguistics, 22,* 32–51.

Lazaraton, A. (2003). Evaluative criteria for qualitative research in applied linguistics: Whose criteria and whose research? *Modern Language Journal, 87,* 1–12.

Markee, N. P. (2001). *Conversation analysis.* Mahwah, NJ: Lawrence Erlbaum Associates.

Tashakkori, A., & Teddlie, C. (2003). *Handbook on mixed methods in social and behavior science.* Thousand Oaks, CA: Sage.

Internal Validity Evaluation Inventory

	Risk Factor			Precautions Taken
	Low	Medium	High	
1 History				
2 Maturation				
3 Differential selection				
4 Statistical regression				
5 Subject attrition				
6 Control group contamination				
a. Control group rivalry: John Henry effect				
b. Experimental treatment diffusion (Compromise)				
c. Compensatory equalization of treatments				
d. Demoralization (boycott) of the control group				
7 Testing				
a. Instrumentation				
b. Measurement–treatment interaction				
c. Pretest				
d. Posttest				
e. Time of measurement effects				
8 Experimenter effect (due to particular experimenter)				
9 Pygmalion effect				
10 Hawthorne effect				
11 Novelty and disruption effect				
12 Accumulative treatment effect (multiple-treatment interference)				
13 Treatment fidelity				
14 Treatment strength/time interaction				

Understanding Data Gathering

CHAPTER OVERVIEW

Once researchers determine the research design, they need to decide exactly how they will gather their data. A brief look at research articles in applied linguistics quickly reveals that there are many procedures used for collecting data. Some people argue that certain procedures are superior to others. However, I argue, along with others (e.g., Tashakkori & Teddlie, 1998, chap. 2), that the value of a data-gathering procedure depends on how well it provides answers to the research questions. As a consumer, you should become familiar with as many of these procedures as possible so that you will not be limited in your search for answers to your questions.

This chapter attempts to condense a body of information that could fill an entire course. For this reason, it is important for you to pause and complete each of the three exercises presented at each major break. Similar to the Sample subsection (chap. 4), the information typically provided about the strategy used for data collection in a research study does not occupy much space. However, the underlying issues in proper data collection can make or break the value of a study. As with chapter 5, this chapter is one that you will want to review periodically as you read articles that use different procedures.

The chapter is divided into two sections. The first provides a survey of the different methods by which data are collected and a discussion of the strengths and weaknesses of each. The second section summarizes the qualities needed to gather valid data. These form the criteria that you, the consumer, need for evaluating whether the data-gathering procedures have been appropriately used.

SECTION 1: PROCEDURES FOR DATA GATHERING

This section summarizes a number of data-collection procedures that are commonly used in applied linguistic research (see Table 6.1 for an overview). I group these under two general headings: *observational* and *instrumental* procedures. Under these two headings, I list either *who* or *what* is used to collect data (cf. chap. 4). Below each of these subheadings, a further breakdown is made where needed. Finally, advantages and disadvantages of each procedure are summarized in the two right columns. In the

TABLE 6.1
Data-Collection Procedures

Method	Potential Strengths	Potential Weaknesses
Observational procedures	Discover new phenomena, flexible	Time-consuming, observer effects
Self	Firsthand information, inner thoughts	Possible bias
Introspection	Immediate access, accesses inner states	Intrusive, difficult to validate
Retrospection	Not intrusive	Memory loss
Outside observer		
Full participant	Elicits natural behavior, not intrusive	Possible bias, deceptive, memory loss
Partial participant	Not deceptive	Possible bias
Nonparticipant	Objective	Disruptive
Interviewer	Ability to probe, monitors comprehension, 100% feedback	Needs training, standardization, handling data
Judges/raters	Expert opinion	Subjectivity, fatigue, halo effect, ambiguous rubrics
Instrumental procedures	Large coverage, time-efficient	Inflexible
Questionnaires		
Closed-form	Objective, broad coverage, easy to interpret	Restrictive, low returns
Open-ended	Information revealing	Subjective
Tests		
Discrete item	Objective scoring, broad coverage, easy to score	Guessing, difficult to construct
Constructed response	Allows for individuality, limits guessing	Limited coverage, subjective scoring, training of scorers

following discussion, each of these procedures is expanded and illustrations from published research are given.

Observational Procedures

The procedures under this heading involve capturing data through visual observation. The use of human observers as data collectors is as old as research. It has long been known that the main advantage of human observation of data, over some form of impersonal instrument, is that the former allows the researcher flexibility when exploring what new, and sometimes unexpected, phenomena might be uncovered.

On the other hand, some believe that observational procedures suffer from three disadvantages. The first is that they generally take more time than instrumental procedures. Consequently, they are usually more costly. Second, they are more limited in the numbers of participants/objects that are used for data gathering. Third, they allow for varying degrees of *subjectivity*. That is, the influence of factors such as attitude, temporary emotional and physical states, and so on can distort the observer's perception. However, others believe that these three weaknesses are, in fact, strengths of this category of procedures. The fact that it takes more time, they argue, means that there is a better chance to obtain quality information despite the cost. Using fewer subjects is not a problem if the purpose is to observe information-rich samples. Last, *subjectivity* is viewed as positive because the researcher becomes personally involved with the data collection. In addition, if multiple observers are used and compared to one another for degree of agreement, subjectivity is controlled. When all is said and done, I believe that most everyone would agree that observational procedures are powerful means for gathering data.

Observational procedures have many different formats. First, the one doing the observing can vary considerably. Observers can consist of a researcher, someone employed to make the observation, or the subject observing him or herself. Second, observers might be very involved with the purpose of the study or totally oblivious to why they are being asked to observe. Third, observers might be recording information that requires no interpretation of the observations or be required to give their own evaluative judgments as to what their observations mean. Fourth, the observation process may or may not be backed up with recording devices. Researchers often use recording devices (audio or video) to aid in further analysis.

In the following discussion, I show how these different formats are used by surveying the most common observational techniques with their strengths and limitations. This section is based on the degree to which the observer is personally involved with who/what is being observed, beginning with the most involved observer, the self. It ends with the least involved but most evaluative, the judge.

Self as Observer.   Using participants as observers of their own behavior has become more common over the past years under the heading of *protocol analysis* (cf. chap. 5), although it was commonly used by psychologists before 1940 (Slezak, 2002). This procedure requires participants to observe their own internal cognitive (or emotional) states and/or processing strategies either during an ongoing task, referred to as *introspection,* or after they have completed the task, known as *retrospection.*

Researchers usually record participants' thoughts on audiotape during a *think-aloud* task, as mentioned in chapter 5. To illustrate, several colleagues and myself did a study where we asked participants to identify what strategies they were using to decode new vocabulary in a reading passage. We recorded their introspections during the reading process by audiotape recorder and analyzed the transcribed data later (Perry, Boraie, Kassabgy, & Kassabgy, 2001).

The strength of the *introspection* technique is that it gets the researcher as close as possible to the inner workings of the participants' minds. The problem, however, lies in validating whether the participants are providing accurate information. If the study is not done carefully, participants may simply tell the researcher what they think the researcher wants to hear. An even greater problem is that the act of reporting what a participant is thinking can be disruptive. These intrusions can interfere with the natural cognitive processes, thus distorting the data and making them less authentic.

Another study using the introspection technique was done by Chamot and El-Dinary (1999). It focused on the research question of whether students of higher ability use different strategies than lower ability students when immersed in a foreign language classroom. Their participants consisted of third- and fourth-grade students who were learning French, Spanish, and Japanese. The researchers used a think-aloud interview to capture the data from the students while they read or wrote. This procedure involved a trained interviewer using a think-aloud interview guide to ask questions of the students in the target language during the reading or writing tasks. The guide was used to ensure that students were asked the same questions. Before the data were collected, the students were given some training to familiarize them with the think-aloud procedure. The students were encouraged to respond in the target language, but allowances were made to use their L1. Their responses were audiotaped, transcribed, and then translated into English. The transcription of each student was then examined by a pair of trained observers using an agreed-on coding scheme to identify the strategies.

I recommend you read Chamot and El-Dinary's (1999) study to see the care they took to make sure their data were as clean as possible. However, as with any study using this approach, there are questions about the final data prior to analysis. First, did the students provide accurate descriptions regarding what strategies they actually used? Second, did the presence of an interviewer asking questions in the midst of reading or writing disturb what the students reported? Third, did trying to relate the strategies in the target language interfere with what the students reported? That is, although the students could fall back on English, did the students with more assertive personalities attempt to relate their strategies in the target language more than students with more conservative personalities? Last, was any information lost by translating the students' output in the target language back into English?

However, let me add that the questions I have just raised about the Chamot and El-Dinary (1999) study should not be interpreted as criticisms. Rather, they should give us an appreciation for the complexity of trying to obtain data fresh out of the minds of participants. This is as close as we can get to authentic data. As Chamot and El-Dinary clearly understood, their study is just part of the overall picture. In fact this study was part of a larger 9-year study where other methods of obtaining data were used. As we keep approaching our research questions from different angles (i.e., triangulation), we begin to form a picture of what is actually happening.

To eliminate the possible intrusive effect of the introversion technique that might have occurred in the prior study, some researchers use retrospection. In this case, the participant is required to wait until after the task before reflecting on what they had done cognitively. However, as you might have realized, a different problem can potentially affect the data (i.e., loss of memory). If the task is complicated or takes a lot of time, the participant can forget some of the mental processes that occurred. The tendency found in the psychology of memory is that participants remember the first and last parts of the information and forget what is in between.

The study by Wesche and Paribakht (2000) illustrates not only the use of think-aloud, but illustrates the use of two forms of retrospection: *immediate* and *delayed.* Before discussing this study, however, I want to mention here that this is an interesting study for another reason. The researchers used a qualitative/exploratory/applied approach to follow up a previous quantitative/exploratory/applied study (Paribakht & Wesche, 1997). Typically, the reverse is the normal pattern: qualitative results followed by a quantitative study. The reason is that qualitative methods of data collection often look for information-rich data to build theoretical hypotheses. Based on these hypotheses, larger quantitative studies are performed to test the hypotheses and generalize the findings to larger populations.

However, in the quantitative study by Paribakht and Wesche (1997), a difference was found between a group that used normal reading strategies and one that used *reading plus* for vocabulary learning. Wesche and Paribakht (2000) wanted to know why there was a difference. To do this, they replicated both methods separately using introspective techniques. The part of the study that I discuss here looked at the reading plus method. The researchers purposely used three introspective techniques to take advantage of the strengths of each and, at the same time, control for their weaknesses. First, they trained the participants on using the think-aloud procedure. Next, they had the participants read the target text and complete eight vocabulary tasks. During the tasks, the participants were to verbalize what they were thinking and doing. Immediately after completing each task, the participants were individually asked to retrospect on the strategy they used (i.e., immediate retrospection). After all the tasks were finished, the participants were interviewed regarding the exercises and their use for learning vocabulary (i.e., delayed retrospection). All output by the participants was audiorecorded and transcribed for analysis.

Several concerns come to mind as I read this study. First, an interviewer was present during all of the introspection output to either prompt the participants to keep talking during the introspection protocol or to guide the two types of retrospection. Wesche and Paribakht (2000) felt that this was an advantage in that "the interviewer observes, describes, and confirms certain behaviours which learners would not otherwise report and can elicit learner comments on specific issues of research interest" (p. 208). However, in light of the possibility of a researcher effect, the question must be asked regarding whether the participants' verbal output was not distorted by the prompting and guiding by the interviewers. It looks like a case of "you're damned if you do and damned if you don't." If they had not used prompts or guiding questions, would they have obtained the same data? Yet having used these eliciting techniques, did they alter the output in a way that distorted their findings?

Outside Observers. The more traditional form of the observational procedure is found in research that uses people other than the participants to make observations. I refer to this type as *outside observers* (see Table 6.1). Whereas the self-observer is the best source to try to access the inner workings of the mind, the outside observer is better used for observing the outward behavior of the participants under study.

However, the outside observer varies in how close (i.e., personally involved) s/he gets to the people or events that s/he is observing and how aware the people being observed are that they are being observed. The closer the observer gets and/or more aware the observed person is, the more the observer participates in who or what is being observed. Technically, the continuum ranges from full to nonparticipant observer (cf. Table 6.1).

The *full-participant observer* is one who is or becomes a full member of the group to which the participants/events being observed belong. This is a procedure commonly used to observe a group/event with someone who is either a member or pretending to be a member as an *informant* (i.e., a person who supplies the information). The group is usually unaware that it is being observed.

The obvious advantage of using a full participant is that the other members of the group will behave naturally, thus providing a clear picture of the objective of the observation. The disadvantages are that (a) the observer may be so much a part of the group that s/he cannot remain objective in his or her observations, (b) the researcher(s) is using deception to obtain the data, and (c) the observer may forget information if he or she has to wait until after the encounter with the group before recording the data. In the case of disadvantage (a), limited and/or biased data may be reported by the observer. For (b), the observer might become ostracized from the group when it learns that s/he was informing on it. Problem (c) simply results in incomplete data.

I can imagine a study where the researcher enlists the help of one of the foreign language students in the group being studied to find out what attitudes the group has toward the language program they are in. The student is the informant (i.e., a full-participant observer). Of course the researcher could simply give an attitude survey to the group, which s/he may plan to do as well. To ensure that the members of the group do not paint a rosy picture on the survey to please the researcher, one of the students is asked to gather information predetermined by the researcher and unknown to the other members. By law in the United States, the other members of the group need to be informed that they were observed and their permission obtained before the data are used—especially if anonymity was not guaranteed. Depending on the sensitivity of the information, this could be threatening to the full-participant observer who then may not want to be totally honest in his or her reporting.

An example of the use of full-participant observers is found in Atkinson and Ramanathan's study (1995), where they explored whether there were differences in attitudes and behaviors between L1 and L2 academic writing programs. Because one of the researchers was currently a teacher in the L2 program and the other was a teacher in one of the L1 programs, they considered themselves full-participant observers. Because they belonged to the group, one might say, they believed they avoided the problem of deception. They designed the study so that the L1 researcher used the L2 researcher as an informant in the L2 program, and the L2 researcher used the L1 researcher as an informant in the L1 program. They collected six types of data: observations from teacher orientation sessions, interviews with administrators, interviews with experienced writing teachers, over 20 hours of observation in classes of each of the two programs, samples of writing from the students, and random observations of their own programs. (Now that is what I call a lot of data!) The data were collected over a 10-month school year.

By being full-participant observers, Atkinson and Ramanathan could easily move among the students and fellow teachers, collecting data with the minimum disturbance. In addition, they tried to control for their observations being influenced by being full members of the two programs by alternating between one playing the role of the observer while the other was the informant.

Another example of a study that used participant observers is the Spielmann and Radnofsky (2001) study discussed in chapter 5. Recall that they studied the role of *tension* in language learning apart from the construct of *anxiety* with a beginning French class at Middlebury College Language Schools. The two researchers considered themselves participant observers due to their 5 years of experience with the program they were studying. I would not call them full-participant observers, but they were close. However, their design gave them ample access to the students, faculty, staff, and the facilities, which they believed facilitated obtaining data. Their approach was *ethnographic* in that they gathered as much data from as many sources as possible in a natural setting. Their observations were made during informal and formal interactions with various individuals in the program, after which they took extensive notes. Their records included questions and interpretations in the form of an extensive notation system. They were careful not to rely only on their observations, however. To check for subjectivity creeping in to distort their data, they used a number of other methods for gathering data (i.e., triangulation).

At the other end of the degrees of participation continuum is the nonparticipant observer who does not personally interact with the participants in any manner. The best use of this method is when the observer makes observations of participants' outward behavior. For example, an observer may measure the amount of time a teacher talks versus the amount of time students talk in a language classroom. In this case, the observer has no need to interact with either the teacher or students to obtain these data.

The principal advantage of this strategy is that it is more *objective*[1] than the other participant methods. On the down side, the presence of an unknown observer, or any recording devices, may have a disruptive effect on the participants, causing them to deviate from their normal behavior. To avoid this, the observer needs to desensitize the participants to his or her presence before collecting the data to be used for the study. To do this, a common method is for the observer to attend the sessions long enough for the participants to disregard the observer's presence.

---

[1] *Objective* is at the other end of the continuum from *subjective*, in that the observer's observations are not influenced by bias due to attitude, temporary emotional states, and so on. In actual fact, there is no 100% purely objective or subjective observation.

A study that used this nonparticipant method was done by Viechnicki (1997), whose aim was to analyze the participants' intentions in discussions carried on in a graduate seminar. She observed the verbal interactions of the students in a graduate-level linguistics seminar by sitting in the class and recording what she saw. She also used a tape recorder at the same time to help capture as much of the verbal output as possible. To be as unobtrusive as possible, she was present in the seminar with her recorder some weeks prior to recording the data.

The interesting thing about the prior study is that Viechnicki tried to assess the discourse intentions of the participants without actually asking them what their intentions were. In line with the conversation analysis approach (cf. chap. 5), she observed the outward behavior of the interaction process, including facial gestures and the direction of the speaker's gaze. Based on these, she made inferences about what was going on in the speakers' heads regarding their intentions. Interviewing the participants after making her inferences would have been an excellent way to check on the validity of her conclusions. It is possible that later studies have done this.

Somewhere between the full-participant and nonparticipant observers lie varying degrees of partial-participant observation (cf. Table 6.1). The advantages are several over the nonparticipant observer. First, access to less obvious data, such as attitudes or intentions, is more available. Second, the closer the participant feels the observer is to him or her, the less the chance of falsifying the data. However, the closer the participant is to the observer, the greater the possibility of bias on the part of the observer.

The partial-participant observer also has advantages over the full-participant observer. First, there is less danger that the observer will become so involved with the participants that s/he loses objectivity. Second, the participants usually know that they are being observed, so there is no deception. However, the partial-participant observer may be denied access to more private information that only the full-participant observer would be able to access.

To illustrate the use of a partial-participant observer, Harklau (2000) used this strategy with an ethnographic case study to investigate how student identities change when moving from one language program to another. She observed three ESL students over a 1-year period as they made the transition from high school to a nearby community college. She collected data from several sources.

In all, the data reflect over 50 formal interview sessions with students and instructors as well as over 25 other informal interviews with students' instructors, 10 days of high school classroom observations and over 50 hours of community college classroom observations, and over 5,000 pages of written materials collected from students and from the study sites over the course of the year in which the study took place. (p. 44)

Harklau was a partial-participant observer, in that she met with students and teachers in places like lunch rooms and teacher lounges where she held informal interviews. She most likely did this to establish personal rapport with her participants to ensure more authentic responses. I understand that she won the Newbury House 2000 Research Award for this study, which she no doubt deserves due to this giant undertaking.

Except for Viechnicki (1997), one thing common to the Atkinson and Ramanathan (1995), Spielmann and Radnofsky (2001), and Harklau (2000) studies is that the researchers did not limit themselves to only one procedure for gathering data. Rather, they all used a multiprocedural approach, as referred to previously as *triangulation*. Researchers who want to protect their research from the weakness of only one approach, yet profit from the strengths of that approach, will build into their study several different data-collecting procedures. Researchers may use full, partial, or nonparticipant observers to gather data, but they should triangulate their findings with those of other procedures to increase credibility of their findings.

The consumer of research may ask, which of the previous procedures is most appropriate? As previously stated, the answer depends on the research question and the nature of the data needed to best provide the answer. If the research question requires information that cannot be obtained by observing outward behavior, then a method needs to be used where the observer can get closer to the participants. Where easily observed outward behavior is sufficient, there is no need for closeness. Each approach has its strengths and weaknesses.

Regardless of what type of observer is used, observers need training to provide useful data. Of course, if the researcher is doing the observing him or herself, there is no need for training because s/he knows what s/he is looking for. In addition, to ensure that there is no bias, the researcher should keep his or her observer(s) blind to the purpose of the study, especially if any hypothesis is being tested. (This sounds like an oxymoron: keeping your observer blind.) If s/he fails to keep them *blind*, the observers might unconsciously see only what the researcher wants to be seen. A well-written study will be very clear about whether training was given to the observers and whether the observers were aware of the ultimate purpose of the study.

The last set of studies we have looked at use the researcher(s) as the observer(s). However, a study done by Bejarano, Levine, Olshtain, and Steiner (1997) used observers other than themselves when looking at the use of *interaction strategies*. They videotaped 34 students in subgroups of 4 to 5 at two different times: before and after treatment. The videotapes were then observed by two independent observers who were to count the number of turns taken in the various discussions within each group, identify and count the number of turns taken where no strategy was used, and identify and count the number of interactive strategies used. The observers were trained to use an observation-tally form designed specifically for this study. The videotaping made it possible for the observers and researchers to review the participants' verbal behavior to decrease the chances that anything was missed. The one concern is whether the videotaping influenced the participants' behavior. However, the training in use of the tally form helped regulate the many judgments that the observers had to make. The use of all of these precautions by the researchers added greatly to the validity of their findings.

The Interviewer. As seen in the studies discussed earlier, interviews were used to obtain data as well (cf. Table 6.1). This method is a combination of observation under highly structured conditions and paper-and-pencil data recording. The difference between the observer and interviewer is that the interviewer personally interacts with the participant through a series of questions to obtain data, whereas with the observer data are collected as they occur without probing with questions. The difference between an interview and a questionnaire (which is discussed under the Instrument section) is that an interpersonal connection is formed between the interviewer and interviewee. This connection allows for direct monitoring for comprehension of the questions and modification in the case of misunderstanding.

The quality of the data coming from an interviewer is determined by the care taken to ensure that the same procedures are used for each interviewee. Strict adherence to directions as to what questions are to be asked and in what order they are to be asked need to be observed. Otherwise the answers cannot be compared.

However, an interview can range from highly structured to semistructured to open structured. The *highly structured* interview follows a predetermined set of questions with no allowance for variation. The *semistructured* interview has a set of predetermined questions, but the interviewer is free to follow up a question with additional questions that probe further. The *open-structured* interview has a general interview plan, but is not tied to predetermined questions. This allows the interviewer to explore whatever path seems appropriate at the time.

All of these techniques are commonly used in research. For example, Chamot and El-Dinary (1999) used a highly structured interview guide when asking students to think aloud during their reading and writing tasks. Harklau (2000) used what she referred to as *loosely structured* interviews (i.e., semistructured) to be free to generate more questions as the research progressed. Atkinson and Ramanathan (1995) employed the open-structured interview, which they labeled *ethnographic interviews*, so they could ask anything they thought appropriate to ask.

When evaluating research studies that use one of the interview techniques, ask yourself these questions: Did the researcher pretest the interview questions with the interviewers? Were the interviewers trained and tested before they gave the interviews? Were the interviews audio- or videotaped to prevent the loss of information? Would the data be the same if another interviewer did the interview? If you answer yes to all of these questions, then the study followed sound interviewing procedures.

The Judge/Rater. Another type of observational technique to gather data in applied linguistics research is the use of judges/raters. (From now on, I refer to both as judges.) Not only do judges observe the outward behavior of the participant(s), but they make evaluative judgments regarding the behavior. They do this by giving verbal explanations or using some form of rating scale that ranges from low to high, poor to excellent, and so on and may be expressed verbally or numerically.

Judges vary considerably in their ratings for reasons other than quality of performance, as was seen from the 2002 Winter Olympics figure skating results. However, in applied linguistics research, judges are used to rate such things as writing or oral proficiency of participants, or the distortion of meaning caused by the strength of a participant's accent, much less high stakes than a gold medal. So there should be no reason to allow such things as vote swapping for nationalistic reasons to influence one's rating.

However, the challenge with using judges in research continues to be *subjectivity*, which is defined here as the influence of a judge's particular preferences and beliefs that differ from the criteria that s/he is supposed to use when judging. For example, I and some of my colleagues examined what criteria judges used when rating the writing ability of people trying to enter our university based on a ½-hour essay test. We found that some judges used grammar as their main criteria, whereas others used the quality of *organization*. There were a few others who were heavily influenced by *writing mechanics*. Obviously, the rating of one judge did not mean the same thing as the rating of another due to using different criteria. The assumption should hold that when rating, the judges use the same criteria. If this is not the case, then any interpretation of the data has no real meaning.

To control for subjectivity, three precautions need to be taken: the use of a *rubric, training*, and *multiple judges*. First, the rubric of the rating scale needs to be clearly defined. A well-written rubric clearly defines what each level of the scale means. The quality of these definitions helps judges apply the rubric in a consistent and meaningful way.

One of the most well-known rubrics used today was developed by the American Council on the Teaching of Foreign Languages (ACTFL). You can access their Web site (www.actfl.org) to see their rubrics for writing and speaking. Their most recent version is a four-level scale: Superior, Advanced, Intermediate, and Novice. For each of these levels, a short paragraph is provided that defines what a speaker or writer should be able to do in relation to several language abilities (e.g., grammar, vocabulary, etc.).

Related to having a good rubric, the second method for controlling subjectivity in a judge's decision is training in the use of the rubric. The judge has to keep in mind each level of the rubric with its definition while rating participants. This is a formidable task and needs training to produce consistent results. The validity of the ratings will only be as good as the mastery of the rubric by the judges. A well-planned study will report how the judges were trained on the rubric.

Third, at least two judges need to be used when making judgments. By having multiple judges, the researcher is able to check whether the judges are using the same criteria. In addition, the judges can be checked for the *severity* of their judgments. If one judge is consistently rating participants higher than other judges, then s/he is too lenient. If s/he rates the participants consistently lower than the others, then s/he is too severe. If there were only one judge making the judgments, the researcher could not know whether the ratings were too lenient or severe.

A study that took into account the three precautions outlined earlier when using judges was done by Way, Joiner, and Seaman (2000). They addressed the question of whether novice foreign language students' writing was affected by different writing tasks and/or different prompts. One of the four variables that they examined was *overall quality* of each participant's writing. They used two 8-point, four-category rubrics for their scales, but did not provide copies of the rubrics in their paper for the reader to peruse. The two rubrics were similar, but were adjusted for the two levels of language ability in their sample. They reported training three raters in the use of the rubrics until the raters were close enough in their ratings to conclude the raters were using the same criteria. Finally, they used different combinations of two raters for each writing sample and averaged the two ratings for the data. As you can see, the researchers followed good procedures in gathering their data.

Besides subjectivity, there are two other obstacles that researchers need to attend to when using judges: *fatigue* and *halo effect*. Regarding the first, judges become tired if they have to evaluate too many participants at any given time. The judgments made in the early part of rating a large number of participants may be different from those judged later due to judges simply becoming tired. The study by Way, Joiner, and Seaman (2000) may have had this problem. I estimate that the three judges divided 990 writing samples so that any one judge had to rate 660 samples. It would be interesting to know how the researchers tried to control for the effects of fatigue.

The other obstacle, *halo effect*, is caused by the carryover effect of judging the work of one participant onto the work of the following participant. When judging the quality of writing, for instance, exposure to a well-written (or poorly written) passage may have a positive (or negative) influence on the judgment of the following passage. This is usually controlled for by making sure that the people or things being rated are not in the same order for the two raters. If any precautions are taken, the researchers should mention them to help the reader rule out such effects.

Before moving on to nonpersonal data-gathering methods, I suggest you do the following exercise to help instantiate what we have covered in the first part of Section 1. The following provides an outline of what to look for.

Exercise 6.1

1. Find a recent study that used one of the observational techniques mentioned in the prior discussion.
2. State the research question.
3. State any hypotheses, predictions, or even expectations if they are present.
4. Describe the data being observed.
5. Summarize the observational procedure used in the study.
6. Describe what was done to avoid the potential weaknesses described in Table 6.1.

Instrumental Procedures

The other general method of collecting data is using some form of impersonal instrument that requires participants to supply data to the researcher. Table 6.1 lists two general instrument types that encompass a wide range of devices used to collect data: *questionnaires* and *tests*.

The advantage of using instrumental procedures over observational ones is that the researcher can gain access to many more participants in a timely and economical way. However, the main disadvantage is that, once they are put into print, they cease to be flexible during the data-collection process. Any new thoughts the researcher might have will have to wait until the next study.

Questionnaires. Questionnaires are surveys that can capture a lot of information in a short amount of time. They consist of lists of questions or statements presented on paper or through some other media such as computers. Questionnaires are considered instrumental equivalents to interviews. They have two main advantages over interviews. First, they are useful for collecting data from larger numbers of people in fairly short amounts of time. Second, they are more economical to use than interviews because they do not take as much time or require trained interviewers to administer. As mentioned previously, the main disadvantage is that questionnaires are not flexible in comparison to interviews, in that the questions cannot be modified once they have been given to the respondent, nor can the questionnaire probe the respondent for further information.

The items (i.e., questions or statements) in a questionnaire can be closed form or open form. *Closed-form* items provide a set of alternative answers to each item from which the respondent must select at least one. For example, a question might require a participant to choose either *yes* or *no*, *agree* or *disagree*. A statement might be given requiring participants to indicate their level of agreement on a 5-point scale. This scale is often referred to as a Likert scale, named after R. A. Likert, who used it for measuring attitude (Likert, 1932). The main advantage of using the closed form is that the data elicited are easy to record and analyze with statistical procedures.

Open-form items allow participants to give their own answers without restrictions. This type works best when there could be a wide variety of answers that participants might give to a question, such as "How old are you?" Another common use is when the researcher is exploring what possible answers might be given, as when asking participants what they think is good about the language program they have just completed.

Typically, most questionnaires contain both open- and closed-form items. Demographic information about the respondent (e.g., gender, nationality, etc.) and the program (e.g., course level, etc.) uses both formats. Even when the rest of the items in the questionnaire are closed form, the last item is almost always open form to capture any other comment by the respondent.

A well-prepared questionnaire should be *pilot-tested* before administered in the main study. That is, it is tried out on a group of people similar to the target group who will eventually get it. The resulting feedback can provide useful information to make sure that all the items are clearly understood and the entire questionnaire is user-friendly.

One of the challenges in using questionnaires is getting them back from potential respondents. *Response rate* is important because losing respondents is a form of attrition of the sample, which can result in a biased sample (Brown, 2001). Typically, the response rate is much less than the number of people who received the questionnaire. Trying to chase after people to return questionnaires is almost impossible because, to ensure anonymity, questionnaires usually do not require respondents to identify themselves.

The rule of thumb is that the researcher should get a response rate of at least 70% before the data are considered representative of a target population.[2] However, if the number of questionnaires that is sent out is small, the return rate needs to be higher to maintain representativeness. A well-written study should report the number of questionnaires sent out and the return rate to aid the reader in applying this criterion.

An example of the proper use of a questionnaire is found in Camiciottoli's (2001) study, which investigated the attitudes and reading habits of Italian EFL students at an Italian university. She administered a 22-item *closed-form* questionnaire to 182 students. To develop the questionnaire, she interviewed 20 students to guide the selection of options for each item. She then gave a draft of the interview to six colleagues with the task to classify the items according to whether they fit the dependent variables and independent variables. She also controlled for *automatic response patterns*, which might occur when a respondent selects only one choice throughout the questionnaire, such as all 4s. Camiciottoli controlled this by omitting the neutral option in the choices and by changing the order of the options for different sets of items. Anyone not paying attention would have been detected and discarded from the data. She controlled for response rate by administering the questionnaire during class time, which guaranteed a 100% response. To ensure complete understanding of the items, the questionnaire was given in the students' first language. As an added bonus, Camiciottoli provided a copy of the questionnaire at the end of the article for us to see.

Another study by Timmis (2002) examined what students and teachers thought about conforming to English native-speaker norms. He gave a questionnaire to students and a similar one to teachers. However, he did not report about how many questionnaires were distributed in total. He did report that 400 responses were obtained from students from 14 countries. This looks like a large number of respondents. Yet without knowing how many were distributed, we cannot determine the response rate or whether the sample of 400 was representative of the target population. The teacher questionnaire was distributed to teachers on a participant list at a conference in Dublin, and over 180 were returned. Again, Timmis did not report how many were given out in total or the response rate. Regarding both the questionnaires, no additional information was given about the number of items.

However, on a more positive note, Timmis (2002) presented sample items in the Results section, which gives a good idea what the contents were about. In addition, he stated that both questionnaires were "extensively pi-

---

[2]Go to http://nces.ed.gov/statprog/2002 and search for Survey Response Rate Parameters.

loted before use, and the results subjected" (p. 241) to a validity check before they were used. He also interviewed 15 students from one university to
get an idea about the reasons that lie behind the student answers. He was
careful to note that the interview responses were only suggestive due to the
sample not being representative. Timmis commented that, due to limited
space he was given in the journal, he had to trim some information about
the methodology. Possibly the missing details mentioned earlier were ones
that were not included. However, they would have added weight to the
study.

Tests. Tests, also popularly referred to as *assessments,* are the other main
type of instrumentation commonly used in research. Although I am sure no
one needs to be told what a test is due to years of experience taking them, I
simply state that a *test* is an instrument designed to assess what participants
can remember or do physically and/or mentally. Because a single test can
do all three, depending on the test items that make up the test, I use the
term *test items,* rather than simply *tests* or *assessments.*

Test items come in all formats and modalities. They can be administered
via paper, computer, or face to face with an examiner. They can assess language abilities through observing outward behavior, as when testing oral
proficiency via an oral interview, or they can assess cognitive outcomes
through responses on paper or a computer screen.

Test items differ by making different cognitive demands on participants.
Some items require participants to *recall* information. Such items as fill in
the blank and completion serve this purpose. Other items require participants to recall and integrate information, such as a test of writing ability
where they must compose an essay. Such items are also referred to as *open
ended* or *constructed response.* Other test items require participants to *recognize*
from a set of alternatives which is the most appropriate answer. Items such
as multiple choice, matching, and alternative choice are commonly used
for this purpose.

Some people have preferences regarding item type. Yet as with everything else we have discussed so far, the type of test item used in research
should be determined by the question being asked. If a research question
inquires whether participants can identify the meaning of a sentence or
written passage, then recognition-type items are quite appropriate. However, if a researcher seeks to know whether the target information has been
stored in such a way that participants can access the information easily,
then a recall-type item would be better. If the researcher is trying to assess
whether participants can integrate information, then an essay format would
be more appropriate.

Accordingly, there are some practical considerations researchers usually
address when choosing item types. Two that are very much related are *time*

and *cost.* Some item types take longer to administer than others and usually require trained judges to analyze the responses. For example, the open-ended essay prompt that requires a 1- to 2-page response from each participant when assessing writing ability can take 1 or more minutes to score depending on the scoring technique. Not just anyone can evaluate these responses. As with training judges, raters of written compositions also need training. All of this takes time; and whatever takes time usually means greater costs. However, recognition-type items can be given to larger numbers of participants and scored by untrained personnel or even by optical-mark scanning machines in a minimal amount of time.

When evaluating the proper choice of item type, we need to ask ourselves whether the responses from the item type of choice are directly related to answering the research question. To illustrate, if writing ability is being investigated, then multiple-choice items would probably not be appropriate. In contrast, if reading comprehension is the focus of the question, then multiple-choice items could be used effectively. If one's oral proficiency is being assessed, then some form of oral interview would probably be the best approach. In Section 2 of this chapter, it becomes apparent why choice of item type is important.

There are other terms you might encounter when reading the instrument section of a study. One common term is *standardized* test. The word *standardized* means that the test has been designed to be given under strict guidelines for administration and scoring. That is, the same instructions are to be given to the respondents at every administration of the instrument. The amount of time that is allowed to finish the test is also held constant for everyone, and the scoring procedure is the same for everyone. Standardization is important for producing data that can be compared. Research has shown that a change in such things as the instructions given by the test administrator can cause changes in the responses to the tests.

Two examples of standardized tests of English ability used around the world are the Test of English as a Foreign Language (TOEFL),[3] which is produced by the Educational Testing Service in Princeton, New Jersey, and the International English Language Testing System (IELTS),[4] developed by the University of Cambridge. Wherever the paper-and-pencil version of these tests is administered throughout the world, each is given on the same day, with the same instructions, allowing for the same amount of time for completion, and strictly scored according to specific guidelines (independent of one another of course). Any changes in these procedures can render the data useless.

---

[3]See http://www.toefl.org/ for more information. Retrieved Jan. 10, 2004.
[4]See http://www.ielts.org/ for more information. Retrieved Jan. 10, 2004.

Commercially produced (CP) standardized tests, such as the two mentioned before, are usually developed for large-scale assessment and not specifically designed for individual research studies. However, some CP tests are occasionally used by researchers because they are assumed to have been carefully constructed to ensure reliability and validity—issues that are discussed in greater detail in Section 2 of this chapter.

In chapter 5, I discussed Sanz's (2000) study, which examined the effects that bilingual education might have on the learning of a third language. She used two standardized CP tests in her study: the Raven's Progressive Matrices Test to measure the variable of intelligence, and the Comprehensive English Language Test (CELT) to measure English proficiency. However, she used only subcomponents of each test, rather than the complete tests, due to time constraints. Sanz was not measuring achievement due to some treatment, but rather language proficiency—at least grammar and vocabulary knowledge. Assuming that the items in these two subcomponents adequately represent the grammar and vocabulary proficiency domains, we can accept them as appropriate measures. However, this raises the question as to whether using only the structure (grammar) and vocabulary subcomponents of the CELT adequately define language proficiency. Similarly, does using only part of the Raven's test adequately measure intelligence? Both of these issues were recognized by Sanz as limitations that restrict applying her conclusions.

Although it is convenient to use an off-the-shelf CP standardized instrument, it might not be the best instrument to use in a particular research study. The reason is that these tests are designed for specific purposes that often do not match the need of the study. If researchers use the TOEFL exam to measure the effect of a new teaching method on improving English ability over one semester, for example, the results would probably not show any noticeable improvement. However, this lack of improvement may not be due to the ineffectiveness of the new method, but instead to insensitivity of the TOEFL due to its global nature. That is, the limited learning outcomes that are targeted in a relatively short period of treatment are lost in the measurement of the multiple areas of the TOEFL. Nevertheless, the TOEFL would be appropriate for identifying various ability groupings in the English language of the participants to be used for research purposes.

In contrast to using CP standardized tests, many researchers design their own instruments for gathering data. The advantage is that they can streamline the instruments specifically to the needs of the study, however. This does not mean that the instruments should not be standardized. When they are given to more than one group of participants, they should follow strict standardization guidelines, such as extra time allowed to finish the test, or else the data from one group might vary from the other groups.

Kobayashi (2002), for example, mentioned previously in chapter 5, developed her own tests for reading comprehension when examining whether text organization and response format affect performance on tests of reading comprehension. She expressly stated that the study needed texts in the tests that were "specially prepared to maximize control over the variables identified in the pilot study" (p. 199). Obviously, she needed to design her own tests rather than use some off-the-shelf CP test. Eight parallel tests were developed for this study. Items in two components of each test were given in Japanese (L1) to eliminate any variation due to English reading proficiency. She also reported how care was taken to standardize the tests by preparing written instructions for both the test administrators and students.

In addition to the term *standardization*, you will come into contact with two other terms in some Instrument sections of various studies: *norm-referenced* and *criterion-referenced* tests. Both terms relate to how test scores are interpreted. *Norm-referenced* means that scores on the test are given meaning when compared with some norming group. A *norming group* is a body of people that is supposed to represent the population of all those who might take the test. On the basis of the statistics generated on the norming group, a person's score is interpreted in relation to the degree to which it is above or below the average of the norming group.

When using a norm-referenced test in a research study, it is important that the sample to which the test is given comes from a similar pool of participants as the norming group. Otherwise the measurements cannot be interpreted by referring to the norming group. An example of a study that focuses on this issue was done by Arriaga et al. (1998), previously mentioned in chapter 4. They used the MacArthur Communicative Development Inventory (CDI), a standardized/norm-referenced test, as their main instrument to compare language development of low- and middle-income toddlers. They were careful to observe that the developers of the CDI warned that the norms of the test might not represent the low-income group. Consequently, Arriaga et al. checked whether the norming sample provided by the developers was appropriate by doing an independent comparison with a comparable sample of toddlers.

A *criterion-referenced* test does not use a norming group to establish guidelines for interpreting test results. Instead one or more criteria are used to decide how well the examinee has done. These criteria are predetermined before administering the test and are used to establish cut points. A *cut point* is a point on the test score scale used to classify people into different categories such as high, middle, or low ability. For instance, all respondents scoring over 80% correct might be considered high ability, those between 50% and 80% average ability, and those below 50% below average.

Some people confuse the terms *norm-referenced* and *standardized*, but they are not synonymous. The term *standardized* relates to the conditions under which the test is given, whereas *norm-referenced* has to do with how the scores are interpreted. This confusion is most likely due to the fact that most standardized tests are also norm-referenced, such as the TOEFL or the IELTS.

As with a lot of research, Kobayashi (2002) did not use norm-referenced or criterion-referenced interpretations for her reading tests. This is because she was not trying to make decisions about individual respondents. She was looking at the overall effect on the participants as groups who received the different text types. This meant that she compared the averages of the different groups against one another, rather than look at individual scores.

In concluding Section 1 of this chapter, procedures that are commonly used to gather data in research were reviewed. However, there are a number of criteria the consumer needs to understand to determine whether they have been properly used. These criteria are covered in the second section of this chapter. However, to help establish a foundation for understanding the next section, I suggest you take the opportunity to complete the following exercise.

Exercise 6.2

1. Find a recent study that used one of the instrumental techniques listed in Table 6.1.
2. Describe the purpose of the study.
3. State the research question.
4. State any hypotheses, predictions, or even expectations if they are present.
5. Briefly summarize the data-gathering procedure in no more than a paragraph.
6. Describe what was done to avoid any of the potential weaknesses listed in Table 6.1.
7. Evaluate whether you think the procedures used provided the necessary data to answer the research question and/or to test any hypotheses.

SECTION 2: QUALITIES OF GOOD DATA-GATHERING PROCEDURES

When many people think of research, they imagine numbers and statistics. However, the numbers that are gathered are based on various data-gathering techniques as outlined in Section 1 of this chapter. The quality of these procedures is determined by the caliber of the data-gathering strategy. To sharpen our ability to discern between weak and strong research, we must give attention to this aspect of research when evaluating the worth of a study. The purpose of this section is to provide an overview of these qualities and give examples of how they have been applied in research. My goal is for you to be able to use these qualities as criteria to evaluate the quality of the research that you read in a discerning manner.

The two most important qualities of any data-collection technique that have traditionally been considered essential are *reliability* and *validity*. The strong consensus in the measurement community is that the level of confidence we can put into the findings of any given research is directly proportional to the degree to which data-gathering procedures are reliable and valid. I begin by discussing reliability, followed by validity. Some research methodology books place their section on validity before reliability. However, because validity relies heavily on reliability, I discuss the latter first.

Reliability

Reliability has to do with the *consistency* of the data results. If we measure or observe something, we want the method used to give the same results no matter who or what takes the measurement or observations. Researchers who use two or more observers would want those observers to see the same things and give the same or similar judgments on what they observe or rate. Likewise, researchers utilizing instruments would expect them to give consistent results regardless of time of administration or the particular set of test items making up those instruments.

The most common indicator used for reporting the reliability of an observational or instrumental procedure is the *correlation coefficient*. A *coefficient* is simply a number that represents the amount of attribute. A *correlation coefficient* is a number that quantifies the degree to which two variables relate to one another. Correlation coefficients used to indicate reliability are referred to as *reliability coefficients*.

I do not go into the mathematics of this particular statistic, but I want to give enough information to help in understanding the following discussion. Reliability coefficients range between 0.00 and +1.00. A coefficient of 0.00 means there is no reliability in the observation or measurement. That is, if we were to make multiple observations/measurements of a particular variable, a coefficient of 0.00 would mean that the observations/measurements were inconsistent. Conversely, a coefficient of 1.00 indicates that there is perfect reliability or consistency. This means that the observation/measurement procedure gives the same results regardless of who or what makes the observation/measurement.

Seldom, if ever, do reliability coefficients occur at the extreme ends of the continuum (i.e., 0.00 or 1.00). So, you might ask, "What is an adequate reliability coefficient?" The rule of thumb is, the higher the better (Wow, that was a no-brainer!!!), but better depends on the nature of the measurement procedure being used. Researchers using observation techniques involving judges are happy with reliability coefficients anywhere from 0.80 on up. Yet achievement and aptitude tests should have reliabilities in the 0.90s. Other instruments such as interest inventories and attitude scales tend to be lower than achievement or aptitude tests. Generally speaking, reliabilities falling below 60 are considered low no matter what type of procedure is being used (Nitko, 2001).

There are a number of different types of reliability coefficients used in research. The reason is that each one reveals a different kind of consistency. Different measurement procedures require different kinds of consistency. Table 6.2 lists the different types of reliability coefficients, what kind of consistency is needed, and the corresponding measurement procedure. The first one listed, interrater or interobserver reliability, is required any time different observers are used to observe or rate participants' behavior.

Researchers typically determine the reliability of the observers/raters by either computing a correlation coefficient or calculating a percentage of agreement. The study discussed in chapter 5 by Bejarano et al. (1997) used two independent raters for their observational procedures. They reported interrater reliabilities for the three variables as 0.98, 0.86, and 0.96. These figures reveal high agreement among the raters, which I am sure pleased the researchers.

TABLE 6.2
Reliability Coefficients Used in Research

Name of Coefficient	Consistency Over	Measurement Procedure	Statistic Used
Interrater/observer	Different raters/observers	Observation of performance: oral, written	Correlation, percentage
Intrarater/observer	Different times for same rater	Same as above	Same as above
Test–retest	Different times of testing	Standardized tests and inventories	Correlation
Alternate form	Different sets of test items and different times of testing	Multiple forms of the same instrument	Correlation
Split-half (odd/even) Kuder-Richardson 20 & 21 Cronbach alpha	Internal consistency of items within a test	Instruments using discrete items and Likert-type items	Correlation, Spearman-Brown, Alpha, KR20, KR21

Also related to the use of observers/raters is *intrarater* reliability. The type of consistency this addresses relates to observers/raters giving the same results if they were given the opportunity to observe/rate participants on more than one occasion. We would expect high agreement within the same person doing the observing/rating over time if the attribute being observed is stable and the observer/rater understood the task. However, if the observer/rater is not clear about what s/he is supposed to observe/rate, there will be different results, and correlations or percentages of agreement will be low. Although this is an important issue, I have not seen many recent studies report this type of reliability.

One example I did find was Goh's (2002) study, mentioned in chapter 5, which used both inter- and intrarater reliability. Recall that her study looked at listening comprehension techniques and how they interacted with one another. She had two participants read passages with pauses. During each pause, they were to reflect on how they attempted to understand the segment they heard. These retrospections were taped and transcribed. The transcriptions were analyzed by Goh, identifying, interpreting, and coding the data. Commendably, she checked the reliability of her observations by enlisting a colleague to follow the same procedures on a portion of the data and computing an interrater reliability coefficient ($r = 0.76$). In addition, she computed an intrarater reliability coefficient ($r = 0.88$) to make sure there was consistency even within her own observations. As expected, she agreed with herself (intrarater) more than she agreed with her colleague (interrater).

The remainder of the other types of reliabilities in Table 6.2 are used with paper-and-pencil or computer-administered instruments, whether questionnaires or tests. Test–retest reliability is used to measure the stability of the same instrument over time. The instrument is given at least twice, and a correlation coefficient is computed on the scores. However, this procedure can only work if the trait (i.e., construct) being measured can be assumed to remain stable over the time between the two measurements. For example, if the researcher is assessing participants' L2 pronunciation abilities, administering the instrument 2 weeks later should produce similar results if it is reliable. However, if there is a month or two between testing sessions, any training on pronunciation may create differences between the two sets of scores that would depress the reliability coefficient. However, if the time between the two administrations is too little, memory of the test from the first session could help the participants give the same responses, which would inflate the reliability coefficient.

A study that reported a test–retest reliability (Camiciottoli, 2001) was mentioned in Section 1 of this chapter. Camiciottoli used a 22-item questionnaire to collect data on both independent and dependent variables. To measure test–retest reliability, she gave 20 participants from the larger group the same questionnaire 6 weeks later. She then correlated the results from the first administration with that of the second and found a reliability coefficient of 0.89. This is considered fairly high reliability.

Another type of reliability estimate typically used when a test has several different forms is the *alternate-form* procedure. Most standardized tests have multiple forms to test the same attribute. The forms are different in that the items are not the same, but they are similar in form and content. To ensure that each form is testing the same trait, pairs of different forms are given to the same individuals with several days or more between administrations. The results are then correlated. If the different forms are testing the same attribute, the correlations should be fairly high. Not only does this procedure test stability of results over time, it also tests whether the items in the different forms represent the same general attribute being tested.

For example, if researchers were to use the Cambridge Certificate in Advanced English (CAE) test battery[5] in a research study, they would need assurance from the test publisher that, no matter what form was used, the results would reveal a similar measure of English language proficiency. Again researchers should report the alternate-form reliability coefficient provided by the test publisher in his or her research report. The assumption cannot be made by researchers that those who read the study will know that a particular standardized test is reliable even if it is well known. No matter what test is used, the reliability should be reported in any study where applicable.

A practice that you will no doubt see in your perusal of research is that of borrowing parts of commercially produced standardized tests to construct other tests. It seems that researchers doing this are under the assumption that, because items come from an instrument that has good reliability estimates, any test consisting of a subset of borrowed items will inherit the same reliability. This cannot be taken for granted. Test items often behave differently when put into other configurations. For this reason, subtests consisting of test items coming from such larger, proven instruments should be reevaluated for reliability before using them in a study.

Rodriguez and Sadoski (2000), mentioned earlier, in addition to developing their own 15-item Spanish test, took 15 items from the Green and Purple Levels of the Stanford Diagnostic Reading Test for use in their English test. It would have been helpful if they had reported the reliabilities for these smaller tests. If reliability information were not available from the test publishers, they could have calculated their own reliabilities. Without knowing the reliability of a test, there is no way to know how consistent the results are.

---

[5]See http://www.cambridge-efl.org/exam/general/bg_cae.htm for more information. Retrieved Jan. 10, 2004.

The last three methods of estimating the reliability of a test are concerned with the *internal* consistency of the items within the instrument. In other words, do all the items in an instrument measure the same general attribute? This is important because the responses for each item are normally added up to make a total score. If the items are measuring different traits, then a total score would not make much sense. To illustrate, if a researcher tries to measure participant attitudes toward a second language, do all of the items in the survey[6] contribute to reflecting their attitude? If some items are measuring grammar ability, then combining their results with those of the attitude items would confound the measure of attitude.

The first of these three methods presented is known as *split-half (odd/ even)*. It is the easiest of the three methods to compute. As the name suggests, the items in the test are divided in half. Responses on each half are added up to make a subtotal for each half. This can be done by simply splitting the test in half, which is appropriate if the second half of the items is not different in difficulty level or the test is not too long. The reason that length is a factor is respondents might become tired in the latter half of the test, which would make their responses different from the first half of the test. To get around these problems, the test can be divided by comparing the odd items with the even items. The responses on the items for each respondent are divided into two subtotals—odd and even. That is, the odd items (e.g., Items 1, 3, 5, etc.) are summed and compared with the sum of the even items (e.g., Items 2, 4, 6, etc.). The odd/even method is preferred because it is not influenced by the qualitative change in items that often occur in different sections of the instrument, such as difficulty of item or fatigue. Whatever the halving method, the two subtotals are then correlated together to produce the reliability coefficient to measure internal consistency.

The next two methods of computing a coefficient of internal consistency—Kuder-Richardson 20 & 21 and Cronbach alpha—are mathematically related and sometimes symbolized with the Greek letter α (alpha). The first two, Kuder-Richardson 20 & 21, are really two related formulas symbolized as KR-20 and KR-21, respectively. Both are used with items that are scored dichotomously—also referred to as discrete point items—that is, correct/incorrect, true/false, yes/no, and so on. Formula KR-21 is a simpler version of KR-20. In laymen's words, these formulas correlate the responses on each item with each of the other items and then average all the correlations. Laufer (1998) reported KR-21 reliability coefficients of 0.88 and 0.82 for two of the instruments she used in her study on the development of active and passive vocabulary. For tests that are dichotomously scored (i.e., correct/incorrect), both tests had good reliabilities.

---

[6]Attitude surveys require the same internal consistency measures as tests.

The Cronbach alpha (also known as *coefficient alpha*) does the same thing as the KR formulas except that it is used when the items are scored with more than two possibilities. One use of this method is on rating scales, where participants are asked to indicate on a multipoint scale—also referred to as Likert-type scale—the degree to which they agree or disagree. As with the KR formulas, the resulting reliability coefficient is an overall average of the correlations among all possible pairs of items. Scarcella and Zimmerman (1998) calculated a Cronbach alpha reliability coefficient of 0.85 for their Test of Academic Lexicon, which was interpreted to mean that their instrument had good internal consistency.

Both the Cronbach alpha and the KR-20/KR-21 are conservative estimations of internal consistency. The term *conservative* is used because they take into consideration all the relationships among items that usually produce lower coefficients than the split-half method. For this reason, producers of all standardized tests typically report this type to demonstrate internal consistency. Again, a well-written study should include this information in the data-collecting procedure section, but you would be surprised by studies that fail to report this information.

Factors that affect reliability are numerous. One of the major factors is the degree to which the instrument or procedure is effected by *subjectivity* of the people doing the rating or scoring. The more a procedure is vulnerable to perceptual bias, lack of awareness, fatigue, or anything else that influences the ability to observe or rate what is happening, the lower the reliability.

Other factors that affect reliability are especially related to discrete-point item[7] tests for collecting data. One of these is *test length*, which can affect reliability in two different ways. The first involves not having enough items. Instruments with fewer items will automatically produce smaller reliability coefficients. This is not necessarily due to the items being inconsistent, but rather is a simple mathematical limitation inherent to correlation coefficients. However, there is a correction formula known as the *Spearman-Brown prophecy formula* (Nitko, 2001), which is available for use. This is used to project what the reliability estimate would be if the test had more items. When researchers use the split-half reliability coefficient (cf. Table 6.2), they usually report the Spearman-Brown coefficient because the test has been cut into halves, creating two short tests.

Garcia and Asencion (2001) followed this procedure in their study, which looked at the effects of group interaction on language development. They used two tasks for collecting data: a text reconstruction test and a test of listening comprehension. The first test was scored using two raters who were looking at the correct use of three grammar rules. They reported

---

[7]This item tests only one thing and is scored correct or incorrect.

interrater reliability with a correlation coefficient of 0.98: very high. For the listening test, which only consisted of 10 items, they used the split-half method along with the Spearman-Brown adjustment for a short test ($r =$ 0.73). This appears to be moderate reliability, but remember that it was a short test. So, in fact, the correlation is not bad.

The second way that the length of an instrument can affect reliability is when it is too long. Responses to items that are in the latter part of the instrument can be affected by fatigue. Respondents who are tired will not produce consistent responses, which will lower reliability coefficients. When developing an English language test battery for placing students at the university where I teach, my development team and I noticed that the reliability of the reading component was lower than expected. This component was the last test in the battery. On further investigation, we found that a number of items in the last part of the test were not being answered. Our conclusion was that the test takers were running out of time or energy and were not able to finish the last items. We corrected the problem, and the reliability of this component increased to the level we felt appropriate. This is also a problem with long surveys.

The final factor I mention is the *item quality* used in an instrument. Ambiguous test items will produce inconsistent results and lower reliability. Participants will guess at poorly written items, and this will not give an accurate measure of the attribute under observation. Items that have more than one correct answer or are written to trick the participant will have similar negative effects. Scarcella and Zimmerman (1998), for example, dropped 10 items from their Test of Academic Lexicon because these items lowered the Cronbach alpha coefficient. For some reason, these items were not consistently measuring the same attribute as the rest of the instrument. This left them with 40 real-word items, which they considered adequate.

There are other factors that influence reliability coefficients, but they relate to correlation coefficients in general. I raise these issues in the next chapter when discussing correlation coefficients in greater detail.

However, to emphasize how important knowing what the reliability of an instrument is, I introduce you to the *Standard Error of Measurement* (SEM; Hughes, 2003; Nitko, 2001). Don't let this term make you nervous; it is not as bad as it looks. I will attempt to explain this in a nonmathematical way. The reliability coefficient is also used to estimate how much error there is in the measurement procedure—error is any variation in the instrument results due to factors other than what is being measured. By performing some simple math procedures on the reliability coefficient, an estimate of the amount of error is calculated, referred to as the SEM. If there is perfect reliability (i.e., $r = 1.00$), there is no error in the measurement; that is, there is perfect consistency. This means that any difference in scores on the instrument can be interpreted as true differences between participants. However, if there is no reliability (i.e., $r = 0.00$), then no difference between participant scores can be interpreted as true difference on the trait being measured. To illustrate, if I used a procedure for measuring language proficiency that had no reliability, although I might get a set of scores differing across individuals, I could not conclude that one person who scored higher than another had a higher proficiency. All differences would be contributed to error from a variety of unknown sources.

What about the real world, where reliabilities are somewhere between 0.00 and 1.00? A rule of thumb that I give to my students is that a measurement procedure that has a reliability coefficient even as high as 0.75 has a sizable amount of error. With this reliability coefficient, half of the average variation in measurement between individuals can be attributed to error. For instance, if one person scores 55 on an instrument measuring proficiency in grammar and another person scores 60 with an SEM of 5.0, we cannot conclude with much confidence that the second person truly has higher grammar ability. I come back to this in the next chapter when I discuss descriptive statistics. I might add here that few studies, if any, report SEMs, although you might see it if you are reading a study about language testing. However, by using the simple reference point of a reliability equaling 0.75, which means that half of the variation between people being measured is due to error, you will be able to judge how stable the results of a study are. Knowing this can help in deciding how much weight you put on a study to answer your questions.

Validity

As with reliability, the quality of validity is more complex than initially appears. On the surface, people use it to refer to the ability of an instrument or observational procedure to accurately capture data needed to answer a research question. On the other hand, many research methodology textbooks distinguish among a number of types of validity, such as *content validity, predictive validity, face validity, construct validity*, and so on (e.g., Brown, 1988; Gall et al., 1996; Hatch & Lazaraton, 1991). These different types have led to some confusion. For instance, I have heard some people accuse certain data-gathering procedures of being invalid, whereas others claim that the same procedures are valid. However, when their arguments are examined more closely, one realizes that the two sides of the debate are using different definitions of validity.

Since the early 1990s, the prior notions of validity have been subsumed under the heading of *construct validity* (Bachman, 1990; Messick, 1989). These types of validity are now represented as different *facets* of validity under this global title. They are summarized in Table 6.3.

TABLE 6.3
Multiple Facets of Construct Validity

FACETS	Criterion Related		Content Coverage	Face Appearance
Trait accuracy	Capacity to succeed	Current character-istics	Cognitive/behav-ioral/affective change	Consumer satisfaction
Utility	Predictive	Diagnostic, place-ment	Achievement of ob-jectives	Public relations
Procedures				
Types	Aptitude tests	Language profi-ciency tests, atti-tude scales	Tests, quizzes, per-formance assess-ments	All
Examples	MLAT	TOEFL, IELTS	Exercises to test treatment effects	All

In the upper half of Table 6.3 in the left column, validity is shown to be comprised of two main facets: trait accuracy and utility. *Trait accuracy,* which corresponds with the former *construct validity,* addresses the question as to how accurately the procedure measures the trait (i.e., construct) under investigation. However, accuracy depends on the definition of the construct being measured or observed. Language proficiency, for example, is a trait that is often measured in research. Nevertheless, how this trait is measured should be determined by how it is defined. If language proficiency is defined as the summation of grammar and vocabulary knowledge, plus reading and listening comprehension, then an approach needs to be used that measures all of these components to accurately measure the trait as defined. However, if other researchers define language proficiency as oral and writing proficiency, they would have to use procedures to directly assess speaking and writing ability. In other words, the degree to which a procedure is valid for *trait accuracy* is determined by the degree to which the procedure corresponds to the definition of the trait.

When reading a research article, the traits need to be clearly defined to know whether the measurements used are valid in regards to the accuracy facet of validity. These definitions should appear in either the introduction or methodology section of the article. To illustrate, in their search for factors contributing to second language learning, Gardner et al. (1997) defined *language anxiety* as "communication apprehension, test anxiety, and fear of negative evaluation" (pp. 344–345) based on the Foreign Language Classroom Anxiety Scale developed by Horwitz, Horwitz, and Cope (1986; cited in Gardner et al., 1997). This practice of defining traits by using already existing instruments is common among researchers. In effect, the instrument provides the operational definition of the trait.

Regarding the second main facet of validity, *utility* is concerned with whether measurement/observational procedures are used for the right purpose. If a procedure is not used for what it was originally intended for, there might be a question as to whether it is a valid procedure for obtaining the data needed in a particular study. If it is used for something other than what it was originally designed to do, the researcher must provide additional evidence that the procedure is valid for the purpose of his or her study. For example, if you wanted to use the results from the TOEFL to measure the effects of a treatment over a 2-week training period, this would be invalid. To reiterate, the reason is that the TOEFL was designed to measure language proficiency, which develops over long periods of time. It was not designed to measure the specific outcomes that the treatment was targeting.

Note in Table 6.3 that there are three other facets that further qualify the main facets of trait accuracy and utility: criterion related, content coverage, and face appearance. These used to be referred to as separate validities: criterion-related validity, content validity, and face validity (e.g., Brown, 1988). However, within the current global concept of construct validity, they help define the complex nature of validity.

Criterion related simply means that the procedure is validated by being compared to some external criterion. It is divided into two general types of trait accuracy: *capacity to succeed* and *current characteristics*. *Capacity to succeed* relates to a person having the necessary wherewithal or *aptitude* to succeed in some other endeavor. Typically, this involves carefully defining the aptitude being measured and then constructing or finding an instrument or observational procedure that would accurately obtain the needed data. The *utility* of identifying people's *capacity to succeed* is usually for prediction purposes. For instance, if a researcher wants to predict people's ability to master a foreign language, s/he would administer a procedure that would assess whether the examinees had the necessary aptitude to succeed. Predictive utility is determined by correlating the measurements from the procedures with measurements on the criterion being predicted. I do not go into further detail about how this is done; suffice it to say that you can find more about this from any book on assessment (e.g., Nitko, 2001).

A number of measures have been used over the years to predict the success of students in acquiring a second language. One of the most well-known standardized instruments that has been around for many years is the Modern Language Aptitude Test developed by Carroll and Sapon (1959). They developed this test for the purpose of predicting whether people have an aptitude for learning languages. Steinman and Smith (2001) presented evidence in their review of this test that it is not only valid for making predictions, but it has become used as an external criterion for validating other tests.

Others have also been involved in developing systems for predicting language learning aptitude more recently. One of the most comprehensive studies on this matter in my opinion was done by Gardner et al. (1997). They analyzed the predictive power of various combinations of 32 different traits on second language achievement in French. They used instruments to measure a number of traits: language aptitude, attitudes, motivation, learning styles, learning strategies, and self-confidence in comparison with two measures of language achievement. The instruments varied from Likert-type rating scales, fill in the blanks, multiple choice, and essay. In most cases, the researchers clearly reported the reliability coefficient for each instrument. Some estimates of reliability were high (e.g., Self-Confidence, $\alpha = 0.91$), and some were low (e.g., the learning strategy of Compensating for Missing Knowledge, $\alpha = 0.43$). The results show that the five traits used in different combinations predicted achievement: self-confidence with motivation, language learning strategies with motivation, motivation with positive attitude, language aptitude along with learning style, and orientation to learn French. From these data, the researchers provided evidence for the validity of the combined use of 5 out of 32 traits to predict L2 achievement in French.

The second general trait that is validated against an external criterion is *current characteristics* (cf. Table 6.3). Such things as language proficiency, personality, and attitude are considered as characteristics that individuals currently possess. Techniques that measure these are used for (i.e., utility) diagnosing people for placement into different categories such as different language proficiency levels. For instance, Ganschow and Sparks (1996) used the Foreign Language Classroom Anxiety Scale (FLCAS) to identify low-, average-, and high-anxiety participants for their study. They cited several studies done by the developers of the FLCAS as indirect evidence for reliability and validity. The aspect of validity that the developers needed to demonstrate was verification that the FLCAS could accurately identify different levels of language anxiety that participants had at the time of the study. This information was provided.

One method used to provide evidence for being able to identify current characteristics is by whether the diagnoses of the procedure match an expert opinion. For example, Kobayashi (2002) took care to use experts to judge the suitability of the passages for her reading comprehension test as well as for the test items. By doing so, she supplied evidence that her instrument was measuring what she intended to measure.

Another common method for showing the prior facet of validity is to correlate the results of the procedure with performance on another instrument that has been accepted by the research community as a good criterion. Often performance on instruments designed for a particular study are correlated with students' performance on a recognized standardized test such as the TOEFL to estimate validity. Laufer (1998), for instance, used three instruments to measure participants' vocabulary knowledge. She reported how two of them were validated by showing how these measures agreed with participants' levels of language proficiency. By doing so, she was able to provide evidence that the trait was accurately being measured.

The second facet in Table 6.3 is *content coverage*. The general traits being assessed here are *cognitive, behavioral,* or *affective change*. In *experimental* research, the main question looks at cause-and-effect relationships in the form of treatment effects. Often the objective of the treatment is to increase learning or change the participants' behavior or attitudes. This same objective needs to be used when planning the measurement procedure because its main utility is to assess whether the treatment objective has been achieved. Thus, the validity of the measurement procedure is determined by how well its content aligns with the treatment objectives. In this case, validity is not assessed by computing a correlation coefficient, as with other validity procedures, but by matching various components of the measurement procedure with the treatment objectives.

For example, Tsang (1996) examined the effects of reading and writing on writing performance. Tsang's reasoning was based on the thinking that the more one reads and writes, the better one will write. The ESL Composition Profile developed by Jacobs et al. (1981) was used to define and measure writing performance both before and after the treatment. Tsang used this profile, which consists of five scales to define writing performance as: content, organization, vocabulary, language use, and mechanics. For this instrument to have been valid for measuring the effects of the treatments, Tsang needed to show that the treatments were designed to increase participants' writing ability in these five areas. Without this information, there is little way to know whether the measuring instrument was sensitive to any changes due to the treatment. The principle here is that when a study has a treatment that is designed to effect cognitive/behavioral/attitude change, the researcher should show how the measurement procedure is sensitive to change in these areas to establish that the procedure has appropriate utility (i.e., one facet of validity).

The third facet in Table 6.3 that qualifies trait accuracy and utility is *face appearance*, which some refer to as *face validity*. Related to accuracy, the key issue is whether a measurement procedure appears to measure what it is supposed to measure. The closer it looks like it is gathering the correct data, the more valid it looks. In regards to utility, face appearance is important for public relations with examinees as well as with the outside community. Examinees who do not feel that the procedure is measuring what they think it should measure might not be motivated to do their best. This, in turn, will affect the results of the study. People outside a study might not see the relevance of a particular measurement technique and, therefore, not consider the results from such measurement useful for answering the researcher question (i.e., the consumer). Although this facet of construct validity is of lesser theoretical importance from a research perspective, it is the one that many practitioners in foreign language teaching give most attention to. This has led some people to make incorrect conclusions about the validity of data that result from some measurement procedures.

To illustrate how easy it is to allow the facet of *face appearance* to overshadow other aspects of validity, I relate this somewhat bizarre, but true, story. One of my former professors once said something like this:

> If I were to tell you that I found a correlation of +0.95 (a very high correlation) between shoe size and success in learning a foreign language, and that I have found this high correlation in a number of studies with different groups of participants, would you use shoe size as a test to predict future success entrants into your foreign language program?

Most likely you would agree with my professor's rhetorical answer with an emphatic, "No way!" However, I asked, "Why not?" His answer was, "The test is not valid." If you agree with him, what facet of validity do you have in mind? Most likely you would be considering face appearance as he was. I, in contrast, argued that the test is valid on the basis of its predictive utility. Anything, no matter what it looks like, that correlates with something else as high as 0.95 is a powerful predictor. I certainly agree that shoe size does not appear at face value to relate to the ability to learn a language. For prediction purposes, however, face appearance is not necessary, although desired. Understanding *why* something can predict something else does not have to be clear either, although we would certainly try to find out the reason. I would argue that if my data are correct, we should use shoe size as an entrance test because it has been shown to have high predictive validity. Certainly, it would be the cheapest and quickest test to administer, although not very popular with people whose foot size predicts failure.

Before concluding this section of the chapter, I need to point out an important principle. The relationship between validity and reliability is *unidirectional*. There are two aspects to this: (a) reliability does not depend on validity, but (b) validity depends on reliability. Regarding the first, reliability does not require or depend on validity. An instrument or observational procedure can be reliable (i.e., consistent) when measuring something, but not necessarily consistently measuring the right thing. To illustrate, if we measure a person's height with a measuring tape, the results are consistent (i.e., reliable) every time. No matter how many times we measure that person's height, we will get the same results. Yet if we claim that our measurement is an accurate assessment of a person's weight, our procedure is not very valid. Notice that I said *not very* and refrained from using *invalid.* The reason is that height is related to weight: Tall people are usually heavier than short people. Although related, height would not be a valid direct measurement of weight. In other words, a measurement procedure can be reliable, but not valid.

However, the opposite is not true. We cannot have a valid instrument that is not reliable: aspect (b). Accuracy implies consistency, but not vice versa. Obviously, if we cannot depend on a procedure to give us consistent (i.e., reliable) results, then accuracy will also fluctuate. In fact the validity of an instrument can never exceed its reliability. If a measurement procedure has low reliability, its validity will be low as well, regardless of how valid the developer wishes it might be. To return to the Gardner et al. (1997) study mentioned previously, the researchers did not comment on the relatively low reliability of the instrument measuring the learning strategy of Compensating for Missing Knowledge ($\alpha = 0.43$). With such a low reliability coefficient, I would be suspicious about the validity of this instrument. On the other hand, a high reliability coefficient does not automatically mean that the instrument is also highly valid. Therefore, reliability is necessary, but not sufficient for defining validity. Once the instrument is determined reliable, the researcher must then show with separate information that it is valid.

In summary, when you read or hear the term *validity* being used, refer to Table 6.3 and try to determine what aspect of validity is being considered. Then ask yourself if the term is being used correctly. Remember that if a measurement has low reliability, regardless of its face appearance, it also has low validity. However, too few studies report how the validity of the procedures used were determined. Yet the results of a study depend heavily on whether the measurement procedures are valid. The weaker the validity, the less we can depend on the results.

In conclusion, the second section of this chapter has introduced the two principle qualities of data-gathering procedures: reliability and validity. Regardless of what procedure a researcher uses from Section 1 of this chapter, s/he needs to report to the reader evidence that the procedure used provides reliable and valid data. If not, there is no way the reader will know whether the conclusions made based on the data have any credibility. With this basic information in hand, you should now be able to read the section about data gathering with understanding. In addition, you should have enough confidence to evaluate whether the procedure a researcher used provided reliable and valid information.

You are now ready to grapple with how data are analyzed. This is the subject of the next chapter. However, before you leave this chapter, try the following exercise so that you can gain firsthand experience in evaluating the data-gathering procedures used in a study of your choice.

Exercise 6.3

Task: Find a research study of interest in a recent journal related to applied linguistics. Do the following:

1. List the research question(s).
2. Look at the data-collection procedure used (i.e., tests, surveys, raters, observers, etc.). Does the procedure seem appropriate for answering the research question(s)?
3. What information was given relating to reliability?
   a. Type?
   b. Amount?
   c. How reliable was the procedure being used?
4. What facet of validity was examined?
5. How well did the procedure correspond to identifying the trait being measured in your opinion?
6. Did statements about validity correspond to evidence of reliability?

Key Terms and Concepts

Section 1

automatic response patterns
closed-form questionnaire items
constructed response items
criterion-referenced tests
discrete point items
full-participant observer
halo effect
highly structured interviews
informant
instrumental procedures
introspection
judge/rater
nonparticipant observer
norm-referenced test
objective
observational procedure
open-form questionnaire items
open-structured interviews
partial-participant observer
participant observers

Section 2

alternate-form reliability
coefficient
construct validity
content coverage
criterion related
Cronbach alpha
face appearance
internal consistency
interrater reliability
intrarater reliability
item quality
Kuder-Richardson 20 & 21
predictive utility
reliability
reliability coefficient
Spearman-Brown prophecy formula
split-half (odd/even) reliability
Standard Error of Measurement
   (SEM)
test–retest reliability

retrospection
rubric
semistructured interviews
standardized test
subjectivity
think-aloud procedure
triangulation

trait accuracy
utility
validity

Additional Recommended Reading

Bachman, L. F., & Palmer, A. S. (1996). *Language testing in practice: Designing and developing useful language tests.* Oxford: Oxford University Press.

Bailey, K. (1998). *Learning about language assessment: Dilemmas, decisions, and directions.* Boston, MA: Heinle & Heinle.

Brown, J. D. (2001). *Using surveys in language programs.* Cambridge, England: Cambridge University Press.

Brown, J. D., & Hudson, H. (2002). *Criterion-referenced language testing.* Cambridge: Cambridge University Press.

Dörnyei, Z. (2003). *Questionnaires in second language research: Construction, administration.* Mahwah, NJ: Lawrence Erlbaum Associates.

Gass, S. M., & Mackey, A. (2000). *Stimulated recall in second language research.* Mahwah, NJ: Lawrence Erlbaum Associates.

Hughes, A. (2003). *Testing for language teachers* (2nd ed.). Cambridge, England: Cambridge University Press.

Kunnan, A. J. (Ed.). (1998). *Validation in language assessment.* Mahwah, NJ: Lawrence Erlbaum Associates.

Scholfield, P. (1995). *Quantifying language: A researcher's and teacher's guide to gathering language data and reducing it to figures.* Philadelphia, PA: Multilingual Matters.

Understanding Research Results

CHAPTER OVERVIEW

Once researchers collect their data, they must determine whether the results answer their research questions. If they are "What" questions, the answers are in the form of information that (a) describes what variables are important, (b) identifies the context in which certain phenomena occur, and/or (c) uncovers important relationships between phenomena. If the questions are "Why" types, then the results attempt to explain the cause behind certain phenomena. In either case, the analysis of the data is presented verbally, numerically, or a combination of the two.

In this chapter, various types of data and data analysis procedures that appear in Results sections of research studies are discussed. Following a short general introduction to data analysis, there are two main sections: The first relates to how verbal data are presented and analyzed, and the second introduces how numerical data are presented and analyzed. Although somewhat technical, this latter section does not require a background in math. It furnishes you with the concepts needed to understand the statistical procedures found in many Results sections.

By the end of this chapter, my goal is for you to be able to read Results sections of research articles with enough confidence to critically evaluate whether appropriate procedures have been used and correct interpretations have been made.

INTRODUCTION TO DATA ANALYSIS

Numerical Versus Verbal Data

Some people think that numerical data are more scientific—and therefore more important—than verbal data because of the statistical analyses that can be performed on numerical data. However, this is a false conclusion. We must not forget that numbers are only as good as the constructs they represent. In other words, when we use statistics, we have basically transferred verbally defined constructs into numbers so we can analyze the data more easily. We must not forget that these statistical results must again be transferred back into terminology that represents these verbal constructs to make any sense.[1] Consider the following statement by Miles and Huberman (1994) as an argument for the importance of verbal data:

> We argue that although words may be more unwieldy than numbers, they render more meaning than numbers alone and should be hung on to throughout data analysis. Converting words into numbers and then tossing away the words gets a researcher into all kinds of mischief. You thus are assuming that the chief property of the words is that there are more of some than of others. Focusing solely on numbers shifts attention from substance to arithmetic, throwing out the whole notion of "qualities" or "essential characteristics." (p. 56)

Nevertheless, be careful not to swing to the other side of the pendulum, thinking that verbal data are superior to numerical data. Both types of data have their place and are equally important. Miles and Huberman provided a powerful discussion on how the two types of data complement each other. This concurs with my position presented in chapter 5 of this book.

Common Procedure

In almost all studies, all of the data that have been gathered are not presented in the research report. Whether verbal or numerical, the data presented have gone through some form of selection and reduction. The reason is that both verbal and numerical data typically are voluminous in their rawest forms. What you see reported in a research journal are results of the raw data having been boiled down into manageable units for display to the public. Verbal data commonly appear as selections of excerpts, narrative vignettes, quotations from interviews, and so on, whereas numerical data are often condensed into tables of frequencies, averages, and so on. There are

---

[1]See Miles and Huberman (1994, chap. 3) for further discussion.

some interesting differences, however, which I describe in the following two sections.

SECTION 1: PRESENTATION AND ANALYSIS OF VERBAL DATA

Most of the credit in recent years for developing criteria for presenting and analyzing verbal data must go to researchers who have emphasized the use of qualitative research strategies. However, because of the variety of qualitative approaches used, there are differing opinions about the analytical steps that should be followed when analyzing verbal data. For instance, Creswell (1998) identified only 3 out of 13 general analysis strategies common to three different authors of qualitative research methods (Bogden & Biklen, 1992; Huberman & Miles, 1994; Wolcott, 1994). This makes it difficult to set standards for evaluating the Results section of a qualitative research article. Lazaraton (2003) was even more pessimistic. She stated, "Can any one set of criteria be used to judge any or all forms of qualitative research? My thesis, in answer to this last question, is that they cannot" (p. 2).

In addition, unlike work with numerical data, presentation of verbal data and their analyses appear very much intertwined together in Results sections of research reports. That is, separating the data from the analysis is difficult. Numerical data, in contrast, are presented in some type of summarized form (i.e., descriptive statistics) and followed with the analysis in the form of inferential statistics (cf. Section 2 of this chapter).

Consequently, the analysis of verbal data is not quite as straightforward as the analysis of numerical data. The reason is that analysis of verbal data is initiated at the beginning of the data-collection process and continues throughout the study. This process involves the researcher interacting with the data in a symbiotic fashion. Literally, the researcher becomes the "main 'measurement device' " (Miles & Huberman, 1994, p. 7). Creswell (1998, pp. 142–143) likened data analysis to a "contour" in the form of a "data analysis spiral," where the researcher engages the data, reflects, makes notes, reengages the data, organizes, codes, reduces the data, looks for relationships and themes, makes checks on the credibility of the emerging system, and eventually draws conclusions.

However, when we read published qualitative research, we seldom are given a clear description of how this *data analysis spiral* transpired. In Miles and Huberman's (1994) words, "We rarely see data displays—only the conclusions. In most cases we don't see a procedural account of the analysis, explaining just how the researcher got from 500 pages of field notes to the main conclusions drawn" (p. 262).

If the researcher is working alone during the data analysis spiral, serious questions arise concerning the credibility of any conclusions made. First, there is the problem mentioned in chapter 6 regarding possible bias when gathering data through observation and other noninstrumental procedures. However, because analysis begins during the data-collection stage in qualitative research, *analytical biases* become a possible threat to the validity of conclusions. Miles and Huberman (1994) identified three archetypical ones: *holistic fallacy, elite bias,* and *going native.* The first has to do with seeing patterns and themes that are not really there. The second is concerned with giving too much weight to informants who are more articulate and better informed, making the data unrepresentative. The third, *going native,* occurs when the researcher gets so close to the respondents that s/he is "co-opted into [their] perceptions and explanations" (p. 264).

So how are we, the consumers of qualitative research, supposed to determine whether the information in the Results section is credible? Miles and Huberman (1994) listed 13 tactics for enhancing credibility that might be of help (see Table 7.1). Four of these tactics (1, 4, 5, & 6)[2] relate to quality of the data, four (7, 8, & 9)[3] to evaluating any patterns and/or themes proposed by the researcher, and five (11, 12, 13, 14, & 15) to appraising explanations and conclusions.

Creswell (1998) provided eight verification procedures that he and a colleague extrapolated from a number of differing types of qualitative studies. Three of these overlapped with Miles and Huberman's (1994) list—triangulation, negative evidence, and member checks (i.e., informant feedback)—leaving five that I have incorporated into the list in Table 7.1. Two relate to evaluating data quality (2 & 3). The third, *peer review* (10), is useful for checking whether the perceived patterns are credible, although also useful for evaluating explanations. The last two, rich/thick descriptions (16) and external audits (17), are powerful tactics for evaluating explanations. Each of these tactics is further explained next.

Few studies use all 17 of these tactics to enhance credibility. However, the more a study has in each category, the more evidence is put forward for strengthening the credibility of the results. There should be at least one tactic used in each of the three general categories in Table 7.1.

Evaluating the Quality of Data

As with numerical data, verbal data cannot be taken simply at face value. The researcher should provide evidence that the data s/he has used in his

---

[2]Although Miles and Huberman put triangulation with data quality, I place it under patterns and themes based on Creswell's use of the term.

[3]Miles and Huberman originally treated outliers and extreme cases as separate tactics. However, because they stated that the latter was a type of the former, I combined them into one.

TABLE 7.1
Evaluation Tactics for Verbal Data

Checking for . . .	*Tactics*

Data Quality
  1. Representativeness
      Respondents
      Events
  2. Prolonged engagement and persistent observation
  3. Clarifying researcher bias
  4. Check for researcher effects
      Researcher on persons/events
      Persons/events on researcher
  5. Weighting the evidence
      Informants' access and proximity
      Circumstances:
         behavior observed firsthand
         adequate exposure
         informal settings
         trusted field workers
         continuous vigilance in checking for various biases

Patterns and Themes
  6. Triangulation
  7. Outliers and extreme cases
  8. Surprises
  9. Negative evidence
 10. Peer review

Explanations and Conclusions
 11. Spurious relationships
 12. If–then tests
 13. Rival explanations
 14. Replicating findings
 15. Informant feedback
 16. Rich/thick description
 17. External audits

or her study are dependable enough to analyze. The researcher has at least five strategies to choose from to support the quality of the data. They are as follows:

1. *Representativeness:* This is not referring specifically to whether the sample is representative of the population (i.e., external validity) as discussed in chapter 4, although related. This is more to do with whether the veracity of the information is being influenced by the choice of respondents or events (i.e., internal validity or credibility). Related to the *elite bias* mentioned earlier, information coming from one particular segment of a larger group of people can be misleading. Similar to the volunteer problem men-

tioned in chapter 4, the most accessible and willing informants are not usually the best group to provide the most appropriate data.

In addition, the researcher needs to give evidence that the events on which generalizations are based are the most appropriate. A researcher might not be present at all times for data collection. If not, the consumer must ask about the proportion of time the researcher was present. If only a fraction of the events were observed, were they typical of most events? The ultimate question for the consumer is whether the researcher has provided evidence that data have come from observing an adequate number of events to ensure that subsequent inferences and conclusions were not based on the luck of the draw.

2. *Prolonged engagement and persistent observation:* The researcher needs enough time to interact with the respondents and/or the event to gather accurate data. This allows the researcher time to gain personal access to the information being targeted. However, if too much time is spent on the research site, there is the possibility one of the *researcher effects* discussed in Item 4 will set in.

3. *Clarifying researcher bias:* Every researcher has his or her own set of biases. Because the analysis of data in a qualitative study begins and continues during the collection of data, knowing the researcher's particular biases can help the consumer discern why the data are being gathered and interpreted a certain way. Therefore, the researcher should disclose any biases that may have an impact on the approach used and any interpretations made on the data. This helps the consumer determine how the researcher arrived at his or her conclusions.

4. *Researcher effects:* These were discussed in chapter 5 under threats to internal validity. In that chapter, the influence was mainly looking at the unidirectional effect of the researcher on the behavior of the persons from which data were being collected. However, Miles and Huberman (1994) pointed out that there is a reciprocal relationship between the researcher and the persons/events being observed. In one direction, the researcher's presence or actions influence the behavior being observed (chap. 5). In qualitative work, for example, respondents might change their behavior in the presence of the data gatherer to meet perceived expectations and/or hide sensitive information. Miles and Huberman warned that a researcher "must assume that people will try to be misleading and must shift into a more investigative mode" (p. 265). To avoid this, they suggested such strategies as: the researcher spending as much time as possible on site to become unnoticed, using unobtrusive methods, having an informant who monitors the impact the researcher is making, and using informal settings for some data gathering.

In the other direction of the reciprocal relationship, the persons/events being observed can impact the researcher. This can happen when the researcher spends too much time with the people being researched, and the researcher *goes native* by no longer being able to keep his or her own thinking separate from that of the respondents. This leads to a quandary because, to avoid the first problem of researcher-on-respondent impact mentioned earlier, the possibility of the respondents impacting the researcher increases. To avoid the respondent-on-researcher effect, Miles and Huberman (1994) proposed tactics such as: use a variety of respondents, include people outside of the group being observed, control site visits, use an informant to monitor events when not present, use triangulation, use peers to critique the work, and so on.

When evaluating the data collected in qualitative research, the consumer should look for ways the researcher tries to control for, or be aware of the effect s/he might have had on the people or the situation and vice versa. This does not simply mean the effect on the *product*, in the form of the data, but also on the analysis *process*. If such care is taken and reported, the researcher deserves kudos, and the credibility of findings has been enhanced.

5. *Weighting the evidence:* Miles and Huberman (1994) pointed out that some data are stronger (or more valid) than others. They laid down three principles for determining the strength of data. I have summarized them here in the form of questions that the consumer can use to evaluate the strength of the data:

a. What information does the researcher provide about the access and proximity of the informants to the targeted data? The closer to the data, the stronger.

b. To what extent do the data consist of actual behavior, observed firsthand, after adequate exposure, in informal settings, by trusted field workers? The more, the stronger.

c. What effort did the data gatherer(s) make toward checking for various biases (as outlined above) during the data-gathering process? The greater, the stronger.

Evaluating Patterns and Themes

One of the main goals of much qualitative research is to extrapolate patterns and themes from the verbal data. The question for the consumer is whether these patterns are plausible based on the data. Five tactics listed in Table 7.1 can be used to support these patterns proposed by researchers (cf. Creswell, 1998; Miles & Huberman, 1994). The first, triangulation, shows how the same pattern is seen in data coming from different sources. The next three involve atypical data that might not fit the patterns or themes being proposed by the researcher. The temptation is to avoid these *hiccups* in the data, referred to in quantitative analysis as *data smoothing.* However, for the qualitative researcher, these exceptions are excellent means to test the perceived patterns being formulated. The last tactic, peer review, involves getting a second opinion, which corresponds to criterion related validity discussed in chapter 6.

6. *Triangulation* (previously mentioned; cf. chaps. 5 & 6): This proce-dure involves using data from multiple sources to converge on themes and patterns. For the purpose of adding weight to an argument, the more evi-dence coming from independent sources, the better. As in the law courts, one witness is not enough. The more independent witnesses, the stronger the case. The same holds true for qualitative research; the more data com-ing from a variety of sources, the better. This, of course, assumes that data from each source can stand the test of the other data quality criteria in-cluded in this list.

Some qualitative methods, such as conversational analysis (cf. chap. 5), that focus on one set of data coming from one source may have difficulty here. Basically, CA uses one source of data, normally in the form of tran-scripts from audiotapes (Lazaraton, 2003). The researcher(s) repeatedly processes the transcripts until constructs and relationships are perceived. The researcher, typically using the *spiral* technique, continually tests and re-tests until s/he is satisfied with his or her conclusions. Of course more con-versational data collected from the same source at different times and set-tings add to support the interpretations. However, CA studies can use triangulation to support their conclusions, if so desired. The TESOL Web site adds in their set of criteria for publishing that "conversational analysis may be supplemented by . . . the use of triangulated secondary data."[4]

Simply stating, however, that triangulation of different data sources was used in a study does not necessarily increase credibility in the conclusions. The researcher needs to inform us how and why triangulation was used. Questions such as the following need to be answered: How do data from each source contribute to the convergence of a perceived pattern or theme? In what way does the researcher believe this particular combination of data add to the overall credibility of the conclusions? These are questions the researcher is obligated to answer to add weight to the overall credibility.

7. *Outliers/extreme cases:* Examining such data seems to be counterintui-tive to the tactic of checking for representativeness at the top of the list (cf. Table 7.1). However, this is an effective way to check whether the patterns and themes perceived by the researcher are not due to some form of bias. Most qualitative studies limit themselves when it comes to how many people

---

[4]http://www.tesol.org/pubs/author/serials/tqguides2.html#qual. #5. Retrieved Jan. 10, 2004.

or situations are studied. Because of this, the perceived patterns and themes may be unique to the sample being used. However, once these patterns and themes have been formulated from the original sample, comparing them with samples of people or events that considerably differ is an excellent way to check credibility.

In some studies, the opposite might be true. The researcher deliberately uses extreme cases compared to the original sample. The reason to do this is that such samples are information-rich (cf. chap. 4). However, once the patterns and themes have been extrapolated, it seems imperative that the researcher would want to compare his or her findings with a sample that is less extreme. If the patterns and themes hold for the more general sample, they are made more credible.

8. *Surprises:* Another tactic for promoting the credibility of perceived patterns and themes is examining unexpected findings. Reporting unexpected findings gives some confirmation that the researcher is not so focused on what s/he wants to find that s/he cannot recognize any anomalies. Of course once the surprise has been noted by the researcher, s/he needs to explain how it confirms or forces adjustment to the proposed pattern or theme.

9. *Negative evidence:* Here the researcher actively seeks evidence that will go against his or her patterns or themes. One would not think that the researcher would want to find evidence contradicting his or her proposals. It certainly is not something that happens automatically as the data are being analyzed by the researcher. The researcher would have to make a planned effort to do this after beginning to formulate any patterns or themes. Just the fact that the researcher made this effort would be impressive. However, it is not sufficient to simply report that negative evidence was found. The researcher needs to identify the evidence and discuss its implications. This type of information reported by the researcher in a published report adds more weight to the findings of the study.

10. *Peer review:* A *peer* is someone on the same level of the researcher "who keeps the researcher honest; asks the hard questions about methods, meanings, and interpretations" (Creswell, 1998, p. 202). The researcher, especially if doing the study alone, needs someone, such as a colleague, to evaluate proposed patterns as well as themes to prevent influences from such analytical biases as *holistic fallacy* mentioned previously.

Evaluating Explanations and Conclusions

The last phase of evaluating a qualitative study is examining the explanations and conclusions of the study. Table 7.1 presents seven tactics that researchers can use to bolster credibility: five from Miles and Huberman (1994) and two from Creswell (1998). These are useful for consumers of qualitative research for evaluation as well. However, the burden of proof is on the researcher, not the consumer. The more tactics used by the researcher, the more weight is given to the credibility of the interpretations of the findings.

11. *Spurious relationships:* Not all things that appear to be related are directly related. For example, lung cancer and the number of ashtrays a person owns are related. However, this relationship is spurious (i.e., misleading). Another variable directly related to each of these—amount of cigarettes smoked—produces an indirect relationship between ashtray and lung cancer. So when a researcher proposes a direct relationship between constructs, s/he should provide a convincing argument that there are not other variables producing this relationship.

12. *If–then tests:* These tests "are the workhorse of qualitative data analysis" (Miles & Huberman, 1994, p. 271). In the fuller version an *if–then test* is a conditional sentence in the form of, *If the hypothesis is true, then there should be a specific consequence.* Every explanation based on data is a type of hypothesis, usually in the form of relationships among variables, underlying principles, or processes. The researcher tests his or her hypothesized explanation by predicting that some consequent would occur with a novel sample of people or set of events. The next two methods are much related to the if–then test.

13. *Rival explanations:* Eliminating competing explanations is a powerful way to add weight to a theoretical conclusion. The researcher formulates at least one plausible competing explanation and repeats the *if–then* test. The explanation that best explains the data is the most plausible. The researcher can then report how the weaker explanations could not compete.

However, the consumer must beware that the competing explanations offered are not *straw men*; that is, explanations that were not plausible in the first place—easy to refute. This might occur if the researcher is so bent on her or his own explanation that s/he does not address more plausible hypotheses, but still wants to give the appearance that s/he has used this technique to gain credibility.

Another caveat for the consumer is to not conclude that, just because the competing explanations were not as robust as the one proposed by the researcher, the proposed one is the best one. There might still be a better explanation than the one proposed, but it has not been discovered as of yet. In other words, the last person standing may not be the strongest. On a more practical note, the researcher must provide evidence that not only his or her explanations are better than the competition, they are also good in themselves.

14. *Replicating findings:* This strategy is recognized by both qualitative and quantitative researchers as an excellent way to support hypotheses and

theories. The more often the same findings occur despite different samples and conditions, the more confidence we can have in the conclusions. Hypothesized relationships that can only be supported by one sample of individuals in only one setting have little use in the practical world. Occasionally, a researcher will report several replications of the study in the same report. This is a good way to provide evidence for the robustness of his or her explanations.

15. *Informant feedback:* This relates to the reactions that the informants have to the conclusions of the study. Such feedback can be used to check the plausibility of patterns perceived by the researcher. The researcher needs to take care here, however, due to possible *researcher effects.* Respondents may simply agree with the researcher just to please the researcher, or the researcher may give the informant a final report that is too technical. This could result in agreement to hide the embarrassment from not understanding or produce a negative response based on misunderstanding. In either case, the researcher needs to inform the consumer of the report regarding the manner in which the feedback was obtained. The more effort the researcher reports to have made to facilitate the understanding of the informant, the more weight the consumer can give to the feedback.

16. *Rich, thick description:* This involves a detailed description of the participants, context, and all that goes on during the data-gathering and analysis stages. The purpose is to provide the reader of the study with enough information to decide whether the explanations and conclusions of the study are transferable to other similar situations. If the description is vague with a lot of detail missing, it is impossible to know where to apply these findings. Therefore, the consumer should ask him or herself whether enough detail has been given to be able to identify similar contexts to which the conclusions can be applied.

17. *External audits:* A seldom used but powerful method (Creswell, 1998) to increase the credibility of the interpretations of a study is to hire an outsider to evaluate the study. Typically, this is not done due to the added cost. However, a well-funded research project may want to employ such a person to add credibility to the findings and conclusions. Any study that reports using such a person has gained many points on the credibility scale.

I have chosen Harklau's (2000) study to illustrate how a study using verbal data might be analyzed using the 17 tactics presented in Table 7.1. Remember in chapter 6, we looked at Harklau's ethnographic case study, in which she examined how the identities of ESL students change as a result of the *representation* (i.e., stereotype) of different institutional programs. She followed three ESL students over a 1-year period as they moved from their senior year of high school to their first year at a nearby 2-year community college. Information used for the evaluation is listed in Box 7.1. A summary of the evaluation is presented in Table 7.2, followed by an expanded explanation.

BOX 7.1
Summary of Harklau's (2000) Study

Variable of concern: Institutional representations of ESL learners.

Participants
1 Turk
2 S.E. Asians
Upper level/college-bound students
Lived in U.S. 6 to 10 yrs.
A teacher chose the student participants
Teachers: no information given

Data Sources
30–50 min. taped interviews
50 formal interviews with students and instructors
25 informal interviews with instructors
Informal visits with students
10 days of high school classroom observations
50 hours of CC classroom observations
5,000 pages of written materials collected over the year

Institutions
The high school
Ethnically mixed (60% Black, 30% White, 10% other)
45 out of 950 were in ESL program (predominantly S.E. Asian)

The 2-year community college
State-sponsored
Commuter campus
Over 13,000 student body
ESL program 250 international students (predominantly S.E. Asian and Eastern European)
Mainly coming from socially and educationally privileged backgrounds
Mostly new arrivals to the States
Course content: language + acculturation

TABLE 7.2
Evaluation Tactics for Verbal Data Applied to Harklau's (2000) Study

Checking for . . .	Tactics	Check
Data Quality	1. Representativeness	
	2. Prolonged engagement and persistent observation	☺
	3. Clarifying researcher bias	☺
	4. Check for researcher effects	
	Researcher on persons/events	
	Persons/events on researcher	
	5. Weighting the evidence	
	Informants' access and proximity	☺
	Circumstances	☺
	Continuous vigilance	
Patterns and Themes	6. Triangulation	☺
	7. Outliers and extreme cases	
	8. Surprises	☺
	9. Negative evidence	☺
	10. Peer review	
Explanations and	11. Spurious relationships	
Conclusions	12. If–then tests	
	13. Rival explanations	
	14. Replicating findings	
	15. Informant feedback	☺
	16. Rich/thick description	☺
	17. External audits	

☺ means that the tactic was effectively used.

Regarding how *representative* Harklau's (2000) data are for evaluating *Data Quality*, she provided detailed information about the three student participants: 1 Turk and 2 S.E. Asians who were selected by their ESL teacher (cf. Box 7.1). The issue here is whether these three subjects are representative of other U.S. immigrant seniors in high school who go to community colleges after matriculation.

In addition, Harklau gave a clear description of the two institutions (cf. Box 7.1), which would help any consumer compare other institutional environments for possible transference of her findings. The high school had a majority of African-American students with an ESL program for 45 students, predominantly S.E. Asians. It was an upper level program in an inner-city school.

However, it would have been helpful if Harklau (2000) had provided a more detailed description of the teachers used to provide data. Because teacher participants were as important as student participants regarding the nature of the data, a report of their personal characteristics would help the consumer understand how transferable the teacher data are.

The next tactic listed in Table 7.1 to support the quality of data is *prolonged engagement and persistent observation* (#2). Harklau (2000) clearly reported that she had ample opportunity to engage the participants over an extended length of time. She collected her data over a 1-year period as a partial-participant observer.

Regarding Point 3, *clarifying researcher bias*, Harklau (2000) supplied details about her own philosophical and research biases in the study. She stated that her research disposition was derived from "critical theory, social practice, and poststructuralist approaches" (p. 37). She added that her premise is that personal identities are "locally understood and constantly remade in social relationships" (p. 37). To her credit, she declared, "like any researcher, I am a positioned subject who is 'prepared to know certain things and not others' (Rosaldo, 1989, p. 8)" (p. 45). The consumer needs to keep this type of information in mind when evaluating data from such studies.

For Tactic 4, *check for researcher effects*, Harklau (2000) did not discuss whether she monitored any effects she may have had on the participants, nor how the participants affected her. However, due to the long-term contact she had with her three student participants and the teachers, the possibility for either *researcher on persons/events* or *persons/events on researcher* effects were most likely present. One likelihood is that she became so close to the student respondents that the data she was prepared to know were determined by a feeling that the three students were being abused by Harklau's perceived college representation. Had she begun her study at the college level and evaluated these students as they came into the program, I wonder if she would have made the same observations. These are not to be understood as negative comments. One of the positive points that qualitative researchers make is that they *become* part of the study. They too are participants in the study.

Under Tactic 5, *weighting the evidence*, Harklau (2000) provided evidence that gives weight to the quality of her data. Regarding *informants' access and proximity* to data, she used three students and teachers from one high school to identify high school representation. She used the same students in addition to college teachers to assess the college representation. Certainly, these participants had good access and proximity to data. The *circumstances* under which Harklau gathered the data also added to the weight. The data were all gathered firsthand over many occasions in both formal and informal settings.

Once the quality of the data has been evaluated, the next area of verbal analysis is *Patterns and Themes*. The first one listed in Table 7.1 is *triangulation* (Table 7.1, Tactic 6). Harklau made extensive use of this tactic to formulate her constructs of institutional representations. She used data from different sources to provide evidence to support the identification of institutional representation. The high school representation, for example, was supported with data from sources such as excerpts from personal stories, classroom observation, and student and teacher interviews. For the college representation, she used, among other sources, interviews, classroom observation, and assignments.

For Tactic 7, *outliers and extreme cases*, Harklau did not report any. However, she did report *surprises* (#8) in some of her data in an incident where the high school teacher was shocked by one of the participant's behavior that went against the proposed high school representation. Harklau also provided *negative evidence* (#9) where the performance of one of the participants contradicted the high school representation of ESL students' being hard working. All of these contribute to the credibility of her construct of institutional representation that she was aiming to demonstrate.

Harklau's (2000) argument for the *believability* of her interpretations would have been enhanced had she reported a *peer review* (#10) during her construct formation. Based on her article, she seemed to be the only one involved in the process—from data collection to final analysis. By using someone, such as a colleague, to check her interpretations of the data, she would have avoided the possibility of a number of biases, one being *holistic fallacy* previously mentioned. However, Harklau did use the teacher participants to check whether her emerging themes had any validity. She reported meeting with them informally over the semester for this purpose. Although this is not exactly peer feedback, it is *informant feedback* (#15), which is also a good tactic for supporting patterns and themes.

The final stage for evaluating verbal data analysis is *Explanations and Conclusions* (cf. Table 7.1). There are seven tactics under this heading that a researcher can choose from for heightening credibility. Harklau (2000) used two of these in her study: *informant feedback* (#15) and *rich/thick description* (#16). Regarding the first, not only did she share her emerging data themes with teacher participants to get feedback, she also shared her conclusions with the student participants in final interviews along with providing them with a copy of the final report.

Harklau clearly used rich/thick description in her study. This is required if there is any discussion of transferability of the findings of a study. She provided a detailed description of the three participants and the two school environments in a narrative format that gives the reader a sense of being there. However, she did not give a detailed description of the teacher participants. This information would help the consumer search for a match for similar situations to which Harklau's conclusions could be transferred.

Tactic 13, *rival explanations*, is one that few researchers have used, but it is a powerful addition to bolster the credibility of her conclusions. For

Harklau's study, for example, one plausible explanation, in my opinion, might have been that the findings were not due to institutional representations, but rather misalignment of students' abilities with their programs. The college program was geared for new foreign students who needed socialization as well as language training. The student participants of the study were mismatched with a program not meant for them. An alternative explanation could be that the particular U.S. high school used in the study did not prepare their long-term resident ESL students with the study habits needed to compete at the college level. Had Harklau proposed one or two competing explanations such as these and shown how her explanation was superior, she would have contributed greatly to her conclusions.

The example of Harklau's study shows how the 17 tactics drawn from combining the work of Miles and Huberman (1994) and Creswell (1998; cf. Table 7.1) are a reasonable way to evaluate the analysis of verbal data found in the Results section of studies using qualitative approaches. As mentioned previously, not all of the tactics need to be used before the analysis is deemed credible by consumers. However, having some in each of the three categories certainly helps. Harklau (2000) clearly presented credibility evidence in all three areas, which has definitely added to the main argument of her paper.

Exercise 7.1

Use a study that uses a qualitative research design.

1. Begin by stating what qualitative procedure was used by the researcher(s).
2. Use Table 7.1 to complete this exercise. Check which tactics the researcher(s) used. Where information is not available, leave blank.
3. Identify the tactics used by the researcher for evidence regarding the quality of data.
4. Identify the tactics used by the researcher to verify any proposed patterns or themes.
5. Identify any tactics used to add credibility to any proposed explanations and conclusions made by the researcher.

SECTION 2: PRESENTATION AND ANALYSIS OF NUMERICAL DATA

Many researchers try to answer their research questions by first converting their ideas and constructs into some form of numerical data before analysis. The main reason is that numerical data are generally easier to work with than verbal data. Not only are there a number of statistical procedures available to quickly identify patterns and relationships in large sets of data, they are also able to estimate whether the findings are greater than random chance. The purpose of this section is to introduce you to some of the most common procedures used to analyze numerical data and some of the basic concepts that underpin them.

However, before going any further, I want to address some of the reservations people have toward this topic. One word that seems to strike some trepidation in many of my students and some of my colleagues is *statistics*. One friend jokingly refers to it as *sadistics*. I have the strong impression that many avoid reading the Results section of research studies because of the statistical terms they might encounter. They see things like $p < .001$, *df*, Σ^2, *r*s, *t*s, and *F*s and say to themselves, "No way, I'm not going there!"

Typically, I find much of the reluctance toward statistics more a result of some traumatic experience people have had in their past. The result is that they have become *math-phobics* and are developing into *stat-phobics*.

I believe there are two things that turn a lot of people off about statistics: math formulas and a lot of technical jargon. Fortunately, understanding statistical formulas is not necessary for the consumer of research. Instead the important things to know are whether an appropriate statistical procedure was used for answering the research questions and whether the results of the study were interpreted correctly. After reading this section, I trust that you will be able to make these decisions.

The second hurdle that people must cross when dealing with statistics is the jargon statisticians use. This is not as easy as it should be because different terms are used for the same thing depending on the discipline in which the statistician is working—as you see later, alpha (α) does not always mean a Cronbach α. This section gives you a good grasp of the terminology as you see these terms applied in actual research situations.

Overview of Statistics

To understand the basic concept behind statistics, we need to review the concepts of *sample* and *population* discussed in chapter 4. Recall that the population is the entire number of people to which the researcher wants to generalize his or her conclusions. The sample is a subgroup of that total number. Statistics are quantities (or numbers) gathered on a sample. They are estimates of what would be found if the whole population were used. Quantities that are gathered directly from the entire population are referred to as *parameters*. Parameters are the *true* values. They exactly describe the population. Because we are almost always dealing with samples, we use statistics rather than parameters.

However, when statistics (i.e., estimates) are used, we have to make inferences about what exists in the population (see Fig. 7.1 to illustrate this

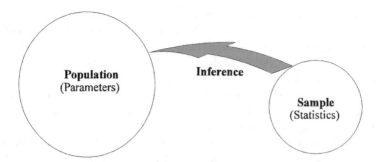

FIG. 7.1. The relationship of the sample to the population.

process). As with any inference, mistakes can be made. Using statistics helps us understand what chance we are taking of making a mistake when inferring from the sample to the population. (Now if you understand what you have just read, you are well on your way to grasping a useful understanding of statistics.)

Statistics can be divided into two main categories: *descriptive* and *inferential.* As the name implies, *descriptive statistics* are those that describe a set of data. They are the fuel used by *inferential statistics* to generate answers to research questions. Inferential statistics not only produce answers in the forms of numbers, they also provide information that determines whether researchers can generalize their findings (i.e., the descriptive statistics) to a target population.

The following subsections of this chapter expand these two general types of statistics. Obviously, they will not exhaust all that there is about these topics. In this regard, I see statistics like an onion: There are many layers. This section only deals with the outer layers at most. However, I have added another layer in Appendix B that takes you a little deeper into some of the more technical aspects of each of these statistical types if you want to gain some deeper insights. I also include in this appendix some less common procedures that you may want to continue with after mastering the following sections. The outer layers presented next give you enough information to be able to understand and evaluate the majority of the studies that you will read. When you come across something not mentioned in the following, it most likely has been treated in Appendix B.

Understanding Descriptive Statistics

There are three basic concerns that should be addressed when using descriptive statistics to describe numerical data: the shape of the distribution, measures of average, and measures of variation (cf. Table 7.3). The first is regarding the shape of the data. The concern is whether the data are sym-

TABLE 7.3
Three Important Areas in Descriptive Statistics

Shape of Data	Averageness	Variance
Symmetrical	Mean	Standard Deviation
Skewness	Median	Semi-interquartile Range
Multimodal	Mode	Range

metrically distributed and approximate a normal curve.[5] The importance of knowing this directly relates to the researcher's choice of the statistics used in his or her study, both descriptive and inferential. This is seldom mentioned in most research articles, but it is important. Suffice it to say here that if a distribution of data is severely skewed (i.e., lopsided), rectangular (i.e., no curve at all), or multimodal (i.e., more than one cluster of data; cf. Table 7.3), certain statistics should not be used. If you want to go to the next level of the onion on this matter, see Appendix B.

Based on the shape of the data, the second concern is which statistic to use to describe average. There are three: mean, median, and mode (cf. Table 7.3). Briefly defined, the *mean* is computed by adding up all the scores and dividing by the total number of scores. The *median* is the middle point in the distribution of data that divides the number of people in half. The *mode* is the most frequent score.

The reason there are three measures used for *average* is discussed more fully in Appendix B. However, for research purposes, the mean is the most common estimate of average used by researchers for numerical data. However, on the occasion that the data distribution does not approximate a normal distribution, other indicators of average more accurately represent the data distribution.

The third concern, also affected by the shape of the data, is what statistic to use to indicate how much the data vary (i.e., the *variance*). There are also three different measures of variation (cf. Table 7.3): standard deviation, semi-interquartile range, and range. The first, related to the mean, is the average deviation of scores from the mean. The second, related to the median, estimates where the middle 50% of the scores are located in the data distribution. The third is the distance from the lowest to the highest scores in the distribution. More detailed discussion is in Appendix B regarding how these three are used and relate to one another. However, because the standard deviation (*SD*) is the one most commonly used in research, it gets more treatment in the following discussions. Similar to the use of the mean,

---

[5]This is a bell-shaped curve that has many properties used by research. There is a more detailed discussion in Appendix B.

the *SD* is only appropriate for describing data if the distribution does not vary too much from normalcy.

Understanding Inferential Statistical Procedures

I began the section on statistics with a discussion of how researchers attempt to infer their findings to a population based on a sample of participants/objects (cf. Fig. 7.1). This inferential process is where inferential statistics play a crucial role. The main goal for the remainder of this chapter is to describe the various inferential statistical procedures that are commonly used, explain why they are used, and provide examples from research published in applied linguistics that have used these procedures. However, before going on to these various procedures, I must first discuss the meanings of *null hypothesis* and *statistical significance*. In my opinion, the need for the consumer to understand these two concepts is more important than remembering the names of the statistical procedures that are described afterward.

The Null Hypothesis

The notion of statistical significance directly relates to the testing of the null hypothesis. Therefore, I first discuss this famous hypothesis (although you may have never heard of it) that all studies test when using inferential statistics, regardless of whether they say so, followed by the meaning of *statistical significance*.

In essence, inferential statistics procedures can be boiled down to answering two types of questions: *are there relationships* between variables or *are there differences* between groups of data? The null hypothesis, as the word *null* suggests, states that there is either *no* relationship or that there is *no* difference between groups. Regardless of whether there is a research hypothesis, the null hypothesis is always there to be tested. In exploratory studies, for instance, where there are no stated hypotheses, behind every relationship being studied there is a null hypothesis that states there is no relationship to be found. For every study that explores whether there is a difference between groups of data, there is a null hypothesis that voices there is no real difference between the groups.

Few published studies in applied linguistics journals explicitly state their null hypotheses these days. Yet whether stated or not, they are always lurking in the background. A good example of a study where a number of null hypotheses are clearly stated without any stated research hypotheses is one by Tsang (1996). Recall from chapter 6 that she investigated whether extensive reading and/or extensive writing affects performance in descriptive writing. She stated five null hypotheses, one being "There is no significant main effect for nature of program . . . as a factor in writing performance of secondary students" (p. 215). The phrase "no significant main effect" means that there are no differences between different programs when it comes to effect on writing performance.

Now why would someone want to state his or her hypothesis in the null form? Why not state the hypothesis in the positive, such as, "There will be a significant difference between programs . . ."? In practice, many researchers state their hypotheses in the positive. However, it is more accurate to state the hypothesis in the negative because it is this hypothesis that inferential statistics test, not the positively stated hypotheses. Be that as it may, the answer to my question lies in making valid logical arguments. For those who would like to understand more about the logical argument that is the basis for using the null hypothesis, go to Appendix B.

Exercise 7.2

1. Look at the Results section of any study that has tables of means and standard deviations and hunt for the phrase "null hypothesis." Ignore all else.
2. When (and if) you find it, note whether it was **rejected** or **failed to be rejected**.
3. If it was rejected, what does that mean in terms of the research question?
4. If it failed to be rejected, what does this mean?
5. How did the researcher(s) interpret these findings?

Statistical Significance

You will encounter the term *statistical significance* more often than *null hypothesis* when reading the Results section of an article; however, the two terms are very much interrelated. When researchers refer to results as *statistically significant*, they are referring to the *null hypothesis* regardless of whether they know it.

Statistical significance has to do with the probability of a mistake being made when inferring that the results found in a sample reflect some truth about the target population (cf. Fig. 7.1). This mistake (or error) is directly related to the null hypothesis. Figure 7.2 should help illustrate this discussion. The heading over the columns of the 2×2 matrix[6] is labeled *Reality*. There are only two possibilities: Either the null hypothesis is true (Column 1) or it is false (Column 2). That is, there is either no true relationship or difference between variables in the population (i.e., the null hypothesis is true), or there is a relationship or difference in the population (i.e., the null hypothesis is false). There is no middle ground.

---

[6]Figure 7.2 is an adaptation of a similar matrix in Hopkins and Glass' (1978) work.

Reality

	Null Hypothesis True in the population	Null Hypothesis False in the population
Fail to reject the Null Hypothesis in the study	CORRECT	TYPE II ERROR p < Beta (β)
Reject the Null Hypothesis in the study	TYPE I ERROR p < alpha (α)	CORRECT (power = 1– β)

SAMPLE

FIG. 7.2. Testing the null hypothesis.

However, in research using samples, it is impossible to know for sure whether the null hypothesis is true unless the research is done on the whole population. This means that the truth about the null hypothesis is inferred from the sample to the population.

The heading for the rows of the matrix in Fig. 7.2 is labeled *Sample*. Again there are only two possibilities: The results from the sample either *fail to reject* the null hypothesis or they *reject* the null hypothesis. If the results show that no relation or difference was found, then the findings fail to reject the null hypothesis (i.e., no statistical significance was found). In this case, no error was made (cf. Fig. 7.2, Column 1, Row 1). However, if the null hypothesis is, in fact, false in the population (i.e., there is a true relationship or difference between variables), the results from the sample are misleading, and an error has been made. This is known as a *Type II error* (Fig. 7.2, Column 2, Row 1). That is, the results of the study fail to reveal that the null hypothesis was false in the population. Moving down to Row 2, the other possible finding from the sample is that the results reject the null hypothesis. Translated, this means that a statistically significant relationship or difference was found in the results. Yet if in the population (i.e., reality) there was no relation or difference (Column 1), then to infer from the sample to the population that the null hypothesis was false would be erroneous. This is referred to as a *Type I error*. However, if the null hypothesis were truly false in the population (Column 2), it would be correct to infer that there was probably a relationship or difference in the population based on the findings from the sample. (At this point, I suggest that you stop and meditate on all of this. Few people grasp these ideas in one reading.)

I am sure you did not fail to notice in Col. 1/Row 2 and Col. 2/Row 1 the $p < $ alpha (α)[7] and $p < $ Beta (β), respectively. These have to do with the probabilities of making a Type I and a Type II error. The most common one cited in Results sections is the probability of making a Type I error ($p < \alpha$). Statistical significance is based on this estimate.

Statistical significance has been somewhat arbitrarily defined by statisticians (and probably some gamblers) as the probability of making a Type I error either equal to or less than 5% (i.e., $p \leq .05$). Translated, this means that there is a 5% chance or less that a mistake has been made when inferring that the null hypothesis (i.e., no relationship or no difference) is not true in the population (i.e., the null hypothesis is rejected). Sometimes you will see other probabilities such as $p < .01$ or $p < .001$. These of course are even smaller than $p < .05$, which means that the probability of making a Type I error is even less (1% or 0.1%, respectively). Tsang (1996), for example, found statistically significant differences between pretests and posttests for reading at the $p < .01$ level. This does not mean that her findings were 99% true—a common misunderstanding of what statistical significance means. What it means is that she can have a lot of confidence that she did not make a Type I error.

Two other misconceptions are common regarding statistical significance. One is to think that because something is statistically significant, there is a strong relationship between variables or a big difference between groups. This may not, in fact, be the case. It is not uncommon to see small relationships or small differences statistically significant. The reason is that statistical significance is directly related to the size of the sample. If the sample size is fairly large, then small relationships or small differences may come out to be statistically significant. When the sample size is smaller, the same statistical value found for a relationship or a difference will not be statistically significant.

Here is where the probability of making a Type II error becomes important. When the sample size is relatively small and the results were found not to be statistically significant (i.e., the null hypothesis failed to be rejected), the probability of making a Type II error is higher than when a larger sample is used. This means that, in reality, the null hypothesis may be false (i.e., there is a relationship or difference), but due to a small sample size the results failed to reveal this. Another way to say this is that the researcher would have found a statistically significant relationship or difference had s/he used a larger sample. For more information on the Type II error and a discussion on the related topic of *power*, go to Appendix B.

The other common misunderstanding regarding statistical significance is to confuse it with *practical significance.* As mentioned earlier, a relationship may be weak but still statistically significant, or a difference between

---

[7]This is not the Cronbach α referred to in chapter 6.

groups may be small but still statistically significant. Here is where we can be misled if we are not careful when reading statistics results. If a relationship is weak or a difference between groups is small, regardless of how statistically significant it is, there may be no practical use for the results. For example, who wants to spend time and money making curricular changes if students using a new method only increase by a few test points compared with those using a traditional method, although the result was statistically significant. This point is illustrated in several research studies mentioned later in the chapter. Related to this is the concept of *effect size*, which some journals require when reporting statistical significance (e.g., *Language Learning*). See Appendix B for more information on this.

Although the previous discussion seems to be beyond what a consumer might need to understand a Results section, the issues discussed earlier are the foundation stones for building an understanding of the statistical procedures about to be outlined. However, before going on to the more interesting stuff, I suggest you do the following exercise to give yourself feedback on how well you have understood this last section. Rushing ahead without grasping what we have just read will hinder understanding the following section.

Exercise 7.3

1. Choose a study that looked for relationships or differences between groups.
2. Look for any mention of a null hypothesis.
3. Now examine the Results section and look for values like $p < .05$, $p < .01$, or less.
4. How does the researcher interpret the results?
5. What is the probability of a Type I error being made in this study?
6. Explain what this means in your own words.

(You might want to go get a cup of coffee or tea at this point and take a break.)

Statistical Procedures

There seems to be no end to all the statistical procedures available for analyzing numerical data. To describe them all would take several large volumes. For this reason, I have selected the most common statistical procedures that are presented in the applied linguistic literature in this section. The procedures presented look at several more layers of the statistical onion, but there are others that lie deeper. For those who would like to go further than what is presented here, a number of issues and procedures are presented in Appendix B, along with a discussion on how they are used.

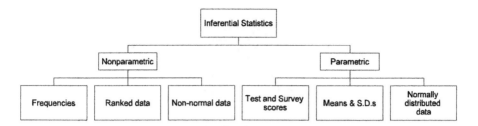

FIG. 7.3. The two main categories of inferential statistics with corresponding data types.

At the end of this current section, the consumer should be able to understand what some common statistical procedures are used for, what their results mean, and whether they are used appropriately. There are no formulas to understand or calculate, only definitions, applications, and interpretations. Examples from published research are given to show how these procedures have been applied.

Inferential statistics can be divided into two general categories: *nonparametric* and *parametric* (cf. Fig. 7.3). Nonparametric statistics are used for analyzing data in the form of frequencies, ranked data,[8] and data that do not approximate a normal distribution. Parametric statistics are used for any data that do not stray too far from a normal distribution and typically involve the use of means and standard deviations. Scores on tests and surveys usually fit these criteria.

As previously mentioned, the objectives of most researchers are to find relationships between variables or differences between groups. Under each of these objectives, there are both nonparametric and parametric procedures for analyzing data.

Relationships Between Variables. Figure 7.4 summarizes some of the more frequently used procedures according to the two types of statistical procedures: nonparametric and parametric.

Nonparametric procedures. Under the *relationships/nonparametric* heading on the left side of Fig. 7.4, there are two procedures that are frequently seen in published research: *chi-square* and *Spearman rank correlation* (*rho*). There are several others, but they are less commonly used. All of them have to do with assessing whether a relationship exists between at least two variables.

The Pearson *chi-square* (pronounced Ky-square and portrayed with the Greek symbol, χ^2) is the procedure of preference when dealing with data in

---

[8]Ranked data are data that have been converted into ordinal numbers (i.e., first, second, third, etc.).

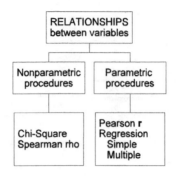

FIG. 7.4.   Statistical procedures for analyzing relationships.

the form of frequencies (or relative frequencies in the form of percentages). In its simplest form, the chi-square procedure compares the observed frequency (or percentages) of the different levels of a variable with what would be expected if no relationship existed (i.e., the null hypothesis).

For example, if a researcher asks the question, "Is there a relationship between gender and success in learning English as a foreign language?", s/he would compare a random sample of males and females on their success rate. Figure 7.5 illustrates what the data might look like if there were 40 females and 40 males sampled. Note that the null hypothesis would be: There is no relationship between gender and success rate, therefore there will be no difference between the number of males and females who pass or fail. If this were true, then the expected frequency should be 20/20 for each sex, which is indicated by the numbers in parentheses. However, in our fictional data, the researcher found that 27 females versus 17 males passed as opposed to 13 females versus 23 males failed. Can the researcher conclude that there is a relationship? Although the frequencies appear to differ, do they differ from what would be expected if the null hypothesis were true? Rather than rely on an "eyeball" analysis, the researcher

	Passed	Failed	Total
Males	17 (20)	23 (20)	40
Females	27 (20)	13 (20)	40

FIG. 7.5.   Comparison of males versus females who passed and failed in frequencies.

would do a chi-square analysis. Out of curiosity, I did an analysis on these data and obtained a chi-square value 5.05, which is statistically significant at $p = .02$. The null hypothesis is rejected with a 2% probability of making a Type I error. The researcher can therefore conclude that there is most probably a relationship between gender and success rate at learning ESL.

To illustrate, recall that Silva's (2000) second research question (cf. chap. 5) was concerned with the relationship between longevity in an L2 environment and the pragmatic transfer of NNSs' and NSs' emotional responses to directives that begin with, *Why don't you.* She predicted that there would be a relationship: The longer the time in the L2 environment, the less accurate Brazilians would be in judging the appropriate use of directives in Portuguese. To test this, she performed a series of chi-square analyses where she compared the percentages of accurate judgments of Brazilians who lived in America, both short and long term, with Brazilians who never left Brazil. She found that the percentage of accurate judgments declined for those who lived in America longer. For example, for one situation, 27.3% longer term Brazilians voted directives as not appropriate, compared with 83.7% Brazilians who never lived in America. This resulted in a chi-square of 20.83, statistically significant at $p < .05$. In this case, the null hypothesis was rejected, giving support to her research hypothesis.

The second method for examining relationships under nonparametric statistics is the *Spearman rank-order* correlation coefficient, also known as the Spearman *rho* correlation coefficient. This procedure analyzes data in the form of ranks, and the correlation coefficient is symbolized by either r_{rank} or the Greek symbol ρ_{rank} (rho). This coefficient ranges from $\rho_{rank} = -1.0$ to $\rho_{rank} = +1.0$. The first value (-1.0) means that there is a perfect negative relationship: As ranking of one variable goes up, the other goes down. The value of +1.0 is a perfect positive relationship where both variables' rankings correspond perfectly in the same direction. A coefficient of 0.00 means there is no relationship. As a coefficient increases between 0.00 and 1.00, despite whether + or − is in front of it, the relationship between the two variables increases: The + increases in a positive direction, and the − increases in a negative direction.

Ferris and Tagg (1996) used the Spearman rho procedure in their needs-analysis study, which examined the expectations instructors had toward students' listening and speaking performances. They specifically used this statistic when examining relationships between demographic variables and the items in their survey. They found that level of class negatively correlated with small groups (rho = -0.19, $p < .003$). Interestingly, although the researchers interpreted this result to be counterintuitive, nothing was said about how low this correlation is, even though statistically significant. Based on what was stated previously about statistical significance, such a low correlation was significant because Ferris and Tagg used a fairly large sample

($N^9 = 234$). Large samples can produce statistically significant correlation coefficients even though small. The question becomes, despite the correlation being statistically significant, is a correlation this small of any practical use? More is stated about this under parametric procedures.

There are other nonparametric measures of relationships that you will occasionally see in research such as the Cohen's Kappa, phi-coefficient, Cramer's V, Somer's d, and so on. To give proper treatment to all of these procedures would require a separate book. However, if you are interested in knowing more about these other procedures, you can do a search on your favorite Web browser by entering *nonparametric statistics* or enter the name of the specific procedure.

Before moving over to some parametric procedures for relationships, I suggest you look at a study related to your interest that has used some form of nonparametric statistic to examine a relationship. The following exercise gives you steps to follow to guide you in this task. Enjoy!!

Exercise 7.4

1. Find a study that looked for a relationship between two or more variables using either chi-square or the Spearman rho in its statistical analysis.
2. What form are the data in (frequencies, percentages, ranks)?
3. What is the null hypothesis being tested (explicit or implicit)?
4. Are the results statistically significant? At what level? What does this mean regarding making inferences?

Parametric procedures. One of the most common statistics used to examine relationships between variables is the *Pearson product–moment correlation* (PMMC) *coefficient.* With a name like this, no wonder people do not like to look at statistics. It is more commonly referred to as the Pearson *r* after Karl Pearson who developed it in the UK. You will also see it reported simply as r or r_{xy}. This coefficient, like the Spearman rho, is computed on two variables for every participant, such as measures of grammar and writing ability. The end product is an r that ranges from -1.00 to $+1.00$, indicating a perfect negative or perfect positive relationship, respectively. As with all coefficients of correlation, a 0.00 means no relationship. The null hypothesis usually states that the relationship is 0.00 in the population.

A study done by Schmitt and Meara (1997) examined how knowledge about words (associations and suffixes) changes over time. Among other statistical procedures, they also obtained PMMC coefficients to test rela-

---

[9]The letters N and n usually stand for sample size.

tionships. They correlated measures of knowledge of word associations and derivative suffixes with vocabulary size and participants' TOEFL scores. They found statistically significant correlations for a number of comparisons. For instance, one result was a Pearson $r = 0.62$ ($p < .05$) for vocabulary size and productive word associations at the second time of testing. As the p $< .05$ indicates, this correlation was statistically significant. Note that $r < 0.62$ is positive and a little over halfway between 0.00 and 1.00. This should be interpreted as a moderate positive relationship, which suggests that as vocabulary size increases so do productive word associations to some degree.

Using the prior results, I want to illustrate a misapplication of the correlation coefficient that occasionally appears in the literature (cf. chap. 5)—correlation means causation. Although Schmitt and Meara did not draw this conclusion, someone might think—and people commonly do—that because vocabulary size correlated positively with knowledge of word associations, we should increase students' vocabulary size to increase their knowledge of word associations. To suggest this is to state that vocabulary size causes (i.e., influences, increases, changes, etc.) knowledge of word associations. Although this might be the case, correlations do not directly show this. Why? Because correlations are bidirectional (i.e., symmetrical), which means that both of the following statements are correct: A correlates with B, and B correlates with A. In other words, Schmitt and Meara could have stated that knowledge of word associations positively correlates with vocabulary size. To show a causal relationship, they would have had to use an experimental design where a treatment was given to increase the participants' vocabulary followed by some assessment of their knowledge of word associations. At most a correlational analysis can find whether there is a potential causal relationship before going to the more arduous task of doing a full-blown experiment. If there is no statistically significant correlation, a causal relationship can be ruled out right from the start.

The second important misuse of the correlation coefficient is assuming that, because a correlation coefficient is statistically significant, it means that it has important practical use. Schmitt and Meara (1997) found another correlation of $r = 0.27$ between vocabulary size and knowledge of derivative suffixes to be statistically significant at the $p < .05$ level. They were quick to state that this revealed a weak relationship, although statistically significant.

Is a correlation of $r = 0.27$ of any practical use (cf. Ferris & Tagg, 1996)? The answer is made clear when you square the correlation coefficient. This is signified by r^2 and is a measure of the percentage of common variance between the two variables. Another way to say this is that r^2 represents the amount of variation that the two variables have in common. This value is commonly used to determine the importance of the relationship. We can see clearly in this case that $r = 0.27$ becomes $r^2 = 0.07$, or that the two variables only have 7% in common—not much to warrant any practical significance. However, the other correlation Schmitt and Meara (1997) found (i.e., $r = 0.62$) shows more potential for practical use. The $r^2 = 0.36$ indicates 36% common variance.

The issue of amount of common variance is important because some people may try to push their own agenda based on statistically significant correlations that are not strong enough to justify an agenda that cost time and money to implement—Schmitt and Meara did not do this by the way. Therefore, when you want to make your own evaluation of the strength of a correlation coefficient, simply square the correlation and interpret the result as the strength of the relationship.

The next common statistical procedure used to explore relationships is *regression analysis*. This is highly related to the PPMC coefficient and r^2. Regression analysis is used to identify variables (referred to as *independent variables*) that either predict or explain another variable (the *dependent variable*). There are two forms of regression analysis: *simple* and *multiple*. In its simple form, there is only one independent variable and one dependent variable. The independent variable is the predictor or the variable that explains, and the dependent variable is the variable being predicted or explained. For example, if we want to find out whether we can predict success in university for foreign students defined by their grade point average (GPA) with their TOEFL results, we would use a simple regression procedure. The TOEFL scores would be the independent variable (i.e., the predictor) and students' GPA after their first semester or year at university. We might want to know how much students' scores on an essay exam (i.e., the DV) can be explained by their grammar ability (i.e., the IV). The first addresses a prediction question, the second an explanation question. It is important to note here that in neither case are we suggesting that the IVs are causing the variation in the DVs.

In its multiple form, regression analysis is used to determine which combination of independent variables best predicts or explains the variation in one dependent variable. For instance, we might want to know what combination of independent variables best predicts or explains success in university. Thus, multiple regression procedure is more common than simple regression in the research that you will come across.

The key statistic for regression analysis is R^2. It means the same thing as the Pearson r^2 mentioned previously. In fact the $R^2 = r^2$ when there is only one predictor variable. That is, the R^2 is the percentage of variance in the dependent variable that is related to the combination of predictor (i.e., independent) variables and ranges from 0% to 100%. The first thing that is tested for statistical significance is the R^2. If it is found to be statistically significant, the null hypothesis that no variance can be predicted (or explained) by the IVs is rejected. When this happens, each predictor variable (IV) in the equation is tested individually for statistical significance to see whether it contributes to the overall prediction (or explanation) of the dependent variable.

An interesting study using multiple regression by Onwuegbuzie et al. (2000), previously mentioned in chapter 4, illustrates this method. The purpose of their study was to test a number of hypotheses regarding the best combination of variables (IVs) that might predict foreign language achievement (DV) among university students. They included six batteries of instruments that measured various components of cognitive, affective, personality, and demographic factors, totaling 18 independent variables. As for their dependent variable, foreign language achievement in four different foreign languages, they used adjusted average grades from their university language courses. As a side note, the researchers pointed out an important principle regarding the number of independent variables one should use in multiple regression. If the ratio of participants to independent variables is too small, the resulting statistics are unstable. Their ratio was 10 participants to every 1 independent variable, which is more than necessary. Onwuegbuzie and his colleagues used a multiple regression procedure to examine all possible subsets of variables to determine which combination best predicts language achievement. For each combination, an R^2 was calculated and tested for statistical significance. Onwuegbuzie et al. found that a combination of two cognitive, one affective, one personality, and one demographic variable resulted in an R^2 of 0.34 ($p < .001$). That is, 34% of the variance of language achievement was predicted by this combination of variables. This is a moderate R^2 in magnitude. Realize that only 34% of the variance of foreign language achievement was accounted for. However, for prediction purposes, this is better than random guessing.

There are more complex methods using correlational procedures for dealing with more specialized questions that I do not cover here. When you come across terms like *factor analysis, discrimination analysis, latent trait analysis, structural equation modeling*, and so on, remember that these involve correlating variables with other variables for the purpose of identifying which variables share common variance. Not only that, some of these procedures are actually used to determine cause-and-effect relationships. You might think I just contradicted myself after all that ranting and raving about correlation not meaning causation. Not really. When these procedures are used to determine cause-and-effect relationships, they are guided by specific theories that instruct the researcher where to place each variable in the equation to manipulate all the variances. If I go any further than this, you might close the book and run, so I will move on.

Exercise 7.5

1. Find a study that looked for relationships between variables using either the Pearson *r* or one of the two regression procedures mentioned previously.
2. What are the variables? (In the case of regression, what are the IVs and the DV?)
3. Describe the data used in the analysis.
4. What is the null hypothesis being tested (explicit or implicit)?
5. Are the results statistically significant? At what level? What does this mean regarding making inferences?

Differences Between Groups of Data. The second type of research objective is to find whether groups of individuals differ from one another. As with relationships, there are both nonparametric and parametric procedures used to analyze these differences (cf. Fig. 7.6).

Nonparametric procedures. Chi-square analysis is also used for finding differences between groups. It is used when data are in the form of frequencies (or relative frequencies in the form of percentages). Returning to Silva's (2000) study for an example, her first research question was concerned with whether NNSs differ from NSs in "sensitivity to appropriate use of directives . . . in Portuguese and English" (p. 162). For this first question, she compared Brazilians in Brazil (BB) with Americans in America (AA) and the latter group with Americans in Brazil (BA)—tasks that required them to judge the pragmatic appropriateness of statements based on five different situations. Her data consisted partly of the percentage of respondents in each group who answered in the negative. She performed a chi-square analysis for each of the five situations. The 10 χ^2s were statistically

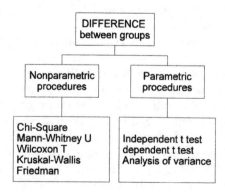

FIG. 7.6.   Statistical procedures for analyzing differences between groups.

significant at the $p < .05$ level. Although Silva did not adjust the probability level for committing a Type I error due to many comparisons, she did report that the majority of her chi-squares were significant at $p < .001$.

By adjusting for the Type I error, I mean that for each comparison (i.e., χ^2 computed) there is a 5% probability of making a Type I error ($p < .05$). When multiple comparisons are made with the same level of 5% for each comparison, the probability of making a Type I error increases. For 10 comparisons, for instance, the overall probability increases to 40% (Hopkins & Glass, 1978). Silva would have been more precise to report what the probability level was for each of the chi-squares instead of lumping them all under $p < .05$. She would have been more accurate if she had limited the overall probability of making a Type I error to a much lower level, such as $p < .001$, for each comparison. Of course this would have meant that some of the statistically significant chi-squares at the .05 level would not have been significant.

When the data are other than frequencies and do not approximate a normal distribution, the difference between two independent samples[10] of participants on some dependent variable is typically analyzed using the *Mann–Whitney U test*. This procedure converts the data into ranks within each group for analysis. There are no means or *SD*s involved. The statistic computed is a U value, which, if statistically significant at the $p < .05$ level, means that the difference between the two groups is statistically significant.

A study done by Vivas (1996) illustrates the use of the Mann–Whitney statistic. She investigated whether reading aloud to young children affected their language comprehension and language expression. She compared children in Home-Based Programs (HBP) with those in School-Based Programs (SBP), along with a control group who was not read to aloud. She recognized in the first part of her Results section that some of her data violated the assumption of normalcy of the distribution and, therefore, used nonparametric statistical procedures. One method she used was the Mann–Whitney test to test the differences among the three groups, one pair at a time. She found that for language comprehension, the HBP group outperformed the control group ($U = 321.5$, $p < .003$), but did not when compared with the SBP group.

When the data in the two groups are not independent, the *Wilcoxon matched-pairs signed rank test* (also known as the *Wilcoxon T test*) is used for comparing two sets of measurements. This means that the two sets of data are dependent or correlated with one another in some way. This can occur in two different situations. The first is when the two sets of data are gathered from the same group of participants. The second occurs when two dif-

---

[10]By *independent samples*, it is meant that the participants in one group are different individuals than those in the other group.

ferent groups of participants are compared on one variable while matched on some other variable. The first situation can occur, for instance, when data are gathered before some treatment is given on a pretest and compared with data from a similar measurement after the treatment on a posttest. Both measurements are made on the same participants. The second situation could occur when the researcher tries to control for (or eliminate) the effects of an extraneous variable, such as intelligence, on the dependent variable by pairing up participants from the two groups based on that extraneous variable.

An example of the first situation is found in Schmitt and Meara's (1997) study mentioned previously, which examined how knowledge about words (associations and suffixes) changes over time. One of their dependent variables was a measure of knowledge about suffixes. They tested the participants once near the beginning of the year and once near the end to see whether there was any gain in knowledge. Therefore, they had two measures on each participant. Although they did not say why they chose to use the Wilcoxon signed rank procedure, my guess is that it was because they were using data in the form of percentages, which is notorious for not fitting the assumptions of normalcy required for a parametric procedure. Usually, the statistic reported would either be in the form of a χ^2 or a z.[11] However, the researchers reported that there was statistical significance by placing an asterisk (*) next to what were either mean or median percentages. (Using asterisks is a common practice for indicating the levels of statistical significance in data. They are usually found at the bottom of a table or in a footnote, such as $* = p < .05$, $** = p < .01$, etc.) Although there was no mention of the null hypothesis, the researchers concluded that for many of the suffixes there was support to indicate that there was increase in knowledge over time.

An example for the second situation occurs when the researcher wants to control for (i.e., eliminate) the effects of an extraneous variable while testing for differences between two groups. S/he would do this by using the Wilcoxon procedure on the dependent variable by matching participants in pairs from the two groups based on the extraneous variable. For this reason, the Wilcoxon procedure is sometimes referred to as the *Wilcoxon matched-pairs signed rank test.* Unfortunately, I have not been able to find an applied linguistics study that has used this matching procedure. However, a quick hypothetical example of using the matching procedure would be to measure attitudes of two different groups of participants (treatment vs. control) toward learning a second language. However, we might want to make sure that our results are not due to differences in language proficiency be-

---

[11]You will see this z statistic quite often. Because it is easier to interpret, some other statistics are converted into this format for easier consumption.

tween the two groups. Thus, we match participants before we begin the treatment by finding two participants with the same language proficiency, however measured, and put one participant into the treatment group and the other in the control group. We do this for the rest of the participants, producing matched pairs. Now we apply the treatment and compare the two groups on a measure of attitude. When using the Wilcoxon method, we would measure the difference in attitude for each matched pair of participants and then compute the Wilcoxon statistic based on those differences.

What happens if a researcher wants to compare more than two sets of data that do not fit the normalcy criterion? The *Kruskal–Wallis test* is typically used for this purpose. This method is an extension of the Mann–Whitney test. However, it compares more than two independent groups of participants using the same procedure of ranking data prior to analysis. The study by Vivas (1996), discussed previously, used the Kruskal–Wallis to test the differences among three groups all at once: school-based (SBP), home-based (HBP), and a control group. She clearly stated the reason for using this nonparametric procedure by reporting that her data did not fit the assumption of normalcy. However, all the Kruskal–Wallis method does when statistical significance is found is to show that somewhere between the groups there is a difference. So when Vivas found a significant Kruskal–Wallis (usually signified with H or put into a χ^2 format), she had to use the Mann–Whitney test to look at the difference between each pair of groups (e.g., SBP vs. HBP, SBP vs. control, and HBP vs. control). The reason she did the Kruskal–Wallis first, rather than going straight to making pair-wise comparisons with the Mann–Whitney, was to control for the Type I error when making multiple comparisons. For each statistical test, there is the probability of making a Type I error. So if one uses the shotgun approach of making all possible pair-wise comparisons, the probability of making a Type I error increases rapidly. Vivas avoided this problem by following the procedure she used.

There is also a nonparametric procedure for testing the difference between three or more sets of dependent data. The Friedman test does exactly this. It is similar to the Wilcoxon T test, in that it tests the differences between different measures on the same set of participants, referred to as *repeated measures* or a *nested design* (cf. Appendix B).

An example of a study using this procedure was done by Al-Seghayer (2001), who investigated the effects of three annotation modalities for presenting glosses on vocabulary acquisition via the computer. Although he clearly hypothesized that the video mode would be superior to the two others (i.e., text only and text with pictures), he also explicitly stated that the null hypothesis of no difference was what was being statistically tested. All of the participants received all three conditions in the study, and three measures of vocabulary acquisition were made, making it a *repeated measures* design (i.e., the variable of modality of presentation was *nested* within the participants). He also clearly stated that he used the Friedman test because his data did not meet the normalcy assumption and the data were ordinal (i.e., ranked data) in nature. Al-Seghayer found a statistically significant difference (Friedman χ^2 = 28.88, p < .001). However, similar to the Kruskal–Wallis test, finding a significant difference only indicated that somewhere there was a difference between data sets. Al-Seghayer followed up this finding with several pair-wise comparisons using the Wilcoxon T test, comparing each modality against the other on measures of vocabulary acquisition. He was also careful to adjust the probability level for making a Type I error due to making multiple comparisons to p < .017 for each comparison—an issue that I discussed previously.

There is a lot more that could be included about nonparametric statistics. In fact there are entire books that only address nonparametric statistics. However, I have introduced you to some commonly used procedures that you will come across in the research. If you see others and want to know more about what they do, you can find needed information by searching the Web. However, before moving on to parametric statistics, the following exercise provides you with an opportunity to find a study of your own to apply what you have read.

Exercise 7.6

1. Find a study that looked for differences between groups of data and that used one of the nonparametric procedures discussed earlier.
2. Describe the data and any reasons that the researcher used the nonparametric procedure.
3. What are the independent and dependent variables?
4. What is the null hypothesis being tested (explicit or implicit)?
5. What statistical procedure is used?
6. Are the results statistically significant? At what level? What does this mean regarding making inferences?

Parametric statistics. When the assumptions regarding the data distribution are met, parametric procedures can be used to analyze differences between groups. The statistical procedures discussed next are almost a mirror image of the ones discussed under the nonparametric section. One difference is in the type of data that are analyzed, and another is that means and *SDs* are being compared.

The parametric equivalent to the Mann–Whitney and the Wilcoxon tests is the *t* test. It is used to test the difference between two sets of measures on one dependent variable. (Just think of the song *Tea for Two* to help remember this.) Corresponding to these two nonparametric procedures, the *t* test comes in two forms: *independent* and *dependent,* respectively. However, the *t* test requires that the distributions of data do not depart too much from normalcy or the variation in each set of data (i.e., *SD*s) does not differ too much.

The *independent t* test analyzes the difference between the averages (i.e., means) on one dependent variable for two independent groups. This is similar to the Mann–Whitney test on the nonparametric side, except that the *t* test deals with means and variances, not rankings. The two independent groups usually represent two levels of one independent variable, such as male and female for the variable of gender, and the measure used for comparison represents one dependent variable, such as the scores on a single reading test.

Laufer (1998) provided an example of this procedure when she examined whether there was a change in active and passive vocabulary development over a year of school instruction. Her one independent variable was *one year of study,* which consisted of two levels: 10th graders and 11th graders. She had one dependent variable called *vocabulary knowledge,* but defined it three different ways: passive, controlled active, and free active. This resulted in three different measures of her one dependent variable. However, because she analyzed them separately, there is only one dependent variable per analysis. Only one of these is discussed here. For instance, she performed an independent *t* test when comparing 10th and 11th graders on passive vocabulary size. She found that the 10th graders had a mean of 24.15 with an *SD* of 8.10, compared with a mean of 48.09 for the 11th graders with an *SD* of 15.86 (Table 1, p. 262 of her study). The *t* test value was 6.57 and was statistically significant at the $p < .0001$ level. The difference between the means suggested to her that passive vocabulary knowledge was acquired over the year of instruction between the 10th and 11th grades.

Just a side note here regarding the difference in the size of the *SD*s between the two groups. Besides the criterion of normalcy of the data distribution, another criterion for using parametric statistics is that the variances are similar (i.e., homogeneity of variance). If you square the *SD,* you have a measure of variance, and in the prior case, they do not look homogeneous (65.1 vs. 251.54). Because the two variances were quite different, Laufer most likely checked whether this assumption was violated. If her data did not violate the assumption of homogeneity of variance, then she followed the correct procedure. Yet if the assumption was violated, she would have most likely used the nonparametric Mann–Whitney test, which would have been a better way to go.

The *dependent t* test (also called the *correlated t test* or *paired t test*) assesses the difference between the means of two sets of scores for either the same group of participants or two groups whose participants have been matched in some way (cf. Wilcoxon T test). An example of the first scenario would be when one group of participants has been given a pretest, followed by a treatment and then given a posttest. The difference between means of the two tests are tested using this procedure.

The second scenario would occur if two groups (e.g., males vs. females) were being tested on reading achievement, but the participants were matched on some other variable such as intelligence. That is, one male is matched with a female based on an intelligence test and then placed in the corresponding group. By doing this, the researcher eliminates any difference between the two groups due to intelligence. The averages for the two groups are then analyzed for difference by the dependent t test. It is comparable to the Wilcoxon test discussed in the nonparametric section, except that means and variances are used.

Schmitt and Meara (1996), already discussed, not only used the Wilcoxon signed rank test when comparing percentage data between Time 1 and Time 2, but also used paired t tests (i.e., dependent t tests). They tested whether there was a difference between means taken at Time 1 and Time 2 on a test of knowledge of word associations: one for productive associations and one for receptive associations. They performed a paired t test for each. Note that there is only one group of participants being compared at two different times using the same test. The time of testing was the IV with two levels (Time 1 & Time 2), and the knowledge of word association was the DV, although they had two forms of it. Only the comparison using the productive modality was statistically significant at the $p < .05$ level, with the mean for Time 2 being greater than for Time 1. This was not the case for receptive knowledge. Note: Anytime a t test is used, the study should include a table with the means and SDs so that readers can see for themselves how great the differences between the means are.

Before moving on to a more complex procedure, use the following exercise to help you apply what you have just read.

Exercise 7.7

1. Find a study that looked for differences between two data sets that used some form of the parametric t test.
2. What are the independent and dependent variables?
3. What form are the data in?
4. What is the null hypothesis being tested (explicit or implicit)?
5. What statistical procedure(s) is used (dependent or independent t tests)?
6. Are the results statistically significant? At what level? What does this mean regarding making inferences?

The statistic that is probably the most commonly used in the applied linguistics literature is analysis of variance (ANOVA). As the Kruskal–Wallis and Friedman tests are to the Mann–Whitney and Wilcoxon T tests, respectively, the ANOVA is to the independent and dependent t test. Whereas the t test compares two sets of data, ANOVA is used to compare more than two sets.

The simplest form of ANOVA involves the use of one independent variable and one dependent variable. This is referred to as a *one-way ANOVA*. The IV may have three or more levels with one DV. The objective is to find whether the means for the groups on the dependent variable differ from one another. For instance, say a researcher wants to study whether there is any difference on reading proficiency (DV) based on nationality (IV). Thus, s/he would take equal random samples from three or more nationalities, obtain measures of reading ability, and perform a one-way ANOVA. In effect, the researcher would compare the means between the groups with one another. The statistic reported is the F *ratio*, which is determined to be statistically significant by the same criterion for all inferential statistics ($p \leq$ .05 or less).

If the F ratio in the prior example is statistically significant, it only indicates that somewhere there is at least one difference between the group means that is statistically significant. It does not identify where the differences are. The researcher must now find out where those differences are by performing pair-wise comparisons. Two of the most common that are used in the literature are the Tukey's HSD and Newman–Keuls[12] (sounds like a brand of cigarettes) tests. You can think of these tests like you would a series of t tests, only they are more stringent regarding making a Type I error for multiple comparisons. There is another procedure used if the researcher wants to combine several groups to compare with one other or with another combination of groups called the Scheffé test.

By now you should realize why we would not simply do a whole bunch of t tests. The reason is that the probability of making a Type I error increases with the number of statistical tests. If we do a lot of t tests at the $p < .05$ level, we multiply this probability by the number of tests made, as mentioned previously in several places. The ANOVA approach, along with subsequent pair-wise procedures, controls for this by keeping the overall probability of a Type I error at the 5% level or less. (There is a repeated measure ANOVA [cf. Friedman test] discussed in Appendix B.)

A good illustration of the use of a one-way ANOVA is a study by Lin (2001), who investigated whether L2 learners' preference of syllable simplification strategies is influenced by formality of task when pronouncing Eng-

---

[12]See http://davidmlane.com/hyperstat/intro_ANOVA.html for more information.

lish consonant clusters. Lin devised four tasks that differed in degree of formality (i.e., one independent variable with four levels), which required participants to pronounce target words. Three types of pronunciation strategies were examined based on the nature of the error made: epenthesis, deletion, and replacement. Each was treated as a separate dependent variable along with the total of all three types of errors as a fourth dependent variable. Lin performed four separate one-way ANOVAs: one for each of the strategies and one for the total number of pronunciation errors. The results for total pronunciation errors were not statistically significant, meaning that overall there were no differences between tasks for number of errors produced. However, the ANOVAs for the individual strategies were statistically significant, supporting Lin's hypotheses. For example, a statistically significant ANOVA was found for the epenthesis strategy, $F(3, 76) = 20.64$, $p < .0001$.[13] This result only shows that somewhere there is at least one difference between the four tasks. Lin correctly performed a post hoc (i.e., after the fact) Scheffé test to compare the various differences. It was found that more of the epenthesis strategy was used for two of the more formal tasks than two of the less formal tasks.

A slightly more complicated form of ANOVA is the *two-way* ANOVA. This approach is used when a researcher wants to look at the effects of two independent variables on one dependent variable at the same time. Each of the independent variables can have two or more levels. For example, the first independent variable may be nationality with four levels (e.g., French, Egyptian, Chinese, and Russian). The second independent variable may also have two or more levels, such as gender (male and female). If this study were found in the literature, the analysis would be referred to as a 4×2 ANOVA, meaning that it has two independent variables, with the first having four levels and the second having two levels.

The order of the independent variables is not important, although in the previous study nationality would come first and gender second. They can be switched around. Thus, in our example, we might have a 2×4 ANOVA (gender by nationality) rather than a nationality (4) by gender (2) ANOVA. However, with any type of ANOVA, you can always assume that there is only one dependent variable.

When a two-way ANOVA is performed on the data, there are three things being tested. The first is the main effect for the first IV, the second is the main effect for the second IV, and the third is the interaction between the two IVs. *Main effect* can be translated into the question, Are there any differences between the levels of an independent variable taken one at a time, ignoring all else? In effect, it is like doing a one-way ANOVA for each independent variable. In our earlier example, the main effect for the IV,

---

[13]The expression (3, 76) is the degrees of freedom. See Appendix B for an explanation.

nationality, would test whether there are any differences on the dependent variable (e.g., test scores for reading ability) among the four nationalities. If there are, and there are more than two levels of the IV, some form of post hoc pair-wise comparison would need to be made to find out exactly where the differences lie. For each main effect, there is a separate F ratio.

The third thing to be tested is whether there is any interaction between the two IVs. The interaction is actually more informative than the main effects, although often they are treated as secondary. The interaction informs us whether the dependent variable behaves differently at the different meeting points of the two IVs. Again using our nationality by gender example, it would be more informative to know whether males and females of one nationality perform differently on reading ability tests than males and females do of other nationalities. A statistically significant interaction would suggest that they do. Figure 7.7 contains two graphs (a and b) that illustrate this. Figure 7.7a shows what data might look like when there is a main effect(s) but no interaction, and Fig. 7.7b shows what a significant interaction might look like. In the top graph, there is a significant main effect for gender, but no significant interaction between gender and nationality. Note that the females outperform the males for all four nationality groups by about the same difference. This graph shows there is probably a statistically significant main effect for nationality as well. The French, in general, performed higher than the Russians and possibly higher than the Chinese.

In contrast, the lower graph illustrates what a significant interaction might look like. Observe that females outperformed males in the French group, but not in the other nationalities, although they were still slightly superior. For illustration's sake, I have added information in the graph that would not normally appear in such a graph in a published article. A significant interaction would be determined by an F ratio for the interaction effect, but this F ratio does not tell the researcher where the difference lies. To find this out, the researcher would have to compare the difference between female/male means for each nationality using some form of post hoc comparison. As you can see, finding this differential effect would be more informative than simply knowing that nationalities or gender differ on reading ability as a whole.

Major et al. (2002) provided a good example of the use of a two-way ANOVA when they investigated the influence of non-native accents on listening comprehension. They performed a 4×4 ANOVA on their dependent variable, which was a measure of English listening proficiency. The first IV consisted of four levels of language of the listener: Chinese, Japanese, Spanish, and American English. The second IV, language of the speaker, also had four levels representing the same four language groups. Based on the previous discussion, we would expect three things to be tested: main effect for language of the listener, main effect for language of the speaker,

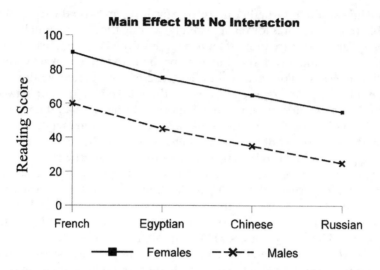

FIG. 7.7a.   Illustration of a main effect between gender and ethnic group with no interaction.

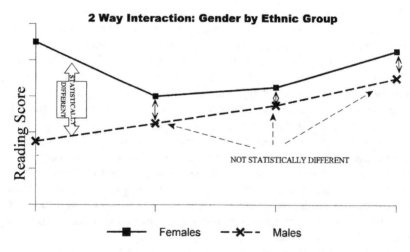

FIG. 7.7b.   Illustrations of an interaction between gender and ethnic group.

and a test for the interaction between the two IVs. They found a significant main effect for language of the speaker ($F = 28.560$, $p < .0001$) and a significant interaction between language of the speaker and language of the listener ($F = 5.27$, $p < .0001$). They followed these findings with 12 post hoc comparisons between individual groups to tease out what was causing the significant interaction. Because of this, they were careful to change their levels of statistical significance to $p < .004$, rather than keeping it at $p < .05$, to control for the probability of a Type I error. Their findings reveal that, regardless of the speaker's accent, Japanese listeners did not differ in listening ability, whereas other language of listener groups did, especially when it came to the Chinese speakers' accent.

There are many more permutations of ANOVA that are not discussed here. However, in Appendix B, other more complex designs that can be found in applied linguistic research are presented. If you come across the terms three-way or four-way ANOVA, ANCOVA, MANOVA, or MANCOVA, look in Appendix B for brief explanations with some examples. However, before moving on to the last chapter, I suggest you find a study that has used some form of ANOVA and do the following exercise. In my opinion, there is nothing better than finding a study of one's own interest to see how these procedures work.

Exercise 7.8

1. Find a study that looks for differences between different levels of independent variables using either a one-way or two-way ANOVA.
2. Identify the independent variable(s). How many levels are in each IV? Identify the dependent variable.
3. Describe the nature of the data used.
4. What is the null hypothesis being tested (explicit or implicit)?
5. What statistical procedure(s) is used (one-way ANOVA, two-way ANOVA)?
6. Are the results statistically significant? At what level? What does this mean regarding making inferences?

I trust that you have been able to follow through this chapter and feel more confident that you can read through the Results section of a study with some understanding as to what is happening. I promise that as you continue to do so, the information discussed here will become clearer. I have not covered everything there is to cover. To do so would require at least one book by itself, and there are plenty on the market. However, I do believe you have enough information in this chapter to handle about 80%, if not more, of what you will see in the Results sections of the studies you will come across. Now on to the last piece of the typical research study—the discussions and conclusions section.

Key Terms and Concepts

Section 1	*Section 2*
average	analysis of variance (ANOVA)
clarifying researcher bias	chi-square

descriptive statistics
external audits
extreme cases
if–then tests
inferential statistics
informant feedback
mean
median
mode
negative evidence
normal distribution
outliers
parameters
peer review
prolonged engagement
range
replicating findings
representativeness
researcher effects
   persons/events on
     researcher
   researcher on
     persons/events
rich/thick description
rival explanations
semi-interquartile range
skewed distribution
spurious relationships
surprises
triangulation
weighting evidence
   circumstances
   continuous vigilance
   informants access

dependent t tests
F ratio
Friedman test
homogeneity of variance
independent t test
Kruskal–Wallis test
Mann–Whitney U test
multiple regression
nonparametric statistical procedures
null hypothesis
one-way ANOVA
pair-wise comparisons
Pearson product–moment correlation
practical significance
regression analysis
Spearman rank correlation (rho)
statistical significance
two-way ANOVA
Wilcoxon matched-pairs signed rank test
Wilcoxon T test

Additional Recommended Reading

Gonick, L., & Smith, W. (1993). *Cartoon guide to statistics*. New York: Harper Perennial Edition.
Huff, D., & Geis, I. (1993). *How to lie with statistics*. New York: W. W. Norton.
Jaisingh, L. J. (2000). *Statistics for the utterly confused*. New York: McGraw-Hill.
Rumsey, D. (2003). *Statistics for dummies*. New York: Wiley.
Weitzman, E. A., & Miles, M. B. (1995). *Computer programs for qualitative data analysis: A software sourcebook*. Thousand Oaks, CA: Sage.

Chapter 8

Discerning Discussions and Conclusions: Completing the Picture

CHAPTER OVERVIEW

The final section of a research article is the Discussion/Conclusion. This is where researchers interpret their findings, make practical applications, and try to fit them into the big picture to answer their research questions. Therefore, second to the abstract at the beginning of the study, this section is the most read part of the average study.

Many reasons are given as to why the stuff between the abstract and the Discussion/Conclusion is jumped over. I often hear, "Why bother with the rest? Let's just go to the conclusion and find out what we can use for our purposes." However, if this *lazy* route is taken, the consumer will never be able to evaluate whether proper conclusions have been made based on solid research, which in turn will lead to faulty applications. Such slothfulness has resulted in a lot of money and time being wasted based on conclusions that have been drawn from faulty research.

The purpose of this final chapter is to facilitate in developing the consumer's ability to discern whether researchers are making valid interpretations and conclusions based on their data, and whether appropriate applications are being suggested. I first explain what the Discussion/Conclusion section is supposed to do, and then I summarize a number of concerns to which the consumer should give attention. To illustrate these principles, I close the chapter with two examples from two different types of research designs.

THE NEEDED INGREDIENTS

Researchers vary in the format they use to wrap up their studies. Some only have a Discussion section, whereas others have both Discussion and Conclusion sections. You might also see additional subheadings, such as Summary and/or Implications. Some attach their Discussion section to their Results section, labeled something like Results and Discussion followed by a final Conclusion. Regardless of the format they use, they usually include the following components in the Discussion/Conclusion section of their paper:

- *An overview of the study:* The purpose of the study is restated, the questions under investigation are summarized, and any propounded hypotheses are reiterated.
- *Overview of the findings:* The researcher should show how the findings address the research question and/or support or fail to support any hypothesis being proposed.
- *Relation of findings:* The researcher should relate the findings of his or her study to previous research findings and theoretical thinking.
- *Attention to limitations:* The researcher should evaluate his or her own study and point out any weaknesses and/or limitations regarding the study.
- *Possible applications:* The researcher should suggest in his or her conclusions how the results can be applied to practical situations.
- *Future possibilities:* The researcher should suggest topics for future research.

QUESTIONS EVERY CONSUMER SHOULD ASK

When evaluating the Discussion/Conclusion section of a study, there is a set of questions that the consumer should address:

1. *Do the findings logically answer the research questions or support the research hypothesis?* Here is where the consumer must be wary. Many, if not all, researchers have their biases and would love to find answers to their questions or support their hypothesis from the results of their studies. Because this final section gives the researchers the right to conjecture about what the findings mean, it is easy to unintentionally suggest things that the results do not support.

2. *Does the nature of the study remain consistent from beginning to end?* My students and I have noticed that some studies begin as exploratory studies, but end up as confirmatory ones. In such cases, the introduction sec-

tion has one or more research question with no specific hypothesis stated. However, in the Discussion section, we suddenly read, "and so our hypothesis is confirmed by the results." Another variation of this is that the researchers generate a hypothesis in the Discussion section—which is their right—but then go on to suggest that their results now support the hypothesis. This is circular reasoning. We cannot use the same data to support a hypothesis from which it has been formulated. A new study must be made to test this hypothesis.

3. *Are the findings generalized to the correct population or situations?* Most studies, in fact, cannot be generalized to a broadly defined population. The reason is that most samples are not randomly selected, nor are they typically large enough to adequately represent a target population. Consequently, results of such studies are suggestive at most and need to be followed up with a number of replications. If the same findings are repeated using different samples from the target population, then we can have more assurance that we are on the right track. A well-written Discussion section will be careful to warn readers of this problem.

4. *Are the conclusions consistent with the type of research design used?* The main concern here is whether *causation* is being inferred from research designs that are not geared to demonstrate this effect. Having an idea of the type of design being used will help the consumer know whether this error is made when reading the Discussion and Conclusion. Nonexperimental designs such as descriptive or correlational ones cannot be used to directly show causation. Yet, especially in the latter case, some researchers have slipped into concluding that their findings indicate that one variable influences another. When researchers apply their findings, they are often tempted to recommend that people manipulate one variable to cause changes in another. Unless their research design warrants this application, they have made a logical error.

5. *Are the findings and conclusions related to theory or previous research?* To help contribute to the big picture, a well-written Discussion/Conclusion section should attempt to tie the findings and interpretations to any current theoretical thinking or previous research. This might be done through showing how the findings support what has gone before or providing evidence to refute some theory or challenge previous research.

6. *Are any limitations of the study made clear?* There are very few, if any, *perfect* studies in the literature. Regardless of how good a study is, a conscientious researcher will mention what the limitations are to caution the reader from being overly confident about the results.

7. *Is there consistency between the findings and the applications?* As previously mentioned, when discussing inferential statistics, some researchers confuse statistical significance with practical significance. I repeat the warning here.

Just because a finding is *statistically significant,* this does not mean that it has *practical significance.* I have seen relatively small correlations, such as $r = 0.30$, interpreted as an important finding because it was statistically significant, or the difference of 5 points between a treatment and a control group given importance for the same reason. Yet is either of these findings large enough to get excited about? Maybe, but much depends on the cost in time, human resources, and finance to get that 0.30 correlation or those extra 5 points due to the treatment. The consumer needs to be on alert when a researcher advocates costly changes based on statistical significance. This is where *effect size* is applied, as mentioned in chapter 7 and elaborated in Appendix B.

In the following, the Discussion/Conclusion sections of two studies have been evaluated using the prior set of questions. The criteria I used for choosing these articles were that they were used previously in former chapters, and they each represented a different type of research: qualitative and quantitative. Both articles were discussed in chapter 6. The first is an example of a qualitative study using an ethnographic design and verbal data. The second is an example of a causal-comparative study using numerical data.

Atkinson and Ramanathan (1995) did an ethnographic study that addressed two questions. The first was whether there were differences in *conceptual framework* between L1 and L2 academic writing programs. The second was concerned with comparing teacher behavior between the two programs (see chap. 6 for more details). Their Results section consisted of observations from six different sources (i.e., triangulation), and all of their data were in the form of verbal descriptions. In line with a purely qualitative study, no inferential statistics were used in their study. Their Discussion section compared the two writing programs based on their observations as data. Here I draw attention to the exact words they used to indicate how the researchers were trying to draw meaning from their data. This is exactly what a Discussion section is supposed to do. For example, they stated:

> A first potentially problematic difference concerns the kinds of cultural knowledge each program assumes on the part of its students. As a program wholly devoted to NNSs [non-native speakers], the ELP [English Language Program] appears to make two pragmatic assumptions. . . . In contrast . . . the UCP [University Composition Program] seems to assume a significant amount of cultural knowledge. . . . (pp. 557, 558)

Notice the words *potentially, assumes, appears,* and *seems to assume.* Clearly, the authors are speculating here. There is no problem with this. This is what researchers do when they try to make sense out of their findings regardless of whether the data are verbal or numerical. However, be careful when you see the word *significant* in a study apart from *statistical significance.* They are not talking about statistical significance here. Most likely they mean *an important difference.*

Atkinson and Ramanathan continued their discussion by pointing out two more differences between the programs. They followed this by relating their findings to research that had gone before them. Then they proposed an application of their conclusions with the caveat that the rationale behind it was based on the condition of the veracity of their conjectures. They stated, "If the contrast we have drawn above is at all accurate . . . it would seem vitally important for each program to know in detail what the other's goals and expectations are" (p. 562). They were careful to include this warning. Hopefully, the readers will not overlook this point while reading the rest of their article.

Atkinson and Ramanathan finished their paper with a Conclusion and Application section, which summarized their interpretations with a concluding remark regarding the usefulness of their findings. They stated, "In conclusion, we call for purposeful articulation among any and all intra-university writing programs that NNS writers must transit for academic success" (p. 564). I raise two caveats regarding this statement. The first is that their study does not show that articulation between ELP and UCPs is necessary. Although I agree with this conclusion in principle, their data do not warrant this conclusion. The second is, implicit in their conclusion is the suggestion that the differences they found are ubiquitous in all universities with similar programs. To suggest such a broad application across most universities based on the finding at their university is overstretching their findings. In essence, they had a sample of one from which such generalizations cannot be made. At most, they can—and do—suggest that everyone who has a similar program needs to see whether such differences exist in their own program. This last conclusion is valid.

In addition to the previous seven questions, keep in mind the criteria listed in chapter 7, Section 1, under Evaluating Explanations and Conclusions (cf. Table 7.1). They should also be taken into consideration when evaluating the final Discussion/Conclusion section of a qualitative study. However, because interpretations and conclusions are ongoing during the data-collection stage in a qualitative study, these criteria apply both then and in the final discussion.

The second example is by Scarcella and Zimmerman (1998), who used a causal-comparative design (cf. chap. 5). Their primary question was whether ESL males differed from ESL females in their knowledge of academic vocabulary at their university. Their subordinate questions had to do with the contributions of preexisting verbal ability, length of residence in the United States, and age of arrival to any differences found for gender. Remember that the causal-comparative design suggests causation, but does not directly provide evidence for it.

They began their Discussion section by stating their primary question, which was immediately followed by a summary of their results. They found that males scored higher than females even when controlling for other possible factors by using the ANCOVA procedure discussed in Appendix B. They were emphatic that neither their study nor previously reviewed studies show "that gender itself causes differences in the TAL scores" (p. 40). However, they continued, justifiably, to suggest several possible causes behind the gender difference found in their study and listed six research questions for follow-up research. (This is the type of article that up-and-coming graduate student researchers should love to read because it provides ready-made research questions that they could take and use for their theses.)

Scarcella and Zimmerman dedicated three paragraphs under a subheading entitled "Limitations of the Study." Again they repeated their warning about inferring causation. However, they also warned about generalizing their findings to all ESL males and females. The reason they gave was that their sample had not been representative of the whole population of ESL males and females. The second limitation they cited was that their results may have been specific to the particular instrument they had used. They suggested that a similar study be done using procedures other than those they had used.

In their conclusions, Scarcella and Zimmerman again warned about causation and overgeneralization. The main application of their findings was that much more research needs to be done. However, they did not just leave the reader with this ubiquitously bland conclusion; they provided a number of specific research questions, along with some notions on how to investigate them, which is invaluable for the person looking for research ideas.

If there is any constructive criticism to offer regarding this study, Scarcella and Zimmerman should have given more emphasis to the fact that they found differences between males and females despite eliminating variance due to other possible causative factors (i.e., preexisting verbal ability, length of residence, and age of arrival in the United States). This is an important finding. By controlling for these factors, they eliminated three potential factors that could have caused the differences between males and females. However, it is always wise to be more conservative in one's conclusions than liberal. No doubt they chose the former.

As you can see, the Discussion/Conclusion section of an article cannot be treated lightly. Yet to discern its quality, you, the consumer, must be able to evaluate how the preceding sections of a research study logically develop to support the interpretations and conclusions a researcher makes. Without understanding and evaluating each building block leading to the final result, it is impossible to evaluate the end product. Hopefully, the prior discussion has provided you with guidelines to help you determine whether the end product (i.e., the conclusions) is warranted. If it is, you are able to make your own conclusions regarding the worth of the study for answering your own questions. Therefore, the best recommendation at this point is to provide you with an exercise that will help you apply what you have just read.

Exercise 8.1

1. Use one of the recent studies you have used in previous exercises.
2. Assess the Discussion/Conclusion section of the study by answering the following questions. Provide a quick rationale for each answer.
   a. State the research question and/or any hypothesis.
   b. Do the findings logically answer the research questions or support the research hypothesis?
   c. Does the nature of the study remain consistent from beginning to end?
   d. Are the findings generalized to the correct population?
   e. Are the conclusions consistent to the type of research design?
   f. Are the findings and conclusions related to theory for previous research?
   g. Are any limitations made clear regarding the study?
   h. Is there consistency between the findings and applications?

Congratulations! You have come a long way. Welcome to the Consumers of Research in Applied Linguistics Association—*whenever we get around to starting such an organization.* Let me close with this analogy. Research is like scuba diving, which I love to do. Many people are afraid to learn how to scuba dive because they think they will drown or they will be claustrophobic. I find that the opposite is true. When I am underwater, it is one of the most relaxing experiences I have ever had. I get to see the underwater beauty of sea life from a perspective that many will never see. The only danger is not following the principles that I studied when I was training for certification. Studying research is similar. There are those who stand on the edge of the ocean of research afraid to jump in and experience for themselves the treasures that await them. Their excuses are fear of drowning in the sea of data and statistics. But as with diving, if they follow the principles discussed in this book, they will find themselves not only discovering many important pieces of information, but will begin to enjoy swimming in the depths. Now it is your turn to jump into the ocean of research and begin finding the treasures of information that await you. Appendix A provides a set of guidelines for completing your own review of the research literature that will address any research question you might have. May you approach it with great confidence.

Constructing a Literature Review

If you have grasped the content presented in the chapters of this book, you are now ready to complete a review of the research literature that focuses on some topic in which you are interested. Whether you are trying to answer a practical problem in the language classroom, preparing a paper on some topic for colleagues, or trying to fulfill the requirements of a course assignment, the ability to do an effective research review is necessary. The purpose of this chapter is to provide guidelines for developing a useful review for answering whatever research question you might have. First, however, I discuss the importance of producing a good literature review.

WHY DO A REVIEW OF RESEARCH?

The main benefit of doing a literature review is to provide the consumer with a mosaic of what is happening concerning a given topic. No one research study exhausts all there is to know about a given topic. However, when you can integrate various recent research articles into a meaningful picture, you can discover a number of interesting things.

First, you will realize whether there are any plausible answers to your questions when you see the bigger picture. On first blush, your impression might be that there are no clear answers, and you might be tempted to give up your search. However, as you weave the studies together in an integrated review, you might find answers for practical use.

In addition, you might find conflicting results between studies. This might cause you to give up and conclude that no one can agree on anything. However, this is when being a discerning consumer will pay off. On careful scrutiny of the studies, you will begin to see why there are conflicting results. You might realize that the differences in the samples used in the studies produced the differing results. There might have been a difference in the procedures or materials used in the treatment. You now have to decide which study best corresponds to the context surrounding your particular research question. The closer the correspondence, the more applicable the findings might be to your situation.

However, if you find that the same results are replicated over a variety of studies, you can have more confidence that you are on the right track. Here is where *external validity* comes into play. Regardless of the sample, procedures, materials, or type of tests used, if the same findings keep appearing, you can be quite confident that you have a workable answer for your question. Without a well-done literature review, you cannot have this assurance.

Occasionally, you will discover that there is little recent research on a particular question. When this happens, you should take this as a warning to take care. Maybe your research question is stated in such a way that your search accessed only a few studies. If this is the case, you will have to adjust the key concepts in your question to produce more rewarding searches. You might have to go back further in time to see whether there was anything done earlier. Then again, your question may be so novel that there is little research available to date.

To illustrate, one of my students raised a question concerning the usefulness of the *critical period hypothesis*. However, when looking over the past 5 years, he could not find enough research to fill a short 3-page review. He first asked whether this topic had been researched out—that is, had research gone as far as possible, whether by sufficiently answering the question or by being limited due to various constraints. Most probably, in my thinking, the latter might be the case. The variables used to test this hypothesis are beyond our current capabilities to manipulate or measure. If this is the case, we cannot make strong conclusions about children's seemingly superior language learning abilities as compared with adults. Possibly new approaches will be developed that will move research ahead on this topic in the future.

Second, doing a research review is important if you plan to do a study yourself. Such a review will give you an overview of the different kinds of methodologies, instruments for collecting data, and ways in which to analyze data commonly used in the research for a given area. This knowledge can help you decide whether your proposed study is even feasible given your time, material, and financial constraints. Many a fledgling researcher could have saved him or herself needless angst if s/he would have realized that the study s/he was interested in doing required more time and resources than were available before launching into the task.

WHERE TO BEGIN

As described in chapter 2, the first place to begin is searching for studies using *preliminary* sources. These are used to find documents that report research studies or theoretical positions, and I suggest you review chapter 2 regarding how to make the best use of these valuable tools. Most university libraries in the United States and Europe, as well as some public libraries, have such computerized search capabilities. Now that the Internet is available in most countries, you should be able to obtain a list of research studies pertinent to your questions even from your home computer.

Again, as mentioned in chapter 2, your search is as good as the *keywords* (or descriptors) you use. You might have to try different combinations of these words to obtain sufficient results for your review, or you might have to use a *thesaurus* from the preliminary source you are using to identify related keywords to guide your search.

Your goal is to access firsthand research studies (i.e., *primary studies*) that relate to your questions. How many studies you include depends on the nature of your question(s). If you want to do an exhaustive literature review, you will want to cover as many studies as you can find. However, most people want to put some limitations on their literature review, such as time constraints and/or only journal articles, to confine their search to studies with only certain characteristics.

Figure A.1 illustrates the results of a search I made for research articles using the ERIC database on the Internet. I put *time limits* and *location limits* for studies published between 1990 and 2002 in research journals only. I first began with the broad search only using the keyword *ESL*. The results

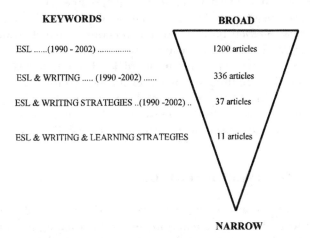

FIG. A.1.   Results of using different combinations of keywords in a literature search using ERIC for years 1990 to 2002.

were 1,200 documents. I then narrowed it down to articles dealing with *ESL* and *writing*, resulting in 336 references. If my question of interest was something like, "What does research say about writing in ESL?", I might want to stop here and scan through all 336 references. (Note that not all of these references are primary research studies. Some could be position papers or literature reviews.)

Most likely, I would want to narrow my search even more. For instance, I am interested in finding research studies about strategies ESL people use when writing. So I restated my search terms to be *ESL* and *writing strategies*. As shown in Fig. A.1, this captured 37 articles.

I could have stopped there, but I wanted to make sure that the way I worded my keywords did not prevent me from seeing some study that might be using different terminology. So I did one more search, adding *learning strategies* to my list of keywords. This reduced the search to 11 articles.

You might ask the question, "How far back in time do you go in your search?" My recommendation is that you begin by looking at the last 5 years of research. Usually this results in enough current research to provide viable information addressing your question(s). I then suggest that you begin with the most recent research and work backward in time. This way you stay abreast with the most recent issues and findings with which researchers are currently working. This can save time by not getting involved with outdated issues with which people in the discipline are no longer concerned.

Once you have identified the studies you want to consider for inclusion in your review, you face the challenge of getting your hands on the actual articles. Hopefully, you will be near a good library that carries the journals so that you can have ready access to the studies. If the library does not subscribe to the journal, it may have a library loan agreement with other libraries that do have the journals. Some journals such as *Language Learning* and *Modern Language Journal* have electronic versions to which your library might have access. In such cases, you can download full articles for reviewing. If all else fails, you can order journal articles through databases such as ERIC, and they will mail them to you either through your library or to your address. If you do this, I strongly suggest that you order the microfiche version to keep the cost down and help save trees. You will need a microfiche reader for this, but these should be available at your library.

ABSTRACTING PRIMARY LITERATURE

In preparation for constructing your review of the research literature, you need to formulate a systematic procedure for cataloging and storing your information for each study. We used to have to put our information on

5″ × 8″ (i.e., 12 cm × 20 cm) cards that were awkward to handle. However, in our computerized day, there are a number of information storage software systems that make this task much easier. The one I favor and have used over recent years is Microsoft® Access 2000 (1999), which is readily available and easy to learn, although there are a number of others that will do the same job. Once you enter the information, which I discuss shortly, you will have created a database of studies from which you can draw information for your literature review. This database will provide you with the ability to sort and aggregate various studies at the click of the mouse based on whatever criteria you decide to use.

When you set up your database of studies for your review, enter the following information in the format (APA, MLA, etc.) that you most commonly use. First, record very accurately the last names and all initials for every author of each study. If you have only one author, it is useful to identify his or her gender as well because you might want to use personal pronouns when summarizing his or her study rather than speaking in the formal *the researcher*. Next, you want to record the exact title of the article. When doing this, use the style (e.g., APA or MLA) that you plan to use for your literature review. This will save you time when you prepare the table of references because you will not have to retype the references. At most you will only have to cut and paste with your word processor software. Following this you will need to record the year published, the exact title of the journal (in italics), the volume number (in italics), the issue number, and the page numbers from the beginning of the article to the very last page.

If you have read a published literature review, you will have noticed that the author basically looks for eight things when summarizing the main body of the study. They are as follows:

1. The focus of the study: What area and/or issue is being studied?
2. The research question(s) being asked.
3. The hypothesis(es) being tested (if any).
4. The size of the sample and important characteristics such as age and gender. Note here how the sample was chosen or assigned to the study, whether randomly or by some other procedure.
5. The variables in the study such as:
   a. Observational
   b. Independent
   c. Dependent
   d. Moderating
6. The procedures followed, including any materials, test instruments, or observational techniques.

7. The overall findings of the study.

8. The conclusion(s) that the researcher draws from the findings.

In addition you will want to add:

9. Any other observations you have made that pertain to your interests.

10. Any concerns you have with the study that you want to point out in your review.

WRITING A REVIEW OF RESEARCH

The outline I recommend for writing a good review of research is one that I have adapted based on chapter 6 of Cooper's (1998) book, *Synthesizing Research*. This pattern seems to be the one followed by many reviewers of research published in journals (e.g., Ellis, 2002; Sparks & Ganschow, 2001). Interestingly, this outline has the same headings that are used in reporting most primary research studies: Introduction, Method, Results, and Discussion.

I. Introduction
   A. The research question that your review addresses.
   B. The importance of the topic.
   C. Historical background of the topic (theory, methodological issues, previous reviews, etc.).
   D. The goal of your review. How you plan to add to the theory and information already available.
II. Method section: Details regarding the makeup of the review.
   A. What years are covered?
   B. What preliminary sources were used to locate the studies?
   C. What keywords guided your search?
   D. Criteria for deciding which studies to review.
      1. Description of the constraints that limited your selection.
      2. Rationale for choosing these constraints.
   E. What studies were excluded and why?
III. Results section: Studies summarized.
   A. An overview of what studies will be discussed and their relation to one another and the review as a whole.
   B. At least one paragraph for each study summarizing the following:
      1. The main point of the study.

    2. The question(s)/hypothesis being studied.

    3. Samples used and how they were chosen.

    4. Procedure(s) used

    5. General findings(results).

    6. Author's interpretations/applications of the findings.

    7. Any concerns to which you might want to alert the reader.

IV. Discussion section

    A. Give an overview of major results of your review.

    B. Compare/contrast the results between studies.

    C. Provide possible reasons for any differences.

    D. Relate results to any theoretical issues you mentioned in the introduction.

    E. Compare with past reviews if any exist.

    F. Explain any difference in findings with past reviews.

    G. Offer application of findings toward future research.

Whenever possible, I recommend that you construct tables to help summarize your findings. What you put in a table will depend on what you are trying to highlight in your review. The purpose of the table is to provide a visual aid that will work with your text in helping the reader understand all of the relationships that you are trying to point out.

Ellis (2002) provided an excellent example of how to make good use of tables to summarize the information he extracted from 11 studies in his review. The question he addressed was stated in the title: "Does Form-Focused Instruction Affect the Acquisition of Implicit Knowledge?" He captured in his first table each study's reference, the samples used, the targeted linguistic structure, the treatment, how acquisition was measured, and the results. In a three-page table, he summarized the issues he wanted to draw the reader's attention to for the 11 studies. He listed six criteria that he used to select the studies he reviewed. His Table 2 summarized the results of this review, which he used to aid his written discussion of his findings. In his Discussion and Conclusion sections, he related his findings to the previous literature reviews and the theoretical issues that he outlined in his introduction. I strongly recommend your perusal of this review as a model for you to follow. However, there are many other well-written literature reviews available that will vary in style, which you may also want to use as a prototype.

Now you should be equipped to go into the world of research and approach any study unabashed. It is your time to decide on a research question based on your own interest and search for a number of studies that address your question. The following exercise will guide you in the experience.

Exercise A.1: Preparing your own review of research literature.

The purpose of this exercise is for you to produce a review of research in an area of your own interest. You are to review whatever number of studies you find relevant in the space allowed. You are to develop an overall picture of what is being studied in your chosen area.
Criteria for the main body of the text:

I.   Introduction: Conceptual presentation
    A. What is your research question(s) that motivates your review?
    B. Why is the answer to your question(s) important to applied linguistics?
    C. What is the historical perspective behind your question?
    D. What is the main aim of your review?
II. Method section
    A. Details of the nature of your search.
        1. What years did you cover in your search?
        2. What preliminary sources did you use?
        3. What keywords guided your search?
    B. Criteria for deciding which studies to review.
        1. What criteria did you use for including a study?
        2. Why did you select these criteria?
        3. What studies did you exclude and why?
III. Results section
    A. An organized summary of the studies: Each study should include the following in your own words:
        1. The main point of the study.
        2. The question(s)/hypothesis being studied.
        3. The sample used and how and why it was selected.
        4. The procedure(s) used for implementing the study.
        5. The general findings (results) in words, not statistics.
        6. The researcher's interpretations/applications of the findings.
IV. Discussion section
    A. Summarize the major results of your review (use tables to provide visual aids in your summary if possible).
        1. Compare/contrast the results between studies.
        2. Provide possible reasons for any differences.
    B. Compare with past reviews if any exist.
    C. Explain any difference in your findings compared with past reviews.
    D. Apply your findings toward answering your future research.

BEST WISHES ON YOUR ADVENTURE IN RESEARCH!!!

Going to the Next Level of Statistics

MORE ABOUT DESCRIPTIVE STATISTICS

Types of Scales

Before looking at statistics in greater detail, you need to understand something about the types of numbers that are used as data. This is important because the type of descriptive or inferential statistic used is dependent on the nature of the data. Numerical data come in one of four forms, referred to as *scales*: *nominal, ordinal, interval,* and *ratio.* Data on the nominal scale are frequencies or relative frequencies in the form of percentages of occurrence. Some variables are measured by simply counting the frequency of occurrence, such as counting how many males and females are present when *gender* is a variable in a study. The word *nominal* means that the levels of a variable are categories. The categories can be identified with words (e.g., *female, male*) or numbers (e.g., 1, 2). The numbers assigned would only be used to identify each level, without having any other meaning. That is, the value 2 for one of the sexes does not mean that one sex had twice as much of gender than the other sex. It is just a numerical name. The frequency of individuals in each category is the data. The frequencies are sometimes converted to relative frequencies (i.e., percentages), but the results are the same. For example, a study may have 60 males and 80 females, or 43% males and 57% females.

Another example of the use of a nominal scale would be when a researcher is interested in knowing whether there are differences in the number of people representing three different nationalities. Nationality is the variable of the study, and the data are the frequency of people for each of the nationalities.

Measurement on other variables can be on an *ordinal scale*. This scale is in the form of some type of ranking. As with the nominal scale, words or numbers can be used. However, in contrast with the nominal scale, the words or numbers have quantitative meaning. For example, the variable of language proficiency might be expressed verbally as low, average, or high ability. It could also be in the form of numbers: 3 = high ability, 2 = average ability, and 1 = low ability.

A commonly used ordinal scale in applied linguistics is known as the *Likert* scale. One use is with measurements of attitude with the rankings: 5 = *Strongly Agree*, 4 = *Agree*, 3 = *Neutral*, 2 = *Disagree*, and 1 = *Strongly Disagree*. This scale has two important qualities: unequal distance between values, and no true zero. What is meant by the first quality is that the distance between a 2 and a 3 on a rating scale, for example, may not represent the same amount of difference in the trait (the attribute) being measured as the distance between the 1 and the 2. What is meant by *no true zero* is that if a 0 were used, it would only represent a level of ability that was lower than a 1. It would not mean that subjects at level 0 were absolutely devoid of the trait being measured.

To illustrate, the following numbers show what the actual amount of a trait might be measured. Note the unequal distances between numbers. The amount of trait measured (or distance) between 1 and 2 differs from that between 2 and 3. The problem is, we do not usually know how much of the trait is being represented by the numbers.

$$1 \underline{\hspace{1cm}} 2 \underline{\hspace{2cm}} 3 \underline{\hspace{2cm}} 4 \underline{\hspace{0.7cm}} 5$$

Many ordinal scales are used in applied linguistic research. In fact any rating scale is almost always an ordinal scale. Besides attitude scales mentioned previously, there are rating scales for writing and oral proficiency, anxiety, and so on. A study that used a number of rating scales (all ordinal) was done by Gardner et al. (1997), mentioned earlier. They measured 13 variables, each using an ordinal scale to examine such traits as attitude, anxiety, interest, motivation, self-confidence, and course and teacher evaluation.

Measurement of a variable can also be in the form of an *interval scale*. Whereas the values used in the ordinal scale represent unequal amounts of the variable being measured, the intervals between the values in an interval scale are equal, as illustrated next.

$$1 \underline{\hspace{0.5cm}} 2 \underline{\hspace{0.5cm}} 3 \underline{\hspace{0.5cm}} 4 \underline{\hspace{0.5cm}} 5 \underline{\hspace{0.5cm}} 6 \underline{\hspace{0.5cm}} 7 \underline{\hspace{0.5cm}} \text{etc.}$$

However, as with the ordinal scale, there is no *true zero*. A common example of an interval scale is the scale that heat is measured on a thermometer. The 1-degree difference between 20° and 21° Celsius in amount of heat is the same as the 1-degree difference between 29° and 30°. In other words, the units of measurement mean the same in terms of the amount of the trait (heat in this example) being measured no matter where it is on the scale. At the same time, there is no true zero. Zero degrees Celsius does not mean the total absence of heat. It is a *relative zero*, in that it is used as a reference point determined by the freezing of water. As we all know, zero degrees Celsius is warmer than zero degrees Fahrenheit (i.e., 0° C = 32° F).

Scores on aptitude or achievement tests are usually treated as if they are on interval scales. Each correct item is considered as one unit of the trait being measured, so that a person scoring a 30 on the instrument is 10 units higher on the trait than one who scores 20. (In fact in the measurement world, this is known to be not true, but that is for another book.) A zero on a test is not a true zero because it does not mean that the subject has absolutely no knowledge of what is being tested, although some teachers might think so. It simply means that the examinee did not answer any of the items correctly. All data that consist of the total of summed scores are usually treated as interval scales.

Finally, there is the *ratio scale*, which is seldom ever used in applied linguistics research. As you might expect, this scale has it all. The units of measurement are equal in amount of trait being measured, and there is a true zero. A good example is using a ruler to measure length. One centimeter means the same thing no matter where it is on the scale. In addition, a zero means that there is no length, which of course means that whatever we are measuring does not exist.

The one ratio scale measurement that I can think of that has been used in applied linguistics is reaction time. This is the time it takes for subjects to react by pressing a button or speaking out after experiencing some form of stimulus. Reaction time is measured in units as small as milliseconds. The millisecond units are equal; if the measurement is zero, there was no reaction to whatever was presented to the subject. Akamatsu (2002), for example, used reaction time to study the effects of L1 orthography on decoding L2 (English) words. The researcher described how fluent ESL readers from different L1 backgrounds were presented with 40 words one at a time on a computer screen. The clock started when the word flashed on the screen and stopped when the respondent spoke the word. The response time (also known as response latency) measured in milliseconds constituted the dependent variable.

At this point, you might want to digest what you have just read by doing the following exercise, not to mention taking a break.

Exercise B.1

1. Take any study and identify the variables under consideration.
2. Identify the type of scale that each variable is on: nominal, ordinal, interval, or ratio.

Shape of the Data Distribution

The shape of the distribution of the data is seldom discussed in Results sections of published research, but it is very important. Based on the shape of the distribution of the data, researchers should choose which estimates of average and variation they will report in their studies. In addition, some inferential statistical procedures require the data to be distributed in certain patterns before they can be used appropriately.

The distribution of data is simply a graphical display of how many (the frequency) participants/objects obtained certain measures beginning from the lowest measure to the highest. To illustrate, Fig. B.1 is a bar graph representing a subsection of data based on the total scores taken from a teacher evaluation scale. The graph shows the frequency of the scores ranging from 70 to 80. The height of each bar corresponds to the frequency (i.e., the number on top of each bar). Note that 5 people scored 70, 8 people scored 71, 16 scored 77, and so on. The shape of the distribution is noted by mentally drawing a line connecting the tops of the bars. These

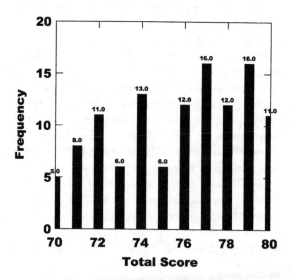

FIG. B.1.   Bar graph of a distribution of data.

data show that there is a tendency for the frequency of people to increase as the total scores increase.

When referring to the shape of the data (cf. Table 7.3), three issues are of concern: symmetricality, skewness, and number of modals (i.e., clusters of data). All of these terms are concerned with how well the shape of the data conforms to a normal distribution. An example is presented in Fig. B.2. A *normal distribution* has specific properties and is used as a reference point for comparing the shapes of data distributions. The reason it is used as the reference for other curves is because many traits that we study are considered by many to be normally distributed in the population.

The distribution of the normal curve is perfectly *symmetrical* and has only one cluster of data in the middle. That is, by drawing a vertical line dividing the graph in half, as seen in Fig. B.2, the shape of the curve on the right side is the exact mirror image of the left half. In addition, notice that the distribution has certain properties. Approximately 34% of the subjects are found from the middle to either the first dotted line above the middle and the one below the middle. That is, 64% of the cases (e.g., people) are clustered in the middle between these two dotted lines. For reference, these off-centered dotted lines are designated by *SD* (i.e., standard deviation). From +1 *SD* to +2 *SD* and −1 *SD* to −2 *SD*, there are approximately 14% of the people being measured. The two ends of the distribution have roughly 2% on each side. To the degree that these distributions stray from being normal, these percentages change accordingly.

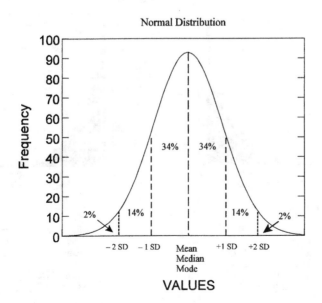

FIG. B.2. The normal distribution.

When a distribution of data is not symmetrical, the issue becomes one of skewness. The *skewness* of the distribution has to do with how much the distribution strays from being symmetrical in terms of lopsidedness. When not symmetrical, a distribution is either *positively* or *negatively skewed*. If it is *positively skewed*, as shown by the distribution on the right of Fig. B.3, the distribution will lean to the left with the skewness index above zero. If the distribution is *negatively skewed*, as illustrated by the left distribution in Fig. B.3, it is lopsided to the right side of the graph, and the skewness index is less than zero depicted by a minus sign. A good way to remember is to look for the long tail. If it is on the right side of the distribution, it is positively skewed. If it is on the left side, it is negatively skewed. The important thing to remember is that if the data are fairly skewed, the researcher should treat the data differently when using either descriptive and inferential statistics. I discuss this further when I come to topics affected by skewness.

One other component is important regarding the shape of the distribution of data: the numbers of *data clusters*. When the data have more than one cluster in the distribution, it means that there are subgroups of data in the data set. This is possible, for example, if the sample of participants consists of two ability groupings. This might be fine for some purposes, but other descriptive and inferential statistics would be drastically affected by such a distribution. How this works practically is discussed next. Besides the

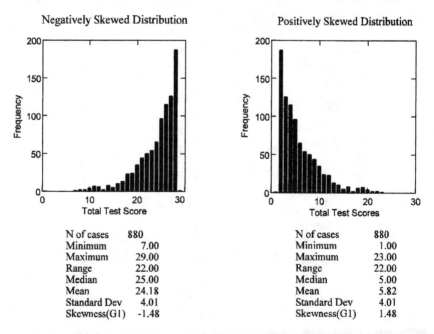

FIG. B.3. Two skewed distributions and descriptive statistics.

shape of the distribution, two other pieces of information are important: average and variation (cf. Table 7.3). They both play a crucial role in the analysis of data.

The Average

To understand the concept of *average*, think about how the word is used by almost everyone in everyday discussion. Teachers refer to their classes or students as average or above/below average. What do they mean? Aren't they saying that they are like the majority of individuals in a group? *Above average* refers to those who are above the majority, and those *below average* measure below the majority. In other words, *average* is used to mean the usual (or normal), and *above* or *below average* is used to mean the unusual (or not normal). In this sense, average should be thought of as an area or zone that encompasses the usual. Figure B.4 illustrates this point. Note the large box in the middle, which represents the average or what people are normally like. The smaller boxes on each side represent people who are above average and below average. The tiny boxes represent people who are exceptionally above (AA+) and below (BA−) average. Note that the boxes overlap to illustrate that the lines among average, above/below average, and exceptionally above/below average overlap. In other words, there is not a clear border between being classified as average or above/below average at these points on the distribution.

Among educators, *the average* is often thought of as a single score on some measures. Those who achieve that score are average, and those who score above or below it are above or below average, respectively. However, this interpretation can be somewhat misleading. As stated in the previous paragraph, average represents an area of scores that are considered *usual*, which means that there is a spread of scores that would fit into the average zone. The single value that is referred to as *the average* is only an indicator of where this average zone might be. Because this zone can change with the

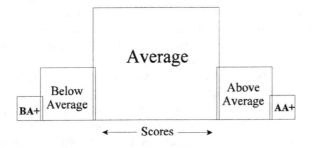

FIG. B.4.   The concept of average.

shape of the distribution, there are three indicators used to mark this zone: *mean, median,* and *mode* (see Table 7.3). These three descriptive statistics are used to represent the average zone, but they should never be thought of as the zone. Statistics books refer to these as measures of *central tendency* for this reason.

Of the three, the *mean* is the most commonly used indicator of the average zone. As you may well know, all the scores are added up and divided by the total number of scores. Many studies that you read will report means in their descriptive data.

The *median* can also be found in some Results sections of research articles, although less often. The median is simply the value that splits the distribution of values in half. It is a point in the distribution of data where 50% of the scores fall above it and 50% below. For example, if you have nine measurements, such as:

$$3 \quad 5 \quad 6 \quad 6 \quad \mathbf{7} \quad 9 \quad 10 \quad 11 \quad 13$$

the value that would divide this distribution in half would be **7** with four scores below and four scores above. The values of the numbers are not added up. We only look for the point that splits the number of scores in half.

So what is the difference between the mean and the median? Often they are equal, in which case the mean is always reported. However, they are not always equal. For example, if you compute the mean by adding up all of the prior values and divide by 9, you get 7.78, which is greater than the median of 7.00. The difference is due to the fact that the prior list of values is not distributed symmetrically. It is slightly skewed to the right (i.e., positively skewed). If the shape of the distribution of data deviates from a symmetrical distribution to a large extent, the median would be the better indicator of averageness.

The third indicator of the average zone is the *mode*, which is the easiest one to understand, but the rarest one used in research. It is simply the most frequent score in the distribution. In the earlier list of values, the mode is 6 because it is the most frequent score, occurring twice. Sometimes there can be more than one mode, as when two different scores have the same most frequent category. The shape of this distribution would be referred to as *bimodal*, where there would be two clusters of data. When there is only one mode, the distribution of values is referred to as *unimodal* (i.e., one cluster of data) as illustrated in Fig. B.2.

Why have three measures of averageness? The answer is based on the shape of the distribution of the data. When the data are perfectly symmetrical and unimodal, the mean, median, and mode are the same value (cf. Fig.

B.2). For example, if a distribution is normally distributed and has a mean of 25, then the median and mode are also 25. In such instances, the mean is always the best indicator of average to report. However, if the distribution is skewed, there will be three different values for the three indicators. You can see from the information under the graph for the negatively skewed distributions in Fig. B.3 that the mean is 24.18, the median is 25, and the mode is 29. For the positively skewed distribution, the mean equals 5.82, the median equals 5.00, and the mode is 1.

You may still be asking, why is this important? The significance of this becomes clearer when a researcher makes comparisons between groups of people using some form of inferential procedure. If the means of the groups are distorted due to skewness, then comparing the means may lead to false conclusions. More is said about this when I discuss inferential statistics. Suffice it to state here that journals should require researchers to include information regarding the shape of any data distributions used to help the consumer judge whether proper statistical procedures were used.

Data Variance

Not only are researchers in some studies interested in averages, they are also interested in how much people vary between one another in relation to the average. In fact understanding variance is at the heart of every research question. Questions such as, On what traits do people vary? How much do they vary? and Why do they vary? are the main foci of most research.

As with the average, there are also three measures of variation (cf. Table 7.3): standard deviation, semi-interquartile range, and range. As Table 7.3 shows, each one corresponds to one of the measures of average. The standard deviation corresponds to the mean, the semi-interquartile range with the median, and the range with the mode. When reporting one type of average, the corresponding measure of variation should be reported as well.

The *standard deviation*, commonly reported as *SD* (cf. Table 7.3), can be thought of as the average deviation from the mean. (Note: Whenever you see the word *standard* in a statistical term, think *average*.) As with the mean, the *SD* is the most common measure of variation reported in published research for describing data. The *SD*s in Fig. B.2 show plus or minus 1 and 2 standard deviations above and below the mean.

The less used measure of variance is the *semi-interquartile range*. In essence, it is used to estimate the central 50% of the subjects in the distribution. Although seldom used, there are studies that report this statistic. Izumi and Bigelow (2000), for instance, realized that their data did not approach a normal distribution, in addition to having a small sample. Instead of using means and *SD*s to describe their data, they used medians and interquartile ranges.[1] Many who use nonparametric inferential statistics should follow Izumi and Bigelow's example.

The last measure of variance is *the range*. This is simply the distance between the lowest value and the highest value in the distribution. In Fig. B.3, the range for both of the distributions is 22. For the data on the left, the minimum score was 7.00 and the maximum score was 29.00. The difference between the two is 22, the range. The principal use of the range is to get a quick idea of how far the distribution stretches and how many *SD*s fit inside the range.

Why is it important for the consumer of research to know anything about the variation of scores? Returning to my first comments in this section on the importance of variance, both the range and *SD* are distorted by data that are highly skewed or that contain unusual patterns of values. If those measures are used in such circumstances, the results of the study are misleading. A well-written research article alerts the reader to any anomalies in the data and explains how these are taken into consideration.

To digest the prior discussion, this might be a good time to take a break by doing the following exercise before moving on to other topics.

Exercise B.2

Locate several research studies and do the following:

1. Determine what types of data are being used in each study.
2. Describe how the data are reported.
   a. What was reported about the shape of the data distribution?
   b. What measure of average was reported?
   c. What measure of variance was reported?
3. In your estimation, were the correct descriptive statistics used?

MORE ABOUT INFERENTIAL STATISTICS

Univariate Versus Multivariate Procedures

Different inferential statistical procedures are determined by the configuration of the independent variables (IVs) and the dependent variables (DVs). A study can have one or more IVs and one or more DVs. If there is

---

[1]The interquartile range is twice the size of the semi-interquartile range and used for the same purpose.

only one DV, then the statistical procedures are labeled *univariate* regardless of how many independent variables there are. However, if a study has more than one DV, then the procedures are referred to as *multivariate*. In other words, the labels *univariate* and *multivariate* are only concerned with the number of DVs without reference to the number of IVs. Recall that an independent variable can have two or more levels. For instance, gender has two levels: male and female. Levels of language ability may have three levels: low, intermediate, and advanced.

Based on this, the following statistical procedures are univariate: regression (simple and multiple), *t* test (dependent and independent), and all forms of ANOVA and ANCOVA. Multivariate procedures commonly used in applied linguistics (i.e., have more than one dependent variable) consist of factor analysis, multivariate analysis of variance (MANOVA), and multivariate analysis of covariance (MANCOVA). The following provides additional procedures to what was presented in chapter 7.

More on Univariate ANOVAs

Multiway ANOVAs. In chapter 7, we left off with 2 × 2 ANOVAs that had two independent variables with two levels each and one dependent variable. The following presents more complex configurations of ANOVA that you will also encounter in the applied linguistic research literature. For example, you might see a three-way or a four-way ANOVA. Again remember that the number in front of the *-way* simply tells you the number of independent variables in the study. To illustrate, Dehaene-Lambertz and Houston (1997) used a three-way ANOVA to study infants' ability to discriminate between native and foreign languages. They used a 2 × 2 × 2 ANOVA, meaning that there were two levels for each of the three factors (i.e., IVs): nationality (2), language of presentation (2), and presence of filtering (2). Note that they had to test for three main effects, three interactions between pairs of variables (i.e., N × LP, N × PF, and LP × PF), and one interaction among all three (i.e., N × LP × PF). Altogether, there were seven things they had to test for statistical significance. As you can imagine, the more complex the configuration, the more complex the statistical analysis.

If the previous study impressed you, look at a study by Goswami, Gombert, and de Barrera (1998), which investigated the development of orthographical representations in children in three different languages: English, French, or Spanish. They used a four-way ANOVA to analyze their data: a 2 × 4 × 2 × 2 ANOVA (Language [2], Age [4], Orthographic Familiarity [2], and Number of Syllables [2]). This means they had four independent variables and one dependent variable. They tested for four main effects, six two-way interactions, three three-way interactions, and one four-way interaction. A group of my colleagues and I once did a study using a similar design. The first thing we did before running our statistical program was to pray that we did not have any complex interactions result in statistical significance. They are very messy to interpret.

Repeated Measures ANOVA.   Another type of ANOVA is one that uses repeated measures. This is similar to the dependent *t* test, in that there are multiple measurements of the same instrument administered repeatedly to the participants. However, if there are more than two administrations, an ANOVA must be done. For example, Marsh, Elfenbein, and Ambady (2003) used a repeated measures analysis in their study that examined whether cultural differences in nonverbal accents were detectable in facial expressions of emotions. They gave 79 adults pictures of nine Japanese nationals and nine Japanese Americans who posed five different emotional states. Participants were to judge the nationality of the poser as either Japanese or Japanese Americans. Marsh et al. used, among other procedures, a one-way repeated measures ANOVA. The results were $F = 6.28$, $p < .001$ (i.e., statistically significant). However, as with a normal one-way ANOVA, once a statistical significance is found, there has to be some form of pair-wise comparison. Marsh et al. used a series of dependent *t* tests to identify where the difference was.

Between-Subjects and Within-Subjects ANOVA.   Some studies use an ANOVA design that has one IV where the levels contain independent groups of participants and another IV that is *within* the participants. For example, if the first IV is gender, there are two separate groups of participants: males versus females. However, the second IV may be time of testing, which might mean that each participant is given a pretest and a posttest. The result is a 2×2 ANOVA, where the first IV is a between-subjects factor and the second IV is a within-subjects factor. In essence, the second variable is a *repeated measure.* In fact some researchers refer to the within-subjects factor as such. Others refer to it as a *nested* variable.

Morris and Tremblay (2002) supplied an example of a study using this type of analysis. They studied whether focusing students' attention on unstressed grammatical words made a difference in morphological accuracy. They used an experimental group that was given a Cloze dictation test to focus attention on the target words and a control group that used the regular curriculum. Therefore, the experimental versus control groups was the between-subjects factor. The researchers gave both groups a story writing task for both a pretest and a posttest. This was the second IV, time of testing, which was the within-subjects factor. As with any 2-way ANOVA, there are two main effects and one interaction. As with most studies with the treatment versus control combined with a pretest versus posttest design, the interaction is the most interesting effect to examine. The reason is seen in the

Morris and Tremblay study, where they found a significant interaction ($F =$ 13, $p < .025$). This meant that the treatment group increased from pretest to posttest more than the control group in morphological accuracy.

Analysis of Covariance (ANCOVA). Recall back in chapter 7 where researchers matched participants on some variable (e.g., intelligence) to eliminate its effect. There is a way to do this using a form of ANOVA as well—it is called *analysis of covariance (ANCOVA).* This procedure removes the variance in the dependent variable that is due to some extraneous variable and then looks at the relation of the independent variable to the remaining variance left in the dependent variable. No, this is not double talk; let me illustrate. Scarcella and Zimmerman (1998) studied whether there were any differences between males and females (i.e., the IV being gender) in terms of their vocabulary knowledge (the dependent variable) defined by the Test of Academic Lexicon (TAL). They first did an independent t test and found that males performed better than females ($t = 3.32$, $p < .001$). However, they did not stop there. They wanted to make sure there were no preexisting differences between the males and females on overall academic ability that could provide an alternative explanation for their results. To eliminate this possibility, they performed an ANCOVA analysis using their verbal Scholastic Aptitude Test (SAT) scores as the *covariate* (the unwanted variable). This eliminated any preexisting difference due to academic achievement ability from both groups before comparing the males with the females on the TAL scores. Again the results were in the same direction, only now they report an F ratio ($F = 5.86$, $p < .05$). Scarcella and Zimmerman followed up this finding by asking whether two other extrinsic variables might be influencing the difference in vocabulary knowledge other than gender (i.e., length of residence in the United States and age of arrival in the United States). They used each of these as covariates in two further ANCOVA analyses and continued to find males outperforming females on their mean scores on TAL even after controlling for these variables. By using ANCOVA, Scarcella and Zimmerman were able to eliminate any competing explanations for their results. This procedure is also useful for controlling variables that creep into a study because of the lack of random sampling.

Multivariate ANOVAs

Whereas univariate statistics have only one dependent variable, multivariate statistical procedures have more than one DV. In cases where a study has one or more IVs and more than one DV, the researcher can perform a separate *univariate* ANOVA on each DV or analyze everything all at once using a *multivariate* approach. The purpose of doing the latter is to control for the Type I error, as with the rationale behind using ANOVA rather than a number of t tests. That is, for every ANOVA, there is an overall probability of making a Type I error.

The most common form found in the literature is the *multivariate analysis of variance* (*MANOVA*). This procedure basically uses any one of the independent variable configurations just discussed regarding ANOVA, only with more than one dependent variable, all at the same time. For example, if we wanted to look at whether people from different cultural backgrounds (IV.1) varied on reading (DV.1) and writing (DV.2) ability, we could do two separate ANOVAs for each DV or we could do one MANOVA that does both at once. The rationale behind this is that the two DVs in this case are related, in that they are both reflective of verbal ability. In actual fact, when using the MANOVA approach, the common factor shared by the DVs is what is being compared in the independent variable. If an overall finding is statistically significant, it would suggest that somewhere in the analysis there is a significant difference. You sometimes see values for *Wilks' lambda* or *Pillai's* trace reported for a statistically significant MANOVA, but they are converted into F ratios and interpreted as any F ratio would be. If a MANOVA is found to be statistically significant, typically separate ANOVAs would then be done on each of the DVs, followed by post hoc pair-wise comparisons to tease out the differences already discussed.

Over the last 10 years, there have been more researchers using MANOVA to analyze complex research designs in applied linguistics. Mehnert (1998), for example, used this procedure along with other procedures when investigating the effect planning time has on L2 speech performance. The research design called for levels of planning time (IV.1), two types of tasks (IV.2), and four different measures of speech performance (four dependent variables). Because these four measures were highly related, Mehnert used the MANOVA procedure. A significant effect (Pillai = 0.92, $F = 2.75$, $p < .005$) was found for planning time on the four dependent variables (or, to be more precise, the overall factor shared by the four dependent variables, which could be defined as *speech performance*). Mehnert did not follow up with a more detailed analysis to identify where the differences were for this common factor. Most likely this was because a series of univariate ANOVAs had been done previously. However, these univariate analyses are only looking at group differences with each individual DV, which is not the same as looking at the differences on the overall common factor of speech performance.

Finally, I close this section with *multivariate analysis of covariance* (MANCOVA), which is a MANOVA with one or more covariates. This is the same as ANCOVA except it has more than one DV, thus MANCOVA. An example of the study done by Tsang (1996), previously referred to in chapter 7, used this procedure. Recall, she looked at the effects of three different levels of language enrichment (IV.1), across four form levels at school (IV.2) on descriptive writing performance, measured by a posttest consisting of six rating scales (the DVs) with a similar pretest used as the covariate. By doing so, she was able to reduce the preexisting differences among the various groups of participants from affecting the results of the posttests. The pretest was used as a measure of preexisting differences between groups that needed to be taken out before looking at the effects of the IVs on the posttest. Tsang followed correct procedures by first looking at the overall MANCOVA, finding it statistically significant, and then moving to more specific analyses to determine where the exact differences lie as outlined previously.

As with the other categories of statistics discussed earlier, there are a number of other multivariate procedures available. Because they are not commonly found in the research literature in applied linguistics, I have not included them here. However, when you do come across some type of statistical procedure that I have not touched on, remember that the same principles apply.

Degrees of Freedom

When you see various inferential statistics reported in Results sections, you might have wondered what the numbers in parentheses mean. For example, what does (3, 76) mean in the ANOVA results of $F(3, 76) = 20.64$, $p < .0001$? These are known as *degrees of freedom* (*df*), which you will see used along with various statistical results. I do not get into the thinking behind this here; but suffice it to say that in the case of the one-way ANOVA, they have to do with the number of *levels* of the *one* independent variable being tested (minus one) and the number of participants being used (minus the number of levels in the IV) in the analysis. In the prior example, there are four levels and 80 participants, therefore (3, 76). It has nothing to do with how many dependent variables there are. The *df*s are used by statisticians to determine whether the F ratio, or whatever statistic being used, is large enough to be statistically significant. If you want to know more about this, consult any elementary applied statistics text or enter the term *degrees of freedom* into your favorite Internet search engine along with the word *statistics*.

Exercise B.3

1. Find a study that looked for differences between groups, but that has more than one dependent variable.
2. Identify the independent and dependent variables.
3. What types of data are being used?

4. What is the null hypothesis being tested (explicit or implicit)?
5. What statistical procedure(s) is used (MANOVA, MANCOVA, etc.)?
6. What follow-up statistics are used?
7. Are the results statistically significant? At what level? What does this mean regarding making inferences?
8. Are the interpretations given by the researcher(s) consistent with the findings?

Type II Error and Power

Recall in chapter 7 that a Type II error is made when the null hypothesis is falsely accepted. That is, a study that fails to find a statistically significant relationship between variables or a difference between groups at the $p < .05$ may have made a mistake (i.e., a Type II error)—there is an actual relationship or difference in the population, but the study missed it. The probability of making this mistake is indicated by Beta (β) (cf. Fig. 7.2). However, the probability of not making a Type II error is $1 - \beta$, referred to as the *power* of the test. That is, the probability of correctly rejecting the null hypothesis increases. Obviously, a researcher wants to have the most power in trying to support his or her hypothesis—usually the opposite of the null hypothesis.

There are three things that affect the power of a statistical procedure. The first is the stringency of the probability of making a Type I error (i.e., the α level). The rule is the lower the α level, the greater the β and, thus, the lower the power $(1 - \beta)$. Enough of the Greek. In plain English, this means that as the probability of falsely rejecting the null hypothesis decreases (e.g., $p < .05$ to $p < .001$), the probability of falsely accepting it increases. Logically, this means that as the probability of falsely accepting the null hypothesis increases, the power of the test decreases (there is less chance of discovering a relationship or difference). In practice, this works out to mean that the researcher should choose the largest α level permissible to increase the chances of a statistically significant finding, although this increases the chance of making a Type I error. Remember, however, that $p = .05$ is as high as one can go for statistical significance.

The other two things that can influence ability of a statistical procedure to detect either a relationship or difference are *sample size* and *direction of the prediction*. Sample size is positively related to power. That is, as sample size increases, so does the power of the procedure and vice versa. Studies that do not find statistical significance and have small sample sizes have low power. Had there been a larger sample, the findings may have been different. Studies with large sample sizes may find statistical significance even with small correlations or small differences between groups of participants. For example, a correlation coefficient of 0.37 is not statistically significant for a study with a sample size of 15, but is for one that has 30 participants.

Direction of prediction is also a factor that can influence the statistical power of a procedure. Studies that test directional predictions have more power than those that do not. What is a directional prediction? If a researcher predicts that there will be a positive relationship between variables (or a negative one), s/he has made a directional hypothesis. Based on theory or previous research, s/he may state that as one variable increases so will the other (positive)—or as one increases the other decreases (negative). However, the researcher may not be able to make a prediction of a directional relationship, but only a prediction of a nondirectional relationship (e.g., one variable relates in some way to the other). If a directional relationship is predicted, then the power of finding this prediction statistically significant increases over one that has no direction in the prediction. The reason is that the critical value[2] of the correlation coefficient is lower for a directional prediction than for the nondirectional prediction. For example, for a study (sample size = 30) that predicts a positive relationship between two variables, any correlation equal to or greater than 0.31 is statistically significant. However, if there is a nondirectional prediction, the study must find a correlation equal to or greater than 0.36.

The same principle as this holds for differences between groups as well. A researcher may predict that the treatment group will do better than the control group (i.e., a directional hypothesis). S/he may only predict that there will be a difference without any direction. The former will have more power in predicting a significant difference than the latter—not because the former is a stronger prediction, but because the critical *t* test value used to test the difference between the means of the two groups does not have to be as great as that of the latter.

Connected to the direction of prediction issue earlier, there are two expressions that you will encounter: *one-tailed* versus *two-tailed* test of significance. Without going into probability theory, the following should be sufficient. If there is a directional hypothesis, you will see the term *one-tailed* test of significance. If there is no direction in the prediction or no prediction at all, you will occasionally find a *two-tailed* test. If there is no statement regarding *tails*, then assume that the procedures are using two-tailed tests. These two terms relate to the issue discussed previously about how the critical value is chosen for determining statistical significance. It is enough to know that the one-tailed test uses the lower critical value and the two-tailed test uses the higher critical value as illustrated before.

---

[2]The critical value is the value that determines whether it is statistically significant.

Effect Size

Increasingly, journals are requiring researchers to include *effect size* with their inferential statistics (e.g., *Language Learning*). As the term suggests, it is an estimate of the extent to which one group differs from another, one variable correlates with another, and so on. This statistic directly relates to the power of a statistical procedure and the practical application of the findings. It relates to power in that the greater the effect size, the greater the power of the statistical test. It relates to practical application in that the greater the effect size, the greater the implications for practical use.

There are a number of statistics used to indicate effect size. The reason is that for every type of statistical procedure used, there is a separate formula to compute effect size. In addition, there may be several ways to compute effect size depending on one's preference. For example, in their study of the relearning of SL vocabulary, Hansen, Umedo, and McKinney (2002) used squared point-biserial correlations (r^2_{pb}) to show the effect size of their t test findings (e.g., $t = 24.19$, $p < .001$, $r^2_{pb} = 0.862$). The r^2_{pb} of 0.862 indicated "a massive effect size" showing that forgotten words were much better learned than pseudowords. Later in the same study, Hansen et al. used another statistic η^2 to show effect size for a one-way ANOVA, which also provided evidence for strong differences.

MORE ON THE NULL HYPOTHESIS

The Logic of Testing the Null Hypothesis

Although a whole chapter[3] on the subject could be written, I try to keep this as brief as possible. Several logical arguments are presented next. Some are valid and some are not. Everything is based on the conditional sentence, *If the hypothesis is true, then the prediction will occur.* The hypothesis is the *antecedent*, and the prediction is the *consequent*.

An important thing to keep in mind is that there might be a number of competing (or alternative) hypotheses that could lead to the same prediction. For example, the hypothesis under investigation might be "Reading improves writing." Based on this, the researcher predicts "students who read more will write better." However, there are alternative hypotheses that could lead to the same prediction, such as "students who are highly motivated will read more and write better." This is why some research books refer to the hypothesis under investigation as the *alternative hypothesis* rather than the research hypothesis.

---

[3]See Giere (2004) for a complete discussion on this topic.

With this in mind, a *valid* argument is one whereby rejecting the consequent (i.e., the prediction failed to occur) leads to rejecting the antecedent (i.e., the hypothesis is refuted). Why is this valid? The reason is that when the prediction fails to happen, not only is the research hypothesis refuted, but all other alternative hypotheses as well, whether known or unknown. For example:

Argument I (valid)

1. *Hypothesis: Reading more improves writing.*
2. *Prediction: Students who read 10 books a month will write better than those who read 2 books a month.*
3. *My research study found that when I gave subjects more reading (10 books), their writing did not improve over those who read 2 books a month (i.e., the consequent was rejected).*
4. *Conclusion: More reading does not improve student writing (i.e., I reject the antecedent/hypothesis).*
5. *Why? Because nothing improved their writing, whether more reading or anything else in my study. This is a valid argument.*

However, an *invalid* argument occurs when, by accepting the consequent (i.e., the prediction occurred), the antecedent (i.e., the hypothesis is supported) is also accepted. For example:

Argument II (not valid)

1. *Hypothesis: Reading more improves writing.*
2. *Prediction: Students who read 10 books a month will write better than those who read 2 books a month.*
3. *My research study found that when I gave subjects more reading, their writing improved over those with less reading.*
4. *Conclusion: More reading improves writing (i.e., I support the antecedent/hypothesis).*
5. *Can I conclude, therefore, that more reading will improve student writing?*
6. *No! Why not? Because something else may have improved their writing other than more reading, such as motivation. For instance, the treatment group (10 books/month) may have been more motivated than the control group (2 books/month).*

Obviously, researchers want to find that their predictions occur to support their hypotheses. However, based on the prior invalid argument, they cannot use this approach. The way around this is to state the research hypothesis in the null form.

Argument III (valid)

1. *Null hypothesis: Reading more does not improve writing.*
2. *Null prediction: Students who read 10 books a month will not write better than those who read 2 books a month.*
3. *However, my research study found that the 10 book group performed better in writing than the 2 book group.*
4. *Therefore, I reject the null hypothesis (the consequent). (Note: A double negative makes a positive.)*
5. *Conclusion: Most probably more reading improves writing performance.*

Notice that I stated most probably. Why? Because some other alternative hypothesis might still be lurking in the background that better explains why writing performance really improves rather than more reading.

As a side note, if my study had found in Argument III that subjects with more reading did not improve in writing, #4 would have been stated differently; that is, *The results of the study failed to reject the null hypothesis.* This does not mean, however, that the null hypothesis is therefore true. To say so would be to make an invalid argument. Like it or not, this is the language that some researchers use in the Results section of a study.

In concluding this section, remember that when dealing with inferential statistics, we are always dealing with *probabilities, not absolute proof.* For this reason, I emphasize that research results *do not prove* anything; they only *support* our hypotheses. History is full of discarded hypotheses caused by new research findings. For this reason, a wise theoretician will present his or her theoretical hypothesis with some humility.

Key Terms and Concepts

univariate ANOVAs
    analysis of covariance (ANCOVA)
    between-subjects and within-subjects ANOVA
    repeated measures ANOVA
multivariate ANOVAs
    multivariate analysis of covariance (MANCOVA)
    multivariate analysis of variance (MANOVA)
Miscellaneous statistical terms:
central tendency
covariate
degrees of freedom (*df*)

effect size
nested variable
normal distribution
one-tailed versus two-tailed test of significance
Pillai's trace
positively or negatively skewed distributions
power
scales: nominal, ordinal, interval, and ratio
Wilks' lambda

Journals Related to Applied Linguistics

Journal/Organization/(Web Site)	*Purpose of Journal*
ACTFL Foreign Language & Education Series National Textbook Company in conjunction with the American Council on the Teaching of Foreign Languages (www.actfl.org)	A different topic is covered in each issue of the series.
Adult Education Quarterly; A Journal of Research and Theory in Adult Education American Association for Adult and Continuing Education (http://www.sagepub.co.uk/journal.aspx?pid=105466)	"... is a refereed journal committed to the dissemination of research and theory in adult and continuing education. Articles report research, build theory, interpret and review literature, and critique work previously published in the journal. Work primarily concerned with the techniques of practice is generally not within the scope of this journal."✤
Advances in Research on Teaching JAI Press Ltd.	[A different overall theme is covered each year in the series.]
American Speech; A Quarterly of Linguistic Usage Duke University Press (http://www.dukepress.edu/americanspeech)	Deals mainly with "English Language in the Western hemisphere also with English worldwide, other languages, general linguistic theory, current usage, dialectology, and the history and structure of English."

(Continued)

Journal/Organization/(Web Site)	*Purpose of Journal*
Annual Review of Applied Linguistics; An Official Journal of the American Association for Applied Linguistics Cambridge University Press (http://journals.cambridge.org/bin/ bladerunner?30REQEVENT=&REQAUTH =0&500002REQSUB=&REQSTR1=Annual ReviewofAppliedLinguistics)	". . . reviews research in key areas in the broad field of applied linguistics. Each issue is thematic, covering the topic by means of critical summaries, overviews and bibliographic citations. Every fourth or fifth issue surveys applied linguistics broadly, offering timely essays on language learning and pedagogy, discourse analysis, teaching innovations, second-language acquisition, computer-assisted instruction, language use in professional contexts, sociolinguistics, language policy, and language assessment, to name just a few of the areas reviewed. It provides over 500 new citations each year."
Anthropological Linguistics Indiana University (http://www.indiana.edu/~anthling/)	"Study of the languages and cultures of the people of the world, especially the native peoples of the Americas." "Cultural, historical and philological aspects of linguistic study."
Applied Linguistics Oxford University Press in cooperation with AAAL, AILA, and BAAL (http://www3.oup.co.uk/applij/)	"Promotion of principled approach to language education and other language-related concerns by encouraging inquiry into relationships between theoretical and practical studies."
Applied Psycholinguistics; Psychological Studies of Language Processes (until 2002) *Applied Psycholinguistics; Psychological Linguistic Studies across Languages and Learners* (from 2003) Cambridge University (http://journals.cambridge.org/bin/ bladerunner?30REQEVENT=& REQAUTH=0&500002REQSUB=& REQSTR1=AppliedPsycholinguistics)	"Psychological processes involved in language; and development, use, and impairment of language in all its modalities, including spoken, signed and written ones with a particular emphasis on cross linguistic studies."
Assessing Writing; An International Journal (http://authors.elsevier.com/ JournalDetail.html?PubID=620369& Precis=DESC)	". . . a refereed international journal providing a forum for ideas, research and practice on the assessment of written language. *Assessing Writing* publishes articles, book reviews, conference reports, and academic exchanges concerning writing assessments of all kinds, including traditional (direct and standardized forms of) testing of writing, alternative performance assessments (such as portfolios), workplace sampling and classroom assessment."

(Continued)

Journal/Organization/(Web Site)	*Purpose of Journal*
Babel Journal of the Australian Federation of Modern Language Teachers Association (http://www.afmlta.asn.au/afmlta/babel.htm)	". . . appears three times a year (in the southern Winter, Spring, and Summer) and publishes articles and reviews on the teaching and learning of languages other than English at primary, secondary, and tertiary levels."
Brain and Language Academic Press (http://www.sciencedirect.com/science/journal/0093934X)	"Concerned with human language or all sorts of communication and related to any aspect of the brain or brain function."
British Journal of Educational Psychology British Psychology Society (http://www.bps.org.uk/publications/jEP_6.cfm)	"Psychological research that makes a significant contribution to the understanding and practice of education."
British Journal of Language Teaching British Association for Language Teaching	"Promoting the cause of language teaching and enhancing the professional practice of those working in the language teaching field."
Calico Journal Computer Assisted Learning and Instruction Consortium (http://www.ritsumei.ac.jp/ec/~nozawa/CALICOJ.html)	"Application of high technology to the teaching and learning of languages."
Canadian Modern Language Review University of Toronto Press (http://www.utpjournals.com/jour.ihtml?lp=cmlrsplash.html)	"Second language teaching and learning."
College Composition and Communication CCC, Conference on College Composition and Communication, National Council of Teachers of English (http://www.ncte.org/store/journals/college/105392.htm)	"Research and theories from a broad range of humanistic disciplines and within composition studies, technical communication, computers and composition, writing across the curriculum, research practice, history of composition, assessment and writing center work."
Cognitive Linguistics Mouton de Gruyter (http://www.degruyter.de/rs/384_86_ENU_h.htm)	"A forum for linguistic research of all kinds on the interaction between language and cognition. Focus is on language as an instrument for organizing, processing, and conveying information. The journal is devoted to high-quality research."
Contemporary Educational Psychology Academic Press (http://www.sciencedirect.com/science/journal/0361476X)	"The application of psychological theory and science to the educational process; descriptions of empirical research and the presentation of theory designed to either explicate or enhance the educational process."

(Continued)

Journal/Organization/(Web Site)	*Purpose of Journal*
Discourse and Society (http://www.sagepub.co.uk/journal.aspx?pid=105519)	"An International Journal for the study of Discourse and Communication in their Social, Political, and Cultural Contexts."
Educational Technology Research and Development The Association for Educational Communications and Technology. (http://www.aect.org/Intranet/Publications/)	"The design and development of learning systems and educational technology applications."
ELR Journal; English Language Research Journal University of Birmingham, UK	[A different overall theme is covered each year in the series.]
ELT Journal; An International Journal for Teachers of English to Speakers of Other Languages Oxford University Press & IATEFL (http://www3.oup.co.uk/eltj/)	"Bridging the gap between the everyday practical concerns of SL/FL ELT professionals and related disciplines. . . . Principles and practice which determine the ways in which English language is taught and learned around the world."
English for Specific Purposes The American University (http://www.sciencedirect.com/science/journal/08894906)	"The majority of papers submitted to and published in *English for Specific Purposes* focus on writing rather than speech. These include papers reporting linguistic analysis and ones describing ESP programmes and teaching methods."
English Journal National Council of Teachers of English (http://www.ncte.org/pubs/journals/ej)	". . . a journal of ideas for English language arts teachers in junior and senior high schools and middle schools. EJ presents information on the teaching of writing and reading, literature, and language. Each issue examines the relationship of theory and research to classroom practice and reviews current materials of interest to English teachers, including books and electronic media."
English Teaching Forum (Forum) U.S. Information Agency (http://dosfan.lib.uic.edu/usia/E-USIA/education/engteaching/eal-foru.htm)	A journal for the teacher of English outside the United States.

(Continued)

Journal/Organization/(Web Site)	*Purpose of Journal*
English Today: The International Review of the English Language Cambridge University Press (http://titles.cambridge.org/journals/journal_catalogue.asp?historylinks=ALPHA&mnemonic=ENG)	". . . provides accessible cutting-edge reports on all aspects of the language, including style, usage, dictionaries, literary language, Plain English, the Internet and language teaching, in terms of British, American and the world's many other 'Englishes.' "
English World-Wide; A Journal of Varieties of English John Benjamins Publishing Co. (http://www.ingenta.com/journals/browse/jbp/eww)	"The focus is on scholarly discussions of new findings in the dialectology and sociolinguistics of the English-speaking communities (native and second-language speakers), but general problems of sociolinguistics, creolistics, language planning, multilingualism and modern historical sociolinguistics are included if they have a direct bearing on modern varieties of English."
Foreign Language Annals American Council on the Teaching of Foreign Languages (http://www.actfl.org/public/articles/index.cfm?cat=27)	"Dedicated to the advancement of foreign language teaching and learning, the journal seeks to serve the professional interests of classroom instructors, researchers, and administrators concerned with the teaching of foreign languages at all levels of instruction."
International Journal of American Linguists University of Chicago Press (http://www.journals.uchicago.edu/IJAL/journal)	"Studies all aspects of the native languages of the Americans: description, history, typology, and linguistic theory."
International Journal of Educational Research Elsevier Science (http://www.sciencedirect.com/science/journal/08830355)	"Investigation of educationally relevant theoretical propositions or conceptual frameworks, evaluation of educational programs, educational policy and practice integration of education with academic disciplines, and advanced research methods and procedures."
International Journal of the Sociology of Language Walter de Gruyter GmbH & Co (http://www.degruyter.de/rs/384_403_ENU_h.htm)	"Development of the sociology of language as an international and interdisciplinary field in which various approaches, theoretical and imperial, supplement and complement each other, contributing thereby to the growth of language-related knowledge, applications, values and sensitivities. . . . Each issue is devoted to a specific topic."

(Continued)

Journal/Organization/(Web Site)	*Purpose of Journal*
International Review of Applied Linguistics in Language Teaching (*IRAL*) Mouton de Gruyter (http://www.degruyter.de/rs/384_392_DEU_h.htm)	"The present editors wish to maintain IRAL's long-term interest in areas of research which concern first- and second-language acquisition (including sign language and gestural systems). . . . We therefore welcome contributions on naturalistic and instructed language learning, language loss, bilingualism, language contact, pidgins and creoles, language for specific purposes, language technology, mother-tongue education, lexicology, terminology and translation."
International Review of Education UNESCO Institute for Education (http://www.kluweronline.com/issn/0020-8566/contents)	Provision of "scholary information on policy issues, educational trends and learning innovation" and concerned with "education and learning throughout life."
Journal of Adolescent & Adult Literacy International Reading Association (http://www.reading.org/publications/jaal/)	". . . peer-reviewed literacy journal published *exclusively* for teachers of adolescents and adult learners. With each issue, *JAAL* gives you the practical solutions you need to overcome your toughest classroom challenges. Newly refocused and revitalized, *JAAL* offers authoritative, classroom-tested advice grounded in sound research and theory."
Journal of Basic Writing City University of New York (http://www.asu.edu/clas/english/composition/cbw/jbw.html)	". . . articles of theory, research, and teaching practices related to basic writing. Articles are refereed by members of the Editorial Board and the Editors."
Journal of Child Language Cambridge University Press (http://journals.cambridge.org/bin/bladerunner?30REQEVENT=&REQAUTH=0&500002REQSUB=&REQSTR1=JournalofChildLanguage)	"Principles and theories underlining the scientific study of language aspects in children."
Journal of Cross-Cultural Psychology Western Washington University (http://www.iaccp.org/JCCP/jccp.html)	"Papers on the inter-relationships between culture and psychological processes. The focus is on ways in which culture and related concepts, such as ethnicity affect thinking and behavior of individuals as well as how individual thought and behavior define and reflect aspects of culture."
Journal of Educational Psychology The American Psychological Association (http://www.apa.org/journals/edu.html)	Publish mainly "original, primary psychological research pertaining to education at all levels" and, second, "exceptionally important theoretical and review articles that are directly pertinent to educational psychology."

(Continued)

APPENDIX C
(Continued)

Journal/Organization/(Web Site)	Purpose of Journal
Journal of Experimental Psychology: Learning, Memory & Cognition American Psychological Association, Inc. (http://www.apa.org/journals/xlm.html)	"Original experimental studies on basic processes of cognition, learning, memory, imagery, concept formation, problem solving, decision making, thinking, reading and language processing."
Journal of Language and Social Psychology Sage Publications Inc. (http://www.ingenta.com/journals/browse/sage/j303)	Concerned with "a wide range of disciplines, including linguistics, cognitive science, sociology, communication, psychology, education, and anthropology."
Journal of Linguistics Cambridge University Press (http://journals.cambridge.org/bin/bladerunner?30REQEVENT=&REQAUTH=0&500002REQSUB=&REQSTR1=JournalofLinguistics)	"Promoting the study of linguistics, providing a forum for discussion, facilitating cooperation in furtherance of interest in linguistics based on original papers of special interests."
Journal of Memory and Language Elsevier Science (http://www.sciencedirect.com/science/journal/0749596X)	"Human memory and language processing."
Journal of Multilingual and Multicultural Development Multilingual Matters Ltd. (http://www.ingenta.com/journals/browse/jbp/eww)	Not mentioned
Journal of Phonetics Academic Press (http://www.sciencedirect.com/science/journal/00954470)	"Promotion of research in the field of phonetics, publishing papers dealing with phonetic aspects of language and linguistic communication processes."
Journal of Pidgin and Creole Languages John Benjamins Publication Co. (http://www.ingenta.com/journals/browse/jbp/jpcl)	"Special emphasis is laid on the presentation of the results of current research in theory and description of pidgin and creole languages, and application of this knowledge to language planning, education, and social reform in creole-speaking societies."
Journal of Pragmatics Elsevier Science (http://www.sciencedirect.com/science/journal/03782166)	"Study of linguistic practice and language as people's main instrument of 'natural' and 'social' interaction."
Journal of Psycholinguistics Research Plenum Publishing (http://www.kluweronline.com/issn/0090-6905)	"Approaches to the study of the communicative process, including: the social and anthropological basis of communication, development of speech and language, semantics and biological foundations; communication between linguists, psychologists, biologists, sociologists, and others."

(Continued)

Journal/Organization/(Web Site)	*Purpose of Journal*
Journal of the International Phonetic Association Cambridge University Press (http://journals.cambridge.org/bin/ bladerunner?30REQEVENT=&REQAUTH =0&500002REQSUB=&REQSTR1=Journal oftheInternationalPhoneticAssociation)	"All aspects of the theory, description, and use of phonetics and phonology."
Journal of Research in Reading Blackwell Publishers for the United Kingdom Reading Association (http://www.ingenta.com/journals/ browse/bpl/jrir)	". . . a refereed journal principally devoted to reports of original, empirical, or theoretical studies in reading and related fields, and to informed reviews of relevant literature. The *Journal* welcomes papers researching issues related to the learning, teaching, and use of literacy in a variety of contexts; papers on the history and development of literacy; and papers about policy and strategy for literacy as related to children and adults."
Language Journal of the Linguistic Society of America (http://www.lsadc.org/language/)	". . . scholarly articles that report on original research covering the field of linguistics broadly, thus treating topics that include, among others, linguistic theory (phonology, morphology, syntax, and semantics); language description; language in its social setting; the history of individual languages; language acquisition; experimentation on language perception, production, and processing; computational modeling of language; and the history of linguistics."
Language Acquisition: Journal of Developmental Linguistics Lawrence Erlbaum Associates, Inc. (http://www.leaonline.com/loi/ la?cookieSet=1)	"Experimental, linguistic, and computational approaches of language acquisition; the development of syntax, semantics, pragmatics, and phonology; and understanding of language growth."
Language and Cognitive Processes Psychology Press Ltd. (http://taddeo.ingentaselect.com/vl= 7234807/cl=18/nw=1/rpsv/cw/psych/ 01690965/contp1.htm)	Addresses mental processes and representations involved in language use.
Language and Communication Elsevier Science (http://www.sciencedirect.com/science/ journal/02715309)	"Integration of language and communicational activity and interactional behaviour; universal/global communication; and investigation of language and its communicational functions."

(Continued)

Journal/Organization/(Web Site)	*Purpose of Journal*
Language and Language Behavior Abstracts (http://www.csa.com/csa/factsheets/ llba.shtml)	Index of abstracts
Language and Speech Kingston Press Ltd. (http://www.ling.ed.ac.uk/~lgsp/)	". . . international forum for communication among researchers in the disciplines that contribute to our understanding of the production, perception, processing, learning, use, and disorders of speech and language."
Language, Culture and Curriculum (http://www.multilingual-matters.com/ multi/journals/journals_lcc.asp?TAG= BW1DPX6X397XX91X5TTL2D&CID=)	". . . a forum for the discussion of the many factors, social, cultural, cognitive and organisational, which are relevant to the formulation and implementation of language curricula. Second languages, minority and heritage languages are a special concern."
Language Forum	"An international journal of language, literature and linguistics."
Language in Society Cambridge University (http://journals.cambridge.org/bin/ bladerunner?30REQEVENT=&REQAUTH =0&500002REQSUB=&REQSTR1= LanguageinSociety)	"Study of speech and language as aspects of social life; preference for general theoretical or methodological interest; social and/or linguistics content predominance."
Language Learning: A Journal of Research in Language Studies University of Michigan (http://www.blackwellpublishing.com/ journal.asp?ref=0023-8333&site=1)	". . . dedicated to the understanding of language learning broadly defined. It publishes research articles that systematically apply methods of inquiry from disciplines including psychology, linguistics, cognitive science, educational inquiry, neuroscience, ethnography, sociolinguistics, sociology and semiotics. It is concerned with fundamental theoretical issues in language learning such as child, second and foreign language acquisition, language education, bilingualism, literacy, language representation in mind and brain, culture, cognition, pragmatics and intergroup relations."
Language Problems and Language Planning John Benjamins Publishing Co., in cooperation with the Center for Research and Documentation on World Language Problems (http://www.ingenta.com/journals/ browse/jbp/lplp)	"Global communication; political, sociological and economic aspects of language and language use; language policy, language management, language international use, and language interaction and conflict; and language communities interaction."

(Continued)

Journal/Organization/(Web Site)	*Purpose of Journal*
Language Teaching Abstracts	Index of abstracts
Language Teaching & Linguistics Abstracts	Index of abstracts
Language Testing Arnold (http://www.arnoldpublishers.com/ Journals/pages/lan_tes/onli.htm)	". . . a forum for the exchange of ideas and information between people working in the fields of first and second language testing and assessment. This includes researchers and practitioners in EFL and ESL testing, and assessment in child language acquisition and language pathology. In addition, special attention is focused on issues of testing theory, experimental investigations, and the following up of practical implications."
Language Variation and Change Cambridge University (http://titles.cambridge.org/journals/ journal_catalogue.asp?historylinks= ALPHA&mnemonic=LVC)	". . . the only journal dedicated exclusively to the study of linguistic variation and the capacity to deal with systematic and inherent variation in synchronic and diachronic linguistics."
Learning and Instruction The Journal of the European Association for Research on Learning and Instruction (http://www.sciencedirect.com/science/ journal/09594752)	"Research in the study of teaching, learning and cognitive development."
Lingua: International Review of General Linguistics Elsevier Science (http://www.sciencedirect.com/science/ journal/00243841)	"Problems of general linguistics."
Linguistic Abstracts	Index of abstracts
Linguistic Inquiry Massachusetts Institute of Technology (http://mitpress.mit.edu/catalog/item/ default.asp?tid=6&ttype=4)	". . . research on current topics in linguistic theory. In this journal, the world's most celebrated linguists keep themselves and other readers informed of new theoretical developments based on the latest international discoveries."
Linguistics and Philosophy A Journal of Natural Language Syntax, Semantics, Logic, Pragmatics & Processing Kluwer Academic Publishers (http://www.kluweronline.com/issn/ 0165-0157/contents)	"Natural language structure and meaning through philosophy of language, linguistics, semantics, syntax and related disciplines."
Linguistics and Language Behavior Abstracts (LLBA)	Index of abstracts

(Continued)

Journal/Organization/(Web Site)	*Purpose of Journal*
Mind & Language Blackwell Publishing (http://www.ingenta.com/journals/ browse/bpl/mila)	"The phenomena of mind and language are currently studied by researchers in linguistics, philosophy, psychology, artificial intelligence, and cognitive anthropology."
Modern English Teacher Oxford University Press (http://www.onlinemet.com/)	"Articles and reviews on language, classroom ideas, exam materials, and technology for teachers of English to speakers of other languages at all levels and ages."
Modern Language Journal National Federation of Modern Language Teachers Association (http://www.ingenta.com/journals/ browse/bpl/modl)	"Devoted primarily to methods, pedagogical research, and topics of professional interest to all language teachers."
Modern Language Quarterly (*MLQ*) Duke University Press (http://thesius.ingentaselect.com/ vl=3041748/cl=33/nw=1/rpsv/cw/dup/ 00267929/contp1.htm)	"The focus of *MLQ* is on change, both in literary practice and within the profession of literature itself. *MLQ* is open to papers on literary change from the Middle Ages to the present and welcomes theoretical reflections on the relationship of literary change or historicism to feminism, ethnic studies, cultural materialism, discourse analysis, and all other forms of representation and cultural critique."
Modern Language Review Official Quarterly Journal of the Modern Humanities Research Association (http://www.ingenta.com/isis/browsing/ AllIssues/ingenta?journal=pubinfobike:// mhra/mlr)	"Modern and medieval languages and literatures."
Monograph Series on Language and Linguistics Georgetown University Press (http://www.blackwellpublishing.com/ journal.asp?ref=0023-8333&site=1)	"It publishes research articles that systematically apply methods of inquiry from disciplines including psychology, linguistics, cognitive science, educational inquiry, neuroscience, ethnography, sociolinguistics, sociology and semiotics. It is concerned with fundamental theoretical issues in language learning such as child, second and foreign language acquisition, language education, bilingualism, literacy, language representation in mind and brain, culture, cognition, pragmatics and intergroup relations."
Natural Language & Linguistic Theory Kluwer Academic Publishers (http://www.kluweronline.com/issn/ 0167-806X/contents)	"Theoretical research—natural language data. . . . Bridges gap between descriptive work and work of a theoretical, less empirically oriented nature."

(Continued)

Journal/Organization/(Web Site)	*Purpose of Journal*
Reading and Writing Kluwer Academic Publishers (http://www.kluweronline.com/issn/ 0922-4777/contents)	"The interaction among various fields, such as linguistics, information processing, neuropsychology, cognitive psychology, speech and hearing science and education pertaining to the processes, acquisition and the loss of reading and writing skills."
Reading in a Foreign Language *Journal of International Education Centre,* *College of St. Mark* St. John, Plymouth, England (http://nflrc.hawaii.edu/rfl/)	"Practice and theory of learning to read and teaching reading in any foreign or second language; and positive and practical improvements of FL reading standards."
Reading Research Quarterly International Reading Association (http://www.ingenta.com/isis/browsing/ AllIssues/ingenta?journal=pubinfobike:// ira/rrq)	"Exchange of information and opinion on theory, research, and practice in reading."
Reading Teacher: A Journal of the International Reading Association (http://www.reading.org/publications/ rt/)	"A peer-reviewed, professional journal published eight times yearly, RT gives thoughtful consideration to practices, research, and trends in literacy education and related fields."
Research in the Teaching of English National Council of Teachers of English (http://www.ncte.org/pubs/journals/rte)	". . . a multidisciplinary journal composed of original research and scholarly essays on the relationships between language teaching and learning at all levels, preschool through adult."
Research on Language and Social Interaction Lawrence Erlbaum Associates, Inc. (http://www.leaonline.com/loi/rlsi)	". . . a journal devoted to research on naturally occurring social interaction. Published papers will ordinarily involve the analysis of audio or video recordings of social activities."
Second Language Research Arnold Journals (http://www.ingenta.com/journals/ browse/arn/slr)	". . . publishes theoretical and experimental papers concerned with second language acquisition and second language performance."
Semiotica International Association for Semiotic (http://www.degruyter.de/rs/384_409_ DEU_h.htm)	". . . features articles reporting results of research in all branches of semiotic studies, in-depth reviews of selected current literature in this field, and occasional guest editorials and reports. From time to time, Special Issues, devoted to topics of particular interest, are assembled by Guest Editors."

(Continued)

Journal/Organization/(Web Site)	*Purpose of Journal*
Studies in Language International Journal sponsored by the Foundation "Foundations of Language" (http://www.benjamins.nl/cgi-bin/ t_seriesview.cgi?series=SL)	". . . a forum for the discussion of issues in contemporary linguistics from discourse-pragmatic, functional, and typological perspectives. Areas of central concern are: discourse grammar; syntactic, morphological and semantic universals; pragmatics; grammaticalization and grammaticalization theory; and the description of problems in individual languages from a discourse-pragmatic, functional, and typological perspective."
Studies in Second Language Acquisition Cambridge Press (http://journals.cambridge.org/bin/ bladerunner?30REQEVENT=&REQAUTH =0&500002REQSUB=&REQSTR1=Studies inSecondLanguageAcquisition)	". . . a refereed journal devoted to the scientific discussion of issues in second and foreign language acquisition of any language. Each volume contains four issues, one of which is generally devoted to a current topic in the field. The other three issues contain articles dealing with theoretical topics, some of which have broad pedagogical implications, and reports of quantitative and qualitative empirical research. Other articles include replication studies, State-of-the-Art articles, responses, book reviews, and book notices."
Studies in Linguistics Southern Methodist University	"All fields of linguistics as an anthropological discipline."
System: An International Journal of Educational Technology and Applied Linguistics Elsevier	"Applications of educational technology and of applied linguistics to all languages and to problems of foreign language teaching and learning."
Southern African Linguistics and Applied Language Studies (*AJOL*) (www.inasp.info/ajol/journals)	". . . publishes articles on a wide range of linguistic topics and acts as a forum for research into ALL the languages of southern Africa, including English and Afrikaans. Original contributions are welcomed on any of the core areas of Linguistics, both theoretical (e.g., syntax, phonology, sematics) and applied (e.g., sociolinguistic topics, language teaching, language policy)."
TESL Canada Journal TESL Canada Federation (http://www.tesl.ca/journal.html)	"Diverse aspects of the teaching and learning of ESL/EFL/ SESD/ FSL including syllabus and curriculum design, testing and evaluation, psycholinguistics, applied linguistics, teacher training, methodology and computerized language learning."

(Continued)

Journal/Organization/(Web Site)	*Purpose of Journal*
(*The Internet*) *TESOL Journal* Teachers of English to Speakers of Other Languages, Inc. (http://iteslj.org/)	"Matters relating to ESL/EFL methodology and technique, materials, curriculum de- sign and development, teacher educa- tion, program administration, and class- room observation and research."
TESOL Quarterly Teachers of English to Speakers of Other Languages, Inc. (http://www.ingenta.com/journals/ browse/tesol/tq)	". . . a refereed professional journal, fosters inquiry into English language teaching and learning by providing a forum for TESOL professionals to share their re- search findings and explore ideas and relationships in the field."
The Linguistic Review Mouton de Gruyter (http://www.degruyter.de/rs/384_406_ ENU_h.htm)	"Syntax, semantics, phonology and mor- phology within the framework of Genera- tive Grammar and related disciplines, as well as critical discussions of theoretical linguistics as a branch of cognitive psy- chology."
TEXT: An Interdisciplinary Journal for the *Study of Discourse* Mouton de Gruyter (http://www.degruyter.com/rs/384_410 ENU_h.htm)	". . . forum for interdisciplinary research on all aspects of discourse (e.g., the situa- tional and historical nature of text pro- duction, the cognitive and sociocultural processes of language practice, partici- pant-based structures of negotiation and linguistic selection)."
Word The International Linguistic Association (http://www.ilaword.org/ilaword.html)	"The structure, function or historical devel- opment of natural languages and related theoretical questions."
World Englishes Blackwell Publishing Ltd. (http://www.ingenta.com/journals/ browse/bpl/weng)	". . . committed to the study of varieties of English in their distinctive cultural, sociolinguistic and educational contexts. It is integrative in its scope and includes theoretical and applied studies on lan- guage, literature and English teaching, with emphasis on cross-cultural perspec- tives and identities."

Note. All Web sites were accessed August 9, 2004.

♣ Text in quotations was taken from the journal or the respective Web site.

Glossary

Accumulative treatment effect: The result of the accumulative effect due to the particular order in which treatments are presented. Also known as the multiple-treatment interference or order effect.

Alternate-form reliability: The degree to which different forms of a test measure the same general attribute.

Analysis of covariance (ANCOVA): A parametric statistical procedure that removes differences among groups prior to treatment.

Analysis of variance (ANOVA): An inferential statistic used to compare the differences among three or more sets of data.

Applied linguistics: A discipline that focuses on practical issues involving the learning and teaching of foreign/second languages.

Applied research: Research that is directly applicable to practical problems in teaching and learning.

Automatic response: Occurs when a respondent selects only one choice throughout the questionnaire without thinking.

Average: A measure that best represents the central core in a distribution of data (i.e., mean, median, mode).

Basic research: Research dealing mainly with highly abstract constructs and theory that has little apparent practical use.

Case: One participant or record in a data set.

Case study: An in-depth study of an example(s) that represents a phenomenon in its natural setting.

Causal-comparative design: Characterized by variation in the independent variable found in nature rather than a result of experimenter manipulations, thus making the findings suggestive of cause/effect at most.

Central tendency: The term used by statisticians for average.

Chi-square: An inferential statistical procedure for comparing observed frequencies with expected frequencies.

Closed-form questionnaire: These items provide a set of alternative answers from which the respondent must select at least one.

Coefficient: A number that represents the amount of some attribute, such as a correlation coefficient.

Compensatory equalization of treatments: Occurs when attempts are made to give the control group extra material or special treatment to make up for not receiving the experimental treatment.

Confirmatory research: A study that is designed to test an explicitly stated hypothesis.

Construct: A concept that a given discipline (e.g., applied linguistics) has constructed to identify some quality that is thought to exist (i.e., language proficiency).

Construct validity: The global concept that encompasses all the facets of validity.

Constructed response items: Test items that require participants to recall and integrate information, such as a test of writing ability where they must compose an essay.

Content coverage: The facet of validity that indicates how well the content of the measurement procedure aligns with the treatment objectives.

Control group contamination: A result of anything that might cause the control group to behave differently than normal.

Convenience sampling: Using participants who are chosen because they are conveniently available for use in a study.

Conversational analysis: A research technique that analyzes verbal output from a totally inductive perspective without any prior knowledge about the context of the participants. Resulting verbal data are seldom coded or transformed into numerical data.

Correlational study: One that investigates relationships between variables.

Covariate: An unwanted variable that is controlled by statistical procedures.

Criterion-referenced tests: Interpretation of the results of such tests is based on one or more criteria for deciding the status of examinees.

Criterion related: The facet of validity that indicates how well a measurement procedure corresponds to some external criterion, such as predicting the capacity to succeed or identifying current characteristics.

Cronbach alpha: An estimate of the reliability of a Likert-type questionnaire (i.e., degree of internal consistency of the items).

Degrees of freedom (*df*): Numbers used to identify the criterion to determine statistical significance—usually associated with number of groups and sample size.

Demoralization (boycott): This potential contaminator occurs when participants in the control group resent the special treatment given to the treatment group and lower their performance.

Dependent *t* tests: An inferential statistic that assesses the difference between the means of two sets of scores for either the same group of participants or two groups whose participants have been matched (also called correlated *t* test or paired *t* test).

Dependent variable: The variable that is analyzed for change as a result of change in another variable (i.e., the independent variable).

Descriptive statistics: Estimates of parameters that describe a population such as means and standard deviations.

Differential selection: The selection procedure results in groups of participants who possess preexisting differences that may affect the variable being investigated.

Discrete-point item: This test item measures only one thing and is scored correct or incorrect.

Effect size: An estimate of the extent to which one group differs from another, one variable correlates with another, and so on. Used for determining practical significance.

Ethnography: A procedure whereby data are gathered from a number of sources in a natural setting, resulting in large quantities of verbal data.

Experimental design: A research design that involves manipulating the independent variable(s) and observing the change in the dependent variable(s) on a randomly chosen sample.

Experimental treatment diffusion (compromise): Occurs when the control group gains knowledge of the factor(s) making up the treatment condition(s) and employs this factor(s) in its own situation, which distorts the results.

Experimentally accessible population: A population that is a subset of a larger population, but more accessible for obtaining a sample.

Exploratory research: A study that seeks to answer research questions without testing any hypothesis.

External validity: The degree to which the findings of a study can be generalized to a target population.

Extraneous variable: A variable that can adversely affect the dependent variable other than the independent variable(s).

F ratio: A value used to indicate statistical significance of differences between groups of data in such inferential statistics such as ANOVA.

Face appearance: The facet of validity that indicates the degree to which a measurement procedure appears to measure what it is supposed to measure.

Friedman test: A nonparametric procedure for testing the differences among three or more sets of data gathered on the same people.

Full-participant observer: An observer who is or becomes a full member of the group being observed.

Grounded theory: A theoretical hypothesis that develops as the data accumulate in a study.

Halo effect: The biasing effect of judging the work of one participant on the work of a following participant.

Hawthorne effect: Occurs when participants behave unnaturally because they know they are in a research study.

Highly structured interview: One that follows a predetermined set of questions with no allowances for variation.

History: Effects due to the influence of events that take place at different points in time on the dependent variable other than the independent variable.

Homogeneity of variance: The degree to which the variances of different groups of data are similar.

Hypothesis: A theoretical statement that proposes how several constructs relate to one another.

Independent t test: An inferential statistic that analyzes the difference between the averages (i.e., means) on one dependent variable for two independent groups of data.

Independent variable: The principal variable(s) being investigated regarding its influence on some dependent variable.

Inferential statistics: Statistics used to make inferences from samples to populations.

Informant: A person from the group being observed who gives verbal information to the researcher.

Information-rich paradigm: A sampling strategy for selecting the best participants for providing the information needed for a particular study.

Instrumental procedures: Procedures that use some form of impersonal instrument for obtaining research data.

Internal consistency: The degree to which all the items in an instrument measure the same general attribute.

Internal validity: The degree to which the results of the study are due to the independent variable(s) under consideration and not due to anything else.

Interrater reliability: The degree to which different observers/raters agree in their observations/ratings of the behavior of participants.

Interval scale: The values represent equal amounts of the variable being measured, but has a relative zero such as temperature on a thermometer.

Intrarater reliability: The degree to which observers/raters give the same results given the opportunity to observe/rate participants on more than one occasion.

Introspection: A procedure that requires participants to observe their own internal cognitive (or emotional) states and/or processing strategies during an ongoing task such as reading.

Item quality: The degree to which an item in a test or questionnaire is understood by the respondents due to the manner in which it is written.

John Henry effect: Occurs when the difference between the control group and the treatment group is due to competition rather than the treatment.

Kruskal–Wallis test: A nonparametric statistical procedure that analyzes the differences between three or more independent groups of participants.

Kuder–Richardson 20 & 21: Two related formulas for calculating the reliability for tests consisting of items that are scored dichotomously (i.e., correct/incorrect, true/false, yes/no, etc.).

Longitudinal study: A study designed to collect data over a period of time.

Mann–Whitney U test: A nonparametric statistical procedure used to analyze the difference between two independent groups of participants.

Maturation: Effects due to natural changes in the participants that take place over time other than due to the variables being studied.

Mean: The most common index of average: the sum of all the scores divided by the number of scores.

Measurement–treatment interaction: Occurs when the results are only found when using a particular type of measuring procedure.

Median: A measure of average: the point that divides the number of scores in half.

Mode: The least used index of average: the most frequent score.

Moderating variable: A variable that moderates the effect(s) of the independent variable on the dependent variable.

Multiple analysis of covariance (MANCOVA): ANCOVA with more than one dependent variable.

Multiple regression: An inferential statistical procedure used to determine which combination of independent variables best predicts or explains the variation in one dependent variable.

Multivariate analysis of variance (MANOVA): ANOVA with more than one dependent variable—all at the same time.

Multivariate statistics: Procedures that analyze more than one dependent variable at the same time.

Multiway ANOVAs: ANOVA procedures with more than two independent variables.

Negatively skewed distribution: Data that are lopsided to the right side.

Nested variable: One where the levels are within the participants rather than between them, such as a repeated measurement on the same subjects.

Nominal scale: One where the values of a variable represent categories, such as 1 = male and 2 = female. Other than identifiers, they have no quantitative value.

Nonparametric statistics: Inferential statistical procedures used for analyzing data in the form of frequencies, ranked data, and other data that do not meet the assumptions for parametric procedures.

Nonparticipant observer: One who does not personally interact with the participants in any manner while making observations.

Nonproportional stratified random sample: A sample of equal numbers of participants randomly sampled from each stratum in the target population.

Normal distribution: A symmetrical, bell-shaped distribution of data that has specific properties and is used as a reference point for comparing the shapes of data distributions.

Norm-referenced test: One where scores are interpreted by comparing them with scores from a body of people who represent the population.

Null hypothesis: One which states that there is no true relationship between variables in a population.

Objectivity: The degree to which the data are not influenced by bias due to attitude, temporary emotional states, and so on of the data collector.

Objects: Inanimate sources of data, such as a corpus of text.

Observational procedure: Any procedure that captures data through visual observation.

Observational variable: A variable that consists of data in the form of observations and descriptions.

One-tailed test of statistical significance: A method for testing statistical significance that is based on one end of the probability distribution. It is used for testing directional hypotheses.

One-way ANOVA: The simplest form of ANOVA involving the use of one independent variable and one dependent variable.

Open-form questionnaire items: Questions that allow respondents to give their own answers without restrictions.

Open-structured interview: One that follows a general plan, but is not restricted to predetermined questions.

Operational definition: One that defines a construct in terms of observable behavior.

Ordinal scale: One where the values represent some type of rank order, such as 1st, 2nd, 3rd, and so on. It represents relative amounts of a variable (e.g., small, large, largest).

Pair-wise comparisons: Procedures that compare the differences between groups of data, two at a time.

Parameters: Measurements on an entire population.

Parametric statistical procedures: Inferential procedures used on data that meet the assumptions of normalcy of distribution and homogeneity of variance.

Partial-participant observer: One who has developed a personal relationship with the group being observed, but is not a full member of the group.

Participant observer: One who has a personal relationship with those being observed by being a member of the group.

Participants: People from whom data are gathered—synonymous with *subjects*.

Pearson product–moment correlation: A parametric statistical procedure that measures the linear relationship between two sets of data, also known as the Pearson r or simply r.

Position paper: A document in which a writer argues his or her particular viewpoint or position on some issues without doing a research study for support.

Positively skewed distribution: A data distribution lopsided to the left side.

Power: The probability of not making a Type II error.

Predictive utility: The aspect of the criterion-related facet of validity that indicates how well an instrument predicts performance.

Preliminary sources: Publications designed to reference and catalogue documents in various disciplines. These are extremely useful for locating primary research.

Pretest effect: Occurs when a test given before the administration of the treatment interacts with the treatment by heightening participants' awareness of importance of certain material.

Primary research: Research performed and reported firsthand by the researcher(s).

Proportional stratified random sampling: A technique that randomly selects cases that represent the proportion of each stratum of the population.

Purposeful sampling: A technique that selects samples based on how information-rich they are for addressing the research question.

Pygmalion effect: A type of researcher effect caused by the bias in the researcher's perception of the behavior of the participants due to preexisting expectations of the participants' performance.

Qualitative research: Research that is done in a natural setting, involving intensive holistic data collection through observation at a very close personal level without the influence of prior theory and contains mostly verbal analysis.

Quantitative research: Any study using numerical data with an emphasis on statistics to answer the research questions.

Quasi-experimental design: One that looks at the effects of independent variables on dependent variables, similar to experimental designs, only the samples are not randomly chosen.

Range: A measure of how much data vary based on the distance from the lowest to the highest scores in the distribution.

Ratio scale: One where the values represent equal amounts of the variable being measured and has a real zero, such as response time.

Regression analysis: A parametric procedure used to identify variables (i.e., independent variables) that either predict or explain another variable (i.e., the dependent variable).

Reliability: The degree to which a data-gathering procedure produces consistent results.

Reliability coefficient: A correlation coefficient that indicates the reliability of a data-gathering procedure.

Replication of research: The repetition of a study typically using a different sample.

Representative sampling paradigm: A strategy for obtaining a sample that represents a target population.

Researcher effect: Occurs when data are distorted by some characteristic of the researcher either in administering the treatment or collecting the data.

Retrospection: A technique that requires participants to wait until after the task before reflecting on what they had done cognitively.

Rubric: A detailed definition of each level of a rating scale.

Sample: A portion of a larger population.

Secondary sources: These summarize other people's research rather than provide firsthand reports by the original researchers.

Semi-interquartile range: An estimate of where the middle 50% of the scores are located in the data distribution—half the distance between the first quartile and the third quartile of the frequency of scores.

Semistructured interview: One that has a set of predetermined questions, but the interviewer is free to follow up a question with additional questions that probe further.

Simple random sampling: Occurs when everyone in the population has an equal chance of being chosen for the sample.

Skewed distribution: One that is lopsided—more scores on one side of the distribution than the other.

Spearman rank-order correlation (rho): A nonparametric correlation that indicates the relationship between sets of data are in the form of ranked data.

Spearman–Brown prophecy formula: A method for estimating the reliability of a test if the number of test items increases.

Split-half (odd/even) reliability: A measure of the internal consistency of a test by correlating one half of the test with the other, usually the odd items with the even ones.

Standard error of measurement (SEM): An estimate of the average amount of error made by a measurement instrument.

Standardized test: A test designed to be given under strict guidelines for administration and scoring across each occasion.

Statistical regression: An effect where the difference between scores on the pretest and posttest is due to the natural tendency for initial extreme scores to move toward the average on subsequent testing.

Statistical significance: Determined when the chances of making a Type I error are equal to or less than 5%.

Stratified random sample: One where a random sample is chosen from each stratum in a population.

Subject attrition (also experimental mortality): Occurs when there is a loss of participants during a research study.

Subjectivity: The degree to which the data are influenced by bias due to attitude, temporary emotional states, and so on of the data collector.

Subjects: People from whom data are gathered (synonymous with *participants*).

Target population: All the members of a group of people/objects to whom the researcher wants to generalize his or her research findings.

Test–retest reliability: An estimate of the stability of measurement results for the same instrument repeated over time.

Theory: An explanation attempting to interrelate large sets of observed phenomena or constructs into a meaningful holistic framework.

Think-aloud technique: A procedure where participants are required to talk about what they are thinking. Usually they are audiorecorded while talking.

Time of measurement: Occurs when the results of a study are not stable over different times of measurement.

Trait accuracy: The facet of validity that indicates how accurately a procedure measures the trait (i.e., construct) under investigation.

Transferability: The extent to which the findings of a study can be transferred to other similar situations.

Treatment fidelity: The degree to which a treatment is correctly administered.

Treatment intervention: Occurs when the results of a study are distorted due to the novelty or disruption of a treatment.

Treatment strength–time interaction: Occurs when the time needed for the treatment to have any noticeable effect is not sufficient.

Triangulation: A procedure using multiple sources of data to see whether they converge to provide evidence for validating interpretations of results.

Two-tailed test of statistical significance: A method for testing statistical significance that is based on both ends of the probability distribution. It is used for testing nondirectional hypotheses.

Type I error: Occurs when the null hypothesis is rejected in a sample while it is true in the population.

Type II error: Occurs when the null hypothesis is not rejected in a sample while it is false in the population.

Utility: The facet of validity that is concerned with whether measurement/observational procedures are used for the correct purpose.

Validity: The degree to which a measurement/observational procedure accurately captures data and is used correctly.

Volunteers: Participants who have been solicited and have agreed to participate in a study.

Wilcoxon matched-pairs signed rank test (or the Wilcoxon T test): A nonparametric procedure for analyzing the difference between two sets of data that are related in some fashion.

Wilks' lambda: A statistic used in multivariate statistical procedures for indicating overall statistical significance.

References

Agresti, A. (1996). *An introduction to categorical data analysis*. New York: Wiley.

Akamatsu, N. (2002). A similarity in word-recognition procedures among second language readers with different first language backgrounds. *Applied Psycholinguistics, 23*, 117–133.

Al-Khatib, M. A. (2001). The pragmatics of letter-writing. *World Englishes, 20*, 179–200.

Al-Seghayer, K. (2001). The effect of multimedia annotation modes on L2 vocabulary acquisition: A comparative study. *Language Learning & Technology, 5*, 202–232.

American Educational Research Association. (2000, April/May). Scientific conduct and human subjects: Guidelines affect educational researchers and universities. *Education, Research & Politics Archives: Research Policy News*. Retrieved December 14, 2001, from http://aera.net/gov/archive/n0400%2D08.htm.

Arriaga, R. I., Fenson, L., Cronan, T., & Pethick, S. J. (1998). Scores on the MacArthur Communicative Development Inventory of children from low and middle income families. *Applied Psycholinguistics, 19*, 209–223.

Arva, V., & Medgyes, P. (2000). Native and non-native teachers in the classroom. *System, 28*, 355–372.

Atkinson, D., & Ramanathan, V. (1995). Cultures of writing: An ethnographic comparison of L1 and L2 university writing/language programs. *TESOL Quarterly, 29*, 539–576.

Azpillaga, B., Arzamendi, J., Etxeberria, F., Garagorri, X., Lindsay, D., & Joaristi, L. (2001). Preliminary findings of a format-based foreign language teaching method for school children in the Basque Country. *Applied Psycholinguistics, 22*, 35–44.

Bachman, L. F. (1990). *Fundamental considerations in language testing*. New York: Oxford University Press.

Bachman, L. F., & Cohen, A. D. (1998). Language testing—SLA interfaces: An update. In L. F. Bachman & A. D. Cohen (Eds.), *Interfaces between second language acquisition and language testing research* (pp. 1–31). Cambridge: Cambridge University Press.

Bachman, L. F., & Palmer, A. S. (1996). *Language testing in practice: Designing and developing useful language tests*. Oxford: Oxford University Press.

Bailey, K. (1998). *Learning about language assessment: Dilemmas, decisions, and directions*. Boston, MA: Heinle & Heinle.

Baker, S. C., & MacIntyre, P. D. (2000). The role of gender and immersion in communication and second language orientations. *Language Learning, 50,* 311–342.

Bejarano, Y., Levine, T., Olshtain, E., & Steiner, J. (1997). The skilled use of interaction strategies: Creating a framework for improved small-group communicative interaction in the language classroom. *System, 25,* 203–214.

Bogden, R. C., & Biklen, S. K. (1992). *Qualitative research for education: An introduction to theory and methods.* Boston: Allyn & Bacon.

Borg, S. (1998). Teachers' pedagogical systems and grammar teaching: A qualitative study. *TESOL Quarterly, 32,* 9–38.

Bracht, G. H., & Glass, G. V. (1998). The external validity of experiments. *American Educational Research Journal, 5,* 437–474.

Brown, J. D. (1988). *Understanding research in second language learning.* Cambridge, England: Cambridge University Press.

Brown, J. D. (2001). *Using surveys in language programs.* Cambridge, England: Cambridge University Press.

Buckwalter, P. (2001). Repair sequences in Spanish L2 dyadic discourse: A descriptive study. *The Modern Language Journal, 85,* 380–397.

Byrnes, D. A., Kieger, G., & Manning, M. L. (1997). Teachers' attitude about language diversity. *Teaching and Teacher Education, 13,* 637–644.

Campbell, D. T., & Stanley, J. C. (1963). *Experimental and quasi-experimental designs for research.* Chicago: Rand McNally.

Camiciottoli, B. C. (2001). Extensive reading in English: Habits and attitudes of a group of Italian university EFL students. *Journal of Research in Reading, 24,* 135–153.

Canale, M., & Swain, M. (1980). Theoretical bases of communicative approaches to second language teaching and testing. *Applied Linguistics, 8,* 67–84.

Carrell, P. L., & Wise, T. E. (1998). The relationship between prior knowledge and topic interest in the second language reading. *SSLA, 20,* 285–309.

Carrier, K. (1999). The social environment of second language listening: Does status play a role in comprehension. *The Modern Language Journal, 83,* 65–79.

Carroll, J. B., & Sapon, S. M. (1959). *Modern Language Aptitude Test and Manual (MLAT).* San Antonio, TX: The Psychological Corporation.

Certificate in Advanced English. (1995). University of Cambridge, Local Examinations Syndicate, Cambridge, UK.

Chamot, A. U., & El-Dinary, P. B. (1999). Children's learning strategies in language immersion classrooms. *The Modern Language Journal, 83,* 319–338.

Chomsky, N. (2000). *New horizons in the study of language and mind.* New York: Cambridge University Press.

Clapham, C. (2000). Assessment for academic purposes: Where next? *System, 28,* 511–521.

Clark, M. M., & Plante, E. (1998). Morphology of the inferior Frontal Gyrus in developmental language-disorder adults. *Brain and Language, 61,* 288–303.

Clarke, M. A. (1980). The short-circuit hypothesis of ESL reading or when language competence interferes with reading performance. *Modern Language Journal, 64,* 203–209.

Cook, T. D., & Campbell, D. T. (1979). *Quasi-experimental: Design and analysis issues for field settings.* Chicago: Rand McNally.

Cooper, H. M. (1998). *Synthesizing research: A guide for literature reviews* (3rd ed.). Thousand Oaks, CA: Sage.

Creswell, J. W. (1998). *Qualitative inquiry and research design: Choosing among five traditions.* Thousand Oaks, CA: Sage.

Creswell, J. W. (2002). *Research design: Qualitative, quantitative, and mixed methods approaches.* Thousand Oaks, CA: Sage.

Cunningham, D. J., Snowman, J., Miller, R. B., & Perry, F. L. (1982). Verbal and nonverbal adjunct aids to concrete and abstract prose memory. *Journal of Experimental Education, 51,* 8–13.

de Beaugrande, R. (2001). Interpreting the discourse of H. G. Widdowson: A corpus-based critical discourse analysis. *Applied Linguistics, 22,* 104–121.

de Groot, A. M. B., & Poot, R. (1997). Word translation at three levels of proficiency in a second language: The ubiquitous involvement of conceptual memory. *Language Learning, 47,* 215–264.

Dehaene-Lambertz, G., & Houston, D. (1997). Faster orientation latencies toward native language in two-month-old infants. *Language and Speech, 41,* 21–43.

Demirci, M. (2000). The role of pragmatics in reflexive interpretation by Turkish learners of English. *Second Language Research, 16,* 325–353.

Denzin, N. K., & Lincoln, Y. S. (Eds.). (2000). *Handbook of qualitative research* (2nd ed.). Thousand Oaks, CA: Sage.

Ehrman, M. E., & Oxford, R. L. (1995). Cognition plus: Correlates of language learning success. *The Modern Language Journal, 79,* 67–89.

Ellis, R. (2002). Does form-focused instruction affect the acquisition of implicit knowledge? *SSLA, 24,* 223–236.

Ericsson, K. A., & Simon, H. (1993). *Protocol analysis: Verbal reports as data* (2nd ed.). Cambridge, MA: MIT Press.

Ferris, D., & Tagg, T. (1996). Academic oral communication needs of EAP learners: What subject-matter instructors actually require. *TESOL Quarterly, 30,* 31–59.

Ferris, D. R. (1995). Student reactions to teacher response in multiple-draft composition classrooms. *TESOL Quarterly, 29,* 33–53.

Fukushima, T. (2002). Promotional video production in a foreign language course. *Foreign Language Annals, 35,* 349–355.

Gall, M. D., Borg, W. R., & Gall, J. P. (1996). *Educational research: An introduction* (6th ed.). White Plains, NY: Longman.

Gall, M. D., Borg, W. R., & Gall, J. P. (2002). *Educational research: An introduction* (7th ed.). Upper Saddle River, NJ: Pearson Education.

Ganschow, L., & Sparks, R. (1996). Anxiety about foreign language learning among high school women. *The Modern Language Journal, 80,* 199–212.

Garcia, P., & Asencion, Y. (2001). Interlanguage development of Spanish learners: Comprehension, production, and interaction. *The Canadian Modern Language Review, 57,* 377–401.

Gardner, R. C., Tremblay, P. F., & Masgoret, A. (1997). Towards a full model of second language learning: An empirical investigation. *The Modern Language Journal, 81,* 344–362.

Giere, R. N. (2004). *Understanding scientific reasoning.* Graton, CA: Wadsworth.

Goh, C. C. M. (2002). Exploring listening comprehension tactics and their interaction patterns. *System, 30,* 185–206.

Goswami, U., Gombert, J. E., & de Barrera, L. F. (1998). Children's orthographic representations and linguistic transparency: Nonsense word reading in English, French, and Spanish. *Applied Psycholinguistics, 19,* 19–52.

Gray, J. (1998). The language learner as a teacher: The use of interactive diaries in teacher training. *ELT Journal, 52,* 29–37.

Guardado, M. (2002). Loss and maintenance of first language skills; Case studies of Hispanic families in Vancouver. *The Canadian Modern Language Review, 58,* 341–363.

Hacquebord, H. (1989). *Tekstbegrip van Turkse en Nederlandse leerlingen in het voortgezet onderwijs* [Text comprehension of Turkish and Dutch students in secondary education]. Dordrecht, the Netherlands: Foris.

Halbach, A. (2000). Finding out about students' learning strategies by looking at their diaries: A case study. *System, 28,* 85–96.

Hansen, L., Umedo, Y., & McKinney, M. (2002). Savings in the relearning of second language vocabulary: The effects of time and proficiency. *Language Learning, 52,* 653–678.

Harklau, L. (2000). "Good Kids" to the "Worst": Representations of English language learners across educational settings. *TESOL Quarterly, 34*, 35–67.

Hasan, A. S. (2000). Learners' perceptions of listening comprehension problems. *Language, Culture and Curriculum, 13*, 137–153.

Hatch, E., & Lazaraton, A. (1991). *The research manual: Design and statistics for applied linguistics.* New York: Newbury House.

Hock, R. (2004). *Extreme searcher's Internet handbook.* Medford, NJ: Information Today.

Hopkins, K. D., & Glass, G. V. (1978). *Basic statistics for the behavioral sciences.* Englewood Cliffs, NJ: Prentice-Hall.

Hu, C. F. (2003). Phonological memory, phonological awareness, and foreign language word learning. *Language Learning, 53*, 429–462.

Huberman, A. M., & Miles, M. B. (1994). Data management and analysis methods. In N. K. Denzin & Y. S. Lincoln (Eds.), *Handbook of qualitative research* (pp. 428–444). Thousand Oaks, CA: Sage.

Hughes, A. (2003). *Testing for language teachers* (2nd ed.). Cambridge: Cambridge University Press.

Izumi, S., & Bigelow, M. (2000). Does output promote noticing and second language acquisition? *TESOL Quarterly, 34*, 239–278.

Jacobs, H. L., Zinkgraf, D. R., Wormuth, D. R., Hartfiel, V. F., & Hughey, J. B. (1981). *Testing ESL composition.* Rowley, MA: Newbury House.

Johnson, D. M. (1992). *Approaches to research in second language learning.* White Plains, NY: Longman.

Kamhi-Stein, L. D. (2000). Looking to the future of TESOL teacher education: Web-based bulletin board discussions in a methods course. *TESOL Quarterly, 34*, 423–455.

Kobayashi, M. (2002). Method effects on reading comprehension test performance: Text organization and response format. *Language Testing, 19*, 193–220.

Koolstra, C. M., van der Voort, T. A., & van der Kamp, L. J. Th. (1997). Television's impact on children's reading and decoding skills: A 3-year panel study. *Reading Research Quarterly, 32*, 128–152.

Krathwohl, D. R. (1998). *Methods of educational and social science research: An integrated approach* (2nd ed.). New York: Longman.

Kunnan, A. J. (Ed.). (1998). *Validation in language assessment.* Mahwah, NJ: Lawrence Erlbaum Associates.

Lam, Y., & Lawrence, G. (2002). Teacher–student role redefinition during a computer-based second language project: Are computers catalysts for empowering change? *Computer Assisted Language Learning, 15*, 295–316.

Larsen-Freeman, D., & Long, M. H. (1991). *An introduction to second language acquisition research.* New York: Longman.

Laufer, B. (1998). The development of passive and active vocabulary in a second language: Same or different? *Applied Linguistics, 19*, 255–271.

Lazaraton, A. (2003). Evaluative criteria for qualitative research in applied linguistics: Whose criteria and whose research? *Modern Language Journal, 87*, 1–12.

Leonard, T. (2000). *A course in categorical data analysis.* Boca Raton, FL: Chapman & Hall/CRC Press.

Likert, R. A. (1932). A technique for the measurement of attitudes. *Archives of Psychology, 140.*

Lin, Y. (2001). Syllable simplification strategies: A stylistic perspective. *Language Learning, 51*, 681–718.

Locke, L. F., Silverman, S. J., & Spirduso, W. W. (1998). *Reading and understanding research.* Thousand Oaks, CA: Sage.

MacIntyre, P. D., Baker, S. C., Clèment, R., & Donovan, L. A. (2002). Sex and age effects on willingness to communicate, anxiety, perceived competence, and L2 motivation among junior high school French immersion students. *Language Learning, 52*, 537–564.

Major, R. C., Fitzmaurice, S. F., Bunta, F., & Balasubramanian, C. (2002). The effects of non-native accents on listening comprehension: Implications for ESL assessment. *TESOL Quarterly, 36,* 173–190.

Marsh, A. A., Elfenbein, H. A., & Ambady, N. (2003). Nonverbal "accents": Cultural differences in facial expressions of emotion. *Psychological Science, 14,* 373–376.

Mehnert, U. (1998). The effects of different lengths of time for planning on second language performance. *SSLA, 20,* 83–108.

Messick, S. (1989). Validity. In R. L. Linn (Ed.), *Educational measurement* (3rd ed., pp. 13–103). New York: Macmillan.

Microsoft® Access 2000. (1999). [Computer software]. Microsoft.

Miles, M. B., & Huberman, A. M. (1994). *Qualitative data analysis: An expanded sourcebook.* Thousand Oaks, CA: Sage.

Morris, L., & Tremblay, M. (2002). The impact of attending to unstressed words on the acquisition of written grammatical morphology by French-speaking ESL students. *The Canadian Modern Language Review, 58,* 364–385.

Nitko, A. J. (2001). *Educational assessment of students* (3rd ed.). Upper Saddle River, NJ: Prentice-Hall.

Norris, E., Mokhtari, K., & Reichard, C. (1998). Children's use of drawing as a pre-writing strategy. *Journal of Research in Reading, 21,* 69–74.

Nunan, D. (1992). *Research methods in language learning.* New York: Cambridge University Press.

Omaggio-Hadley, A. C. (1993). *Teaching language in context* (2nd ed.). Boston, MA: Heinle & Heinle.

Onwuegbuzie, A. J., Bailey, P., & Dailey, C. E. (2000). Cognitive, affective, personality, and demographic predictors of foreign-language achievement. *The Journal of Educational Research, 94,* 3–15.

Ormord, J. E. (1995). *Human learning* (2nd ed.). Englewood Cliffs, NJ: Merrill.

Pailliotet, A. W. (1997). "I'm really quiet": A case study of an Asian, language minority preservice teacher's experiences. *Teaching and Teacher Education, 13,* 675–690.

Paivio, A. (1991). Dual coding theory: Retrospect and current status. *Canadian Journal of Psychology, 45,* 255–287.

Paribakht, T. S., & Wesche, M. (1997). Vocabulary enhancement activities and reading for meaning in second language vocabulary development. In J. Coady & T. Huckin (Eds.), *Second language vocabulary acquisition: A rationale for pedagogy* (pp. 174–200). New York: Cambridge University Press.

Perry, F. L. (1982). Test-like events: An aid to learning. *Singapore Journal of Education, 4,* 44–47.

Perry, F. L., Boraie, D., Kassabgy, N., & Kassabgy, O. (2001). *How EFL learners deal with unknown words.* Paper presented at the American Association for Applied Linguistics Annual Conference, St. Louis, MO.

Perry, F. L., & Shwedel, A. (1979). Interaction of visual information, verbal information and linguistic competence in the preschool-aged child. *Journal of Psycholinguistic Research, 8,* 559–566.

Pichette, F., Segalowitz, N., & Connors, K. (2003). Impact of maintaining L1 reading skills on L2 reading skill development in adults: Evidence from speakers of Serbo-Croatian learning French. *The Modern Language Journal, 87,* 391–403.

Porte, G. K. (2002). *Appraising research in second language learning: A practical approach to critical analysis of quantitative research.* Philadelphia, PA: John Benjamins.

Rodriguez, M., & Sadoski, M. (2000). Effects of rote, context, keyword, and content/keyword methods on retention of vocabulary in EFL classrooms. *Language Learning, 50,* 385–413.

Sanz, C. (2000). Bilingual education enhances third language acquisition: Evidence from Catalonia. *Applied Psycholinguistics, 21,* 23–44.

Sasaki, M., & Hirose, K. (1996). Explanatory variables for EFL students' expository writing. *Language Learning, 46,* 137–174.

Scarcella, R., & Zimmerman, C. (1998). Academic words and gender: ESL student performance on a test of academic lexicon. *SSLA, 20,* 27–49.

Schmitt, N., & Meara, P. (1997). Researching vocabulary through a word knowledge framework. *SSLA, 19,* 17–36.

Schumann, J. (1986). Research on the acculturation model for second language acquisition. *Journal of Multilingual and Multicultural Development, 7,* 379–392.

Silva, R. S. (2000). Pragmatics, bilingualism, and the native speaker. *Language and Communication, 20,* 161–178.

Slezak, P. (2002). Thinking about thinking: Language, thought, and introspection. *Language & Communication, 22,* 373–394.

Sparks, R., & Ganschow, L. (2001). Aptitude for learning a foreign language. *Annual Review of Applied Linguistics, 21,* 90–111.

Spencer-Oatey, H. (2002). Managing rapport in talk: Using rapport sensitive incidents to explore the motivational concerns underlying the management of relations. *Journal of Pragmatics, 34,* 529–545.

Spielmann, G., & Radnofsky, M. L. (2001). Learning language under tension: New directions from a qualitative study. *The Modern Language Journal, 85,* 259–277.

Steinman, L., & Smith, M. (2001). Modern Language Aptitude Test and Manual (MLAT). Carroll, J. B., & Sapon, S. M. (1959). San Antonio, TX: The Psychological Corporation: A review. *Canadian Modern Language Review, 58*(2). Retrieved June 16, 2004, from http://www.utpjournals.com/jour.ihtml?lp=product/cmlr/582/Modern-1.html.

Storey, P. (1997). Examining the test-taking process: A cognitive perspective on the discourse cloze test. *Language Testing, 14,* 214–231.

Su, I. (2001). Context effects on sentence processing: A study based on the competition model. *Applied Psycholinguistics, 22,* 167–189.

Swanborn, M. S. L., & de Glopper, K. (2002). Impact of reading purpose on incidental word learning from context. *Language Learning, 52,* 95–117.

Taguchi, E. (1997). The effects of repeated readings on the development of lower identification skills of FL readers. *Reading in a Foreign Language, 11,* 97–119.

Tashakkori, A., & Teddlie, C. (1998). *Mixed methodology.* Thousand Oaks, CA: Sage.

Tashakkori, A., & Teddlie, C. (2003). *Handbook on mixed methods in social and behavior science.* Thousand Oaks, CA: Sage.

Timmis, I. (2002). Native-speaker norms and international English: A classroom view. *ELT Journal, 56,* 240–249.

Treiman, R., Kessler, B., & Bourassa, D. (2001). Children's own names influence their spelling. *Applied Psycholinguistics, 22,* 555–570.

Tsang, W. (1996). Comparing the effects of reading and writing on writing performance. *Applied Linguistics, 17,* 210–233.

Viechnicki, G. B. (1997). An empirical analysis of participant intentions: Discourse in a graduate seminar. *Language and Communication, 17,* 103–131.

Vivas, E. (1996). Effects of story reading on language. *Language Learning, 46,* 189–216.

Wallinger, L. M. (2002). The effects of block scheduling on foreign language learning. *Foreign Language Annals, 33,* 2–50.

Way, D. P., Joiner, E. G., & Seaman, M. A. (2000). Writing in the secondary foreign language classroom: The effects of prompts and tasks on novice learners of French. *The Modern Language Journal, 84,* 171–184.

Wesche, M. B., & Paribakht, T. S. (2000). Reading-based exercises in second language vocabulary learning: An introspective study. *The Modern Language Journal, 84,* 196–213.

Wolcott, H. F. (1994). *Transforming qualitative data: Description, analysis, and interpretation.* Thousand Oaks, CA: Sage.

Zahar, R., Cobb, T., & Spada, N. (2001). Acquiring vocabulary through reading: Effects of frequency and contextual richness. *The Canadian Modern Language Review, 57,* 541–565.

Zhongganggao, C. (2001, Winter). Second language learning and the teaching of grammar. *Education, 122,* 326–336. Retrieved September 17, 2003, from Academic Search Premier.

References of Web Sites

American Council on the Teaching of Foreign Languages (ACTFL): www.actfl.org

Cambridge Certificate in Advanced English (CAE) test battery: http://www.cambridge-efl.org/exam/general/bg_cae.htm

Department of Education: www.ed.gov/offices/OCFO/humansub.html

Department of Linguistics and Applied Linguistics at the University of Melbourne, Australia: http://www.linguistics.unimelb.edu.au/about/about.html

ERIC search: http://www.eduref.org

International English Language Testing System (IELTS): http://www.ielts.org

Bobbi Kerlin: http://kerlins.net/bobbi/research/qualresearch/bibliography/sampling.html

David M. Lane: http://www.davidmlane.com/hyperstat/sampling_dist.html

National Center for Educational Statistics: http://nces.ed.gov/statprog/2002/appendix b4.asp

Test of English as a Foreign Language (TOEFL): http://www.toefl.org

The Test of English to Speakers of Other Languages (TESOL): http://www.tesol.org/pubs/author/books/demystifygrids.html

TESOL International Research Foundation (TIRF) (criteria for publishing): www.tirfonline.org

TESOL Web site lists of journals: http://www.tesol.org/pubs/author/serials/tqguides2.html #qual. #5.

University of North Florida: www.unf.edu/dept/fie/sdfs/selecting_programs_2004.ppt

Author Index

Subject Index